The Military in American Politics

WITHDRAWN

The Military in American Politics

James Clotfelter

EMORY UNIVERSITY

HARPER & ROW, PUBLISHERS
NEW YORK   EVANSTON   SAN FRANCISCO   LONDON

FOR SALLIE, ETHAN, AND JUSTINE

THE MILITARY IN AMERICAN POLITICS
Copyright © 1973 by James Clotfelter

Standard Book Number: 06-041307-7
Library Of Congress Catalog Card Number: 72-9393

Contents

Preface

The American debate over "national priorities" continues. Attention has been focused on domestic problems such as poverty, the decay of the cities, discrimination against minorities, and environmental pollution. Considerable academic effort has been devoted to exploring these problems, and remedies for basic ills or more immediate methods of social control have been suggested. Less academic attention has been given to the leading competitor for national priorities, the military. However, it has played a central role in political decision-making in the United States—not only in regard to foreign policy but also to the distribution of economic and political resources within the country. As the Vietnam War continued and new military programs were authorized by Congress, some spokesmen for the "dispossessed" elements began to talk more loudly of the military and its civilian allies as their enemy. Frequently the military was unfairly maligned and unwisely defended. The literature spawned in this period, both by the antiwar Left and by the defenders of the Pentagon, often was either polemical or involved special pleading by interested parties.

This book is intended to be nontechnical and nonpolemical. It does not proceed from the assumption that "the military values—loyalty, duty, restraint, dedication—are the ones America most needs today" (S.H. Huntington, *The Soldier and the State*, Harvard University Press, 1957, p. 465); nor from the assumption that the military is engaged in a conspiracy to maintain a high level of international tensions so as to increase defense spending and military control of the government. Balance and fairness are sought.

This book employs material from a wide array of primary and secondary sources: the specialized military literature; case studies; original research; and the general political science literature. The main effort has not been to describe formal bureaucratic and constitutional relationships. I have attempted to describe and analyze behavioral patterns which involve the military and civilian groups. Rather than envisioning the military purely as an actor in international politics and foreign policy, a specialized public administration field, or an esoteric and apolitical field of its own, this book attempts to relate civil-military politics and national security policy to the broader context of American politics. It is hoped that much in these pages will be useful to both college undergraduates and more advanced students.

I would like to acknowledge the assistance of my political science colleagues at Emory University; students in my undergraduate and graduate classes on civil-military politics; Emory University's Research Committee, which granted me a summer research award for 1970; research assistant Ray Chambers; and the military officers who gave me information and guidance. I want to thank Walter Lippincott and Luther Wilson of Harper & Row for their kind patience. I owe a particular debt to John Shingler, who suffered through my first graduate school interest in the military (African); Raymond Dawson of the University of North Carolina at Chapel Hill, from whom I learned much about the American military; and the faculty and graduate students at Chapel Hill between 1967-1969, for miscellaneous intellectual stimulation. Finally, I have been aided greatly by my wife Sallie, who encouraged me to write, and my son Ethan, who didn't.

James Clotfelter

CHAPTER ONE

The Military and National Priorities

"From the people who brought you Vietnam: the antiballistic missile system." Thus read a peace group's newspaper advertisement depicting a circle of Napoleonic militarists and munitions-makers huddled around a missile. "They're mad. They're absolutely mad," the advertisement read. "Everyone can see that things at home are getting worse all the time. . . . The last thing in the world we need is to spend six or seven thousand million dollars for the down payment on an antiballistic missile system. But what can you expect from the type of mind that got us into Vietnam in the first place, and that keeps plunging us back in for one-last-victory-try every time it looks as if we might finally extricate ourselves?" [SANE]

By the early 1970s a decade of military involvement in Vietnam, marked by tens of thousands of American deaths and expenditure of tens of billions of dollars, had brought no victory. Half a million U.S. troops, equipped with everything short of the atomic bomb, had failed to subdue the army of a "fourth-class power" and its peasant-guerrilla allies. Was the American military leadership and its business and civilian governmental allies to blame for (1) initially involving the United States in a land war in Asia; (2) steadily escalating that involvement until April 1968; and (3) resisting de-escalation after that time? Was the Vietnam lesson that the military had gotten out of hand and taken too much control over foreign policy-making from acquiescent or sympathetic civilians?

At home, while the war "dragged on," antiwar governmental and mass media spokesmen sought to organize resentment against the size and scope of the armed forces. Defense spending took 8 to 9 percent of the Gross National Product (GNP) and included such purchases as $1.6 million worth of musical instruments annually. Cost overruns characterized most major weapons systems, although technology and inflation sometimes were the culprits. More

1

seriously, the military proposed an enlarged post-Vietnam wardrobe of weapons, principally the antiballistic missile (ABM) system with an ultimate price of $50 billion, the B-1 bomber, Poseidon and Trident missiles, and a Fast Deployment Logistics fleet. In 1960, with talk of a growing "missile gap" between the U.S.S.R. and the United States, only 18 percent of those queried in a Gallup national sampling favored reductions in the defense budget, and 21 percent favored increased spending. In 1969, however, 52 percent of those interviewed believed that military spending was too high, and only 8 percent believed expenditures should be increased. Even after billions of dollars were cut from budgets and manpower was reduced, the defense budget remained over $70 billion a year, and more than 4.5 million people (in and out of uniform) were directly employed by the defense establishment. With more programs proposed to take up any slack caused by the end of the Vietnam War, had military spending spiraled out of reasonable bounds? How much defense was enough?

Worse, in some people's minds, than the political and monetary damage wrought by war abroad and wasteful spending at home was the possible damage done to the nation's political psyche. What about the people? Had the basic fabric of American democracy been undermined? Had America become, as Harold Lasswell warned before World War II, a "garrison state" in which "the specter of crisis shapes men's minds into the strategic mold of thought [and] other features of social life are given meaning insofar as they can be translated in terms of ultimate fighting effectiveness?"[9]. Widespread insecurity leads (in Lasswell's formulation) to increased public deference toward the military as the only group capable of protecting the country and eventually leads to "the supremacy of the soldier." "The American people," Senator William Fulbright said in 1964, "have come to place excessive faith in military solutions to political problems." By 1969 other opponents of the war and military spending were saying that America had become a militaristic, aggressive nation.

To determine whether the military and military spending have gotten out of hand, we must ascertain the extent of military participation in and its influence over key sectors of American life and explore the attitudes of the general public and the government toward the military. In addition we must study the attitude of the military toward the rest of the political system. How do civilians react to the military and how are they affected by it? Do the president and Defense Department civilians control their military advisers, or are they captives of the expertise of military "specialists on violence"? Has Congress become a rubber stamp for military requests? Have the links between the military and the business community become so close that business and labor are dependent on large hardware programs for continuing high profits and wages, and therefore do they encourage the military to seek larger programs? Have ties to the military corrupted the scientific and academic communities? Has pervasive militarization of American culture affected the mass media, the schools, and public attitudes?

FROM "WASTE" TO "CONTROL"

Civilian control over the military is one of the oldest issues in American politics. It originated in eighteenth-century concerns about the threat to democracy posed by a large standing army. As in past periods of crisis and anxiety brought on or accompanied by external conflicts, the place of the military in American government and society again became a matter of controversy in the late 1960s. But the source of much of the disharmony, the Vietnam War, seemed beyond control. Closer at hand and (because of its size) perhaps more vulnerable, was the military itself. The war in Vietnam and the continued high rate of military spending was emphasized by liberal politicians who spoke of "domestic priorities" sufficiently important to outweigh national defense and containment of Communism; the "crisis of the cities," coupled with racial turmoil, brought the "war" into the streets of America. More money should be put into the cities and into combating poverty at home, they argued, and less into wars and preparation for wars abroad. "There are bombs going off in our cities," the SANE advertisement continued, "but they're not coming from China or the U.S.S.R." The final cost of the Vietnam War will exceed $350 billion—including the continuing burdens of veterans' benefits and interest on the national debt[3]. Although Bruce Russett showed that in the period of 1938-1967 changes in defense spending had less impact on civil public expenditures (education, health, welfare) than on investment and personal consumption, the impact of higher military spending on all civilian sectors was found to be substantial[12].

The crusaders against the "military-industrial complex" had a more fundamental concern than the one that high defense spending and waste had siphoned off funds needed for domestic programs. The crucial task, as John Kenneth Galbraith saw it, "is not to make the military power more efficient or more righteously honest. It is to get it under control"[6]. The ABM, the C-5A plane, and the B-1 were opposed (unsuccessfully) by liberals in Congress, not only because they cost too much or were strategically unnecessary, but because they were seen as symbols of a military-dominated government.

In the early 1960s the efforts of Secretary of Defense Robert S. McNamara and his civilian "whiz kids" had been directed at rationalizing the decision-making processes in the Pentagon. McNamara was widely credited with imposing the tightest civilian control of the military yet seen, through the use of budgetary controls. "He taught the politicians . . . how to understand the military establishment, how its strategies are made, how its weapons are chosen. He took the mystery and witchcraft out of the whole business and thus prepared the way for critical questioning of the military budget"[7]. But, by the end of the decade, liberals attacked McNamara's reforms for being too "successful." Galbraith, Richard Goodwin, and Marcus Raskin wrote:

The Kennedy administration took office in 1961 with the avowed aim of establishing greater civilian control over the military. Yet the harsh fact is that military considerations today play a greater role in determining American policy than at any time in our national history.

In the name of efficiency, we unified the operations of the armed services, introduced the techniques of computer management and encouraged closer interactions between the military and industry. As a result, power once checked by rivalries and inefficiency is now wielded as a single force, defying effective democratic control[8].

The liberals believed that this was accomplished not by military professionals, but by their civilian allies in government and business. Yet the result, they believed, was to give the "complex" greater influence over policy and resource allocation.

Others believed that the military had been made a scapegoat. Conservative columnist William F. Buckley pointed out that the percentage of the GNP devoted to military programs had declined during the 1960s: "What we purchase every year for eighty billion dollars is worth much more to individual New Yorkers than everything contributed by . . . zealous welfarists. What the citizens of New York purchase for their military dollar is the right to speak their minds" [1].

Hans Morgenthau, later a leading opponent of Johnson administration policy in Vietnam, said in 1964 that the military was attacked by people who could not explain changes in the nation's political situation. "The influence of the military has declined in recent years. But people who look for a scapegoat . . . hit upon the military as the cause of all evil. The military takes the place that the munitions makers held following World War I. [The result is] the myth of the all-powerful Pentagon which dominates the life of the nation"[2]. Not only is the military not the villain, Nixon's Secretary of Defense Melvin Laird believed; the military-industrial-labor team is a tremendous asset to the nation, he said.

THE MILITARY IN POLITICS

Politics usually has been conceived in allocative or conflictual terms, or as a combination of the two. In allocative terms there is assumed to be a scarcity of desired values, such as wealth, deference, political power, and safety, and a necessity for mechanisms to decide who is to get what there is of the desired things and who is to be denied them. Resources usually are seen as usable in alternative ways. Thus David Easton defines politics as "the authoritative allocation of values"[5].[1] In conflictual terms some political scientists have

[1] The military is most clearly involved as a participant in the authoritative allocation of these values:

1. Safety or lack of safety: Which cities are given ABM sites or other forms of active defense?
2. Deference or lack of deference: Which scientists and academics are given security clearance? Which congressmen are invited in for special briefings?

identified the distinctive quality of a political system as its relation to coercion, force, and violence—especially "legitimate force," that is, the *rightful* power to punish, enforce, or compel.

Whether allocation or coercion is accepted as the distinctive feature of political behavior, the professional military seems intimately involved in "politics." It might be assumed that the military exercises coercive power only at the direction of civilian leadership, and that allocation of resources within the military and between military and civilian programs is the responsibility of civilians. This assumption is correct in traditional democratic theory and constitutional lines of authority. However, three factors reinforce the view that the military *is* intimately involved in politics: (1) the method of military administration of policy is at least as important as the policy itself; (2) many of the civilians who make authoritative decisions relevant to the military are themselves part of a military-industrial-administrative complex and, in fact, some are former military officers or active reserve officers; and (3) the guiding ethos by which decisions are made was formed in part by military men. These basic values, such as anticommunism, tend to restrict day-to-day decision-making discretion. Therefore, the assumption upon which this book has been based is that the American military and its nonuniformed allies and employees are engaged in political behavior.

EVALUATING THE IMPACT OF THE MILITARY

The expanded role of the military is not peculiar to the United States, although in dollar terms only the U.S.S.R. rivals it. In 1970 world military expenditures reached $204 billion—or 20 percent higher (in "real" dollars, adjusted for inflation) than in 1964. The United States was one of 22 countries that spent more than 5 percent of their GNP on the military[13]. More than 50 million people were in active military service or in military-related jobs throughout the world. The U.S.S.R., China, Israel, and many Middle Eastern, Asian, African, and Latin American nations have armed forces which—by the standards of the society—spend much money and have considerable technical, organizational, and political resources.

In the early 1970s the American military was described as huddling together, on the defensive against the outside menace of "public opinion." Other armies have felt the taste of what they considered to be public ingratitude—most notably the French army after World War II, Indochina, and Algeria. Most Western European armies have been permitted to decline in strength in recent years. The American military has never been a "state within the state" in the way that the pre-Hitler German military was, nor has the

---

3. Wealth or lack of wealth: Where are bases located? Which bases are closed? Which firms are chosen for weapons contracts?
4. Political power: Which civilians in government find the military supporting their foreign-policy positions?

United States had a "man on horseback" tradition as have France and many Latin American nations.

Like all institutions having close ties to counterparts overseas, the American military is subject both to factors affecting the armed forces of all major world powers in the nuclear age and to factors peculiar to American society.

• • •

We are dealing with a political institution whose role in American politics heretofore has been expanded by hot and cold wars. The priorities debate and military controversies of 1969-1971 only illuminated existing conflicts of interest. After World War II the military had kept a large share of national resources, both in terms of the budget and in terms of managerial and technical skills, and military leadership had held a prominent place in decision-making councils. But it took Vietnam and the prospect of heavier military spending after the war to create a significant amount of public uneasiness about civilian control over the military. Had the United States, in creating a vast peacetime standing army as protection against the dangers of the cold war, in fact created a Frankenstein's monster? Or was the military a scapegoat for more complex anxieties?

To better understand the military's place in American government and society, we will discuss the questions posed earlier in this chapter and specify conditions under which these hypotheses would appear to be supported or not supported. Three sets of questions will be asked, and a broad range of quantitative and nonquantitative, objective and judgmental, comparative and case-study forms of data will be employed in the search for tentative answers. The first set of questions involves the economics of defense.

Has military spending spiraled out of control? Have the links between the military and the business community become so close that business and labor are dependent on large hardware programs for continuing high profits and jobs? To answer these questions we need to know: (1) how profitable and irreplaceable defense work is to corporations and labor; (2) how important (in the sense of bringing large payrolls, being irreplaceable, or otherwise benefitting community life) defense spending is to local communities; and (3) what is the exact relationship between the military and business, in personnel and programs, and for whose sake does it operate? Relevant data include:

1. For corporations: Information on the company's return on capital investment and on sales from defense work as compared with returns from investments in commercial business, and "synergistic" benefits (such as technological developments) from defense work which aid commercial business.

2. For localities: Geographical patterns of defense plants and bases, and impact on local economies from significant increases or decreases in the local defense payroll.

3. For the military-industrial relationship: The number and nature of military-business personnel crossovers, cost control and contracting procedures, and information as to the points in the weapons' development process where businessmen play key roles.

The second set of questions directly involves civilian control of the military, or more specifically, *what kind* of civilian control exists?

Do the president and Defense Department civilians control their military advisers, or are they captives of the expertise of the military? Has Congress become a rubber stamp for military requests? Here the "chameleon" problem is troublesome, since military leaders and civilians in the executive and legislative branches of government might follow the same policies either because of independently arrived at conceptions of the national interest or because one group is influencing the other [4]. Relevant data include:

1. For the executive branch: Information on the outcome of known clashes between military men and civilians in the White House, Office of Management and Budget, or Pentagon (for example, what happens when members of the Joint Chiefs carry budgetary disputes to Congress, after having had programs rejected or reduced by the executive?); incidence of differing schools of advice from within the military services; the extent to which the military is perceived as monopolizing relevant expertise in strategic, tactical, and overall defense policy problems, or who are the defense intellectuals; what are the changing role perceptions of Defense Department civilians?

2. For Congress: By using roll call votes, committee reports and testimony, and floor speeches, determine how military requests are treated in different House and Senate committees, at different points in time and in comparison with nonmilitary programs.

The relative importance of Congress, the executive, the military, and business in initiating and gaining approval for strategies and weapons systems will be considered since differing strategies mean differing internal resource allocations.

A third set of questions involves the military's relationship to nongovernmental groups and the public. *Have ties to the military corrupted the scientific and academic communities? Has pervasive militarization of American culture affected the mass media, the schools, and public attitudes?* These questions involve a strong normative element, making proof difficult. Relevant data include:

1. For the scientific-academic sector: Information regarding grants from the services to research programs and the extent to which grants are irreplaceable, the topics of research, and the uses to which research findings are put.

2. For the socialization media: Changing content.

3. For the public from 1936-1971: A descriptive trend analysis of survey data on attitudes toward defense spending, military training, the military's professional status, civilian control of the military in peace and war, and international affairs.

The above are examples of the type of material to be discussed. The first set of questions will be dealt with in Chapter Four. The second set will be examined largely in Chapters Seven, Eight, and Nine. The third set will be dealt with in Chapters Three, Five, and Six.

We will examine the place of the military professional in American society, in an historical and contemporary focus, in Chapters Two and Three. The quality of available data—some of it from case studies, some partially obscured by the nonpublic nature of many of the military's political trans-actions—means that answers to these questions will be circumstantial and approximate. But the questions deserve attention because they are important for the American polity, as political actors debate the continuing question of what is the proper role in a democratic system for the "managers of violence." We will suggest, in succeeding chapters, that the military is not to blame for some things commonly attributed to it but that it is responsible for other things not usually attributed to it.

REFERENCES

1. Buckley, William F., "$80 Billion Better Spent By Military," *The Char-lotte (N.C.) Observer*, July 1, 1969, p. 3-C.
2. "Carolina Symposium Speaker Declares Military Has Become U.S. 'Scapegoat,' " *The Durham Herald*, April 7, 1964, p. 8-A.
3. Clayton, James L., "Vietnam: The 200-Year Mortgage," *The Nation*, Vol. 208 (May 26,1969), pp. 661-663.
4. Dahl, Robert A., "The Concept of Power," *Behavioral Science*, vol. 2 (July 1957), pp. 201-215.
5. Easton, David, *The Political System* (New York: Knopf, 1953).
6. Galbraith, John Kenneth, *How to Control the Military* (New York: Signet Books, 1969), p. 74.
7. Harwood, Richard, , "Hill Wises Up to Pentagon," *The Washington Post*, August 10, 1969, pp. B-1.
8. Harwood, Richard, and Laurence Stern, "McNamara: Debate Puts His Record on Trial," *The Washington Post,* June 15, 1969, pp. A-1, A-10, A-11.
9. Lasswell, Harold, *The Analysis of Political Behavior* (London: Archon Books, 1966.)
10. Lasswell, Harold and Abraham Kaplan, *Power and Society* (New Haven, Conn.: Yale University Press, 1950).

11. "Military Using Cold War for High Budgets," *The Durham Herald*, April 6, 1964, p. 1-A.
12. Russett, Bruce M., "Who Pays for Defense?" *American Political Science Review*, vol. 63 (June 1969), pp. 412-426.
13. *World Military Expenditures 1970* (Washington: United States Arms Control and Disarmament Agency, 1970), pp. 1, 8.

CHAPTER TWO

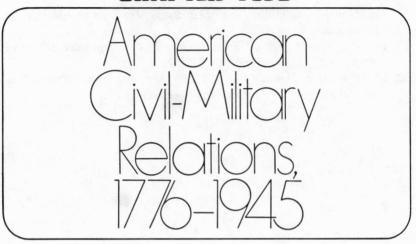

American Civil-Military Relations, 1776–1945

"With respect to a standing army," James Madison said, "I believe there was not a member in the Federal [Constitutional] Convention who did not feel indignation at such an institution." One member felt sufficient indignation to propose that the Constitution limit the size of the national army to no more than 3000 men. George Washington, usually an impartial chairman, whispered an amendment to the motion, making it unconstitutional for any enemy of the United States "to attack us with a larger force than we might lawfully mount"[18, pp. 19-20]. Nothing further was heard of the motion to limit the military to one-thousandth the size of the American forces of 1970, but the defense establishment was in for many lean years nevertheless.

The dangers of military weakness were widely preferred to those of a strong army, "the engine of despotism" and praetorianism in Europe, which was responsible for "men on horseback," such as Bonaparte and Cromwell, who imposed their will on the peoples' representatives. In the eighteenth and early nineteenth centuries a professional standing army was thought by liberal republicans to endanger democracy, liberty, equality, individualism, peace, and prosperity. Thus, despite the presence of European forces and Indian nations to the north, south, and west, the United States started the post-Revolutionary period with an army of 80 men, to guard the stores at West Point and Fort Pitt. "More than magazine guards will be useless if few," Thomas Jefferson said, "and dangerous if many" [14, p. 42].

In its history the United States has been involved in hundreds of armed conflicts and has amassed much of its territory through military conquest. Though it has been a nation given to displays of martial ceremony, and not a notably peaceful nation, it has not been one which honored its military. As Francis Quarles's 1635 poem put it:

Our God and soldiers we alike adore
when at the brink of ruin, not before
After deliverance, both alike requited
Our God forgotten, and our soldiers slighted.[1].

But in America, until recent years, it has been only the citizen-soldier whose prestige rose "at the brink of ruin." The low status of the professional soldier helped to account for the chronic unpreparedness with which the United States is said to have entered all wars through 1945.

In this chapter we shall look at American civil-military relations through World War II and trace the development of these relationships through war and peace, the Industrial Revolution, and upheavals in the social structure and political system. Histories are available elsewhere; here we will try to convey the flavor of civil-military relations at different points in time and relate them to contemporary themes.

THE REVOLUTION AND THE CONSTITUTION

George Washington was the first American commanding general to come into conflict with civilians who wanted to run a war. Through World War II, Congress had established a committee to investigate the conduct of every war (except the Spanish-American War, which was investigated by a presidential commission); the Revolution[1] was no different, and Washington, as commander-in-chief, clashed often with the Board of War. Washington's requests for soldiers and supplies repeatedly were ignored or altered by the Continental Congress. Military historian Emory Upton noted that "nearly all of the dangers which threatened the cause of independence may be traced to the total inexperience of our statesmen in regard to military affairs"[14, p. 33].

The most serious threat to civilian dominance—and one of the few instances in American history where there was even the hint of a military plot to take over the government—came after the Yorktown surrender. The Continental army was held at Newburgh, New York, until the terms of peace were negotiated and Congress made provisions for the army's payment and demobilization. As protests to Congress brought no response, a group of officers in 1783 distributed a petition of grievances, and several asked General Washington to accept a king's crown and lead the army against Congress. Washington discouraged such suggestions and held the army at Newburgh until Congress found funds for soldiers' back pay.

The Continental army's soldiers were citizens away from their homes. They were early subjects of one of the nation's most persistent beliefs, that

[1] One of the charges against King George in the Declaration of Independence was that he had "affected to render the military independent of and superior to the civil power."

America's best defender in time of war was the citizen-soldier, the Minute Man, Cincinnatus come from behind the plow. The myth persisted in the face of contrary facts. Only 3 percent of the population were mobilized in the Revolutionary War[11], compared with 10 percent during World War II. Less than 15 percent of the males of military age served in the Continental army, a minority of which was derived from voluntary enlistment; Washington's peak strength was only 35,000 men. The forces raised by states were "democratic in the extreme, groups of men . . . who elected their own officers, provided their own weaponry. . ."[3, p. 3]. Recruits often went home after the summer's campaign, and some left the field whenever their one-year enlistments were up, regardless of the military situation. Desertion was widespread, and numerous mutinies occurred over the lack of pay and provisions and over discharge demands. In effect, a new army had to be raised each year. Although Americans were proficient weapons-users, they disliked the rank, discipline, and hardships of military service. "It is nonsense to talk of regulars," Jefferson noted. "They are not to be had among a people so easy and happy at home as ours. We might as well rely on calling down an army of angels from heaven!"[14, p. 55]. Thus, because a citizen-volunteer army could not be raised and because a professional army was considered undemocratic even if feasible, conscripted state militias were the answer. The states had always had to depend on bounties and conscription: Between the years 1607 and 1775 the colonies passed more than 600 conscription laws and ordinances affecting men aged 16 to 60, and military service remained unattractive after independence. The Militia Act of 1792 proclaimed a universal military liability to service in state militias (with exceptions). Despite conscription controversies and militia failures in the War of 1812 and the Mexican War and the need for national conscription in the Civil War, the Militia Act stayed on the books for 110 years. The citizen-soldier ideal it reflected, bolstered by Jacksonian suspicion of an army's expertise and professionalism, retained its attraction well into the twentieth century. The Society of Cincinnati, an association of ex-officers, was opposed because it would emphasize the differences between officers and men and between civilians and the military—the latter "distinction," Jefferson said, "it is for the happiness of both to obliterate"[17, p. 99]. The society lost much of its original political force and later was disbanded, leaving the country with no major veterans organization until after the Civil War.

The Revolution also provided the impetus for the expansion of manufacturing enterprises in the colonies. Forges, foundries, ironworks, and gunsmiths were needed to produce guns, powder, and lead, and other firms sold food and clothing to the military. Inventor Eli Whitney received one of the first private-industry military contracts during the Revolution, to produce muskets with interchangeable parts by assembly line. (As with many later contracts, Whitney ran far behind schedule and costs were several times higher than had been estimated.) President Washington, in his annual message to Congress in 1796, addressed himself to the problems of a private sector dependent on defense contracting.

As a general rule, Manufactures on public account, are inexpedient. But where the state of things in a Country, leaves little hope that certain branches of Manufacture will, for a great length of time, obtain; when these are of a nature essential to the furnishings and equiping of the public force in time of War, are not establishments for procuring them on public account, to the extent of the ordinary demand for the public service, recommended by strong considerations of National policy, as an exception to the general rule? . . . If the necessary Articles should, in this mode, cost more in time of peace, will not the security and independence thence arising, form an adequate compensation? Establishments of this sort . . . will, in time of War, easily be extended. . .[10].

In the decades after the Revolution, Coates and Pellegrin noted, "military needs did much to stimulate industrialization. Many inventions and refinements of industrial processes . . . occurred because of military requirements" [4, p. 73]. Thus, metallurgical advances were stimulated by the military's need for improved cannon, and the sewing machine was first used in making army uniforms.

In 1784, despite Washington's support for a 2600-man army, the standing army was virtually abolished. However, fears of insufficient national capability to deal with domestic insurrection from the "debtor classes" (symbolized by Shays's Rebellion in 1786) and with perceived external threats to American mercantilist and expansionist interests supported the contention that a new constitutional framework was needed. There has been dispute as to the relative importance of economic and other motivations in the calling of a Constitutional Convention in 1787, but certainly, military apprehensions played some part. William Riker argued, in his "military interpretation of the Constitution," that the external and internal military dangers facing the new nation were the most important consideration to the founding fathers [16].

Regardless of motivations, the effect of the new Constitution was to strengthen the national government greatly, and a major part of the government's new powers were those of "sword and purse." Congress was given the power to raise and support armies, to make rules and regulations for military forces, to declare war, and to tax the populace in support of these forces. Appropriation periods were limited to two years (one year in practice) to maintain close control. (The navy was under no such restrictions, as a permanent naval force was not seen as a threat to the government; how does one take over Congress with a frigate?) To guard further against national military despotism, states retained control of the appointment of militia officers and militia training, although from 1791 the president could accept companies of volunteers and appoint officers. The separation of powers provisions and the commander-in-chief clause further divided civilian control over the military between executive and legislature, which further limited *civilian* use of military power. Three members of the constitutional convention refused to sign the document because of the lack of restrictions placed on a standing army. In at least 10 states the Constitution's military features were the subject of debate among the ratifiers, and 5 states made direct recommendations to Congress for amendments to lessen the danger of military despotism. Although these amendments were not adopted, congressmen for years afterward shared these fears and kept the army small (Table One). Despite concessions to states rightists and those who feared a standing army, the Constitution did provide the institutional framework for a national force whose size could be increased to meet changing conditions.

A MILITARY FORCE EMERGES

If the Constitution was the conservative institutional structure in which American civil-military relations were formed, as Samuel Huntington argued, Jeffersonian-Jacksonian liberalism was the ideological constant[7]. To the extent that a professional military was necessary, Jefferson felt it should be closely incorporated into civilian society; there should be a fusion between the civilian and the military, and in peacetime, standing forces should be used for civilian purposes. Thus, West Point was established by Jefferson in 1802 not as a professional military academy but as a part of the Corps of Engineers—the English-speaking world's first engineering school. Military

TABLE ONE
Army size, 1800-1939

	Regular army average size	Percentage of national population
1800-1809	3,666	0.069
1810-1819	14,433	0.199
1820-1829	6,359	0.066
1830-1839	8,167	0.063
1840-1849	19,157	0.112
1850-1859	13,695	0.059
1860-1869	393,255	1.251
1870-1879	28,297	0.071
1880-1889	26,495	0.053
1890-1899	51,050	0,081
1900-1909	77,108	0.101
1910-1919	433,266	0.471
1920-1929	154,171	0.146
1930-1939	155,246	0.126

"Average size" for a decade is arrived at by averaging the regular army force levels for each year of the decade. The population data is for the first year of each decade.

officers also were used to explore the frontier and to administer new territories. This was the "technicism" which Huntington posited as one of the
three strands of America's military tradition; the others were popularism and
the professionalism supported by Alexander Hamilton, John Calhoun, and
the South generally.

Jacksonian popularism was associated with both the notion that military skills were not so complex that any freeman could not learn them
quickly and with the citizen-soldier myth. During the War of 1812 state
militias proved highly unreliable, on several occasions refusing to leave their
states to pursue the enemy or to aid other militias and demonstrating
relatively little military training when they did fight. However, Jackson's
victory at the Battle of New Orleans helped to preserve the individualistic
frontiersman as the symbol of American self-defense, much as the atomic
bomb attacks on Japan in 1945 helped to rescue the "strategic bombing"
approach after a succession of failures during World War II. (Another national
legend which somehow survived the War of 1812 was that of America's
unbeaten war record. A century and a half later, during the Vietnam War,
President Nixon was to vow that he would not be "the first American
president to lose a war," although most historians have accorded that distinction to President Madison.) The state-national conflict seen in the War of
1812 surfaced again during the Seminole War in Florida, when General
Jackson appointed cooperative Indians as officers. Angered by Jackson's
violation of the states' prerogative to appoint militia officers, the Senate
investigated.

During the early 1820s, although a small standing army had become a
widely accepted alternative because no one was willing to train and discipline
the militias, the army was reduced in size to about 6000 and the $4.5 million
budget was criticized as a tax burden. By 1828 the Senate was debating the
question of whether two generals were enough or if a third were needed. A
strong navy was becoming an accepted part of national policy; by 1815
negotiations with three nations had been entrusted to navy officers, and in
1841 the administration proposed that American naval strength be at least
one-half that of the strongest foreign nation.

Hamilton had supported a strong military as a means to make the
national government stronger than the states. He also wanted more control of
the military to reside in the executive's hands, as it did during the Alien and
Sedition crisis of 1798-1799. In the early 1820s Secretary of War Calhoun
supported the "expansible army" concept—a standing army composed of
understaffed units capable of being filled out quickly in an emergency—but
the concept was not implemented. By the end of the decade no one advocated a strong national military establishment [18, p. 31]. Through the three
decades after the War of 1812, army pay was low, promotions slow, and
morale was said to be poor. "The military profession . . . has been so poorly
encouraged," the *Army and Navy Chronicle* said in 1839, "that but little

incentive is held out to devote exclusive attention to it" [14, p. 67]. The curriculum at West Point was becoming more professional, and military service was evolving into a social tradition for some Southern families. But proponents of a stronger military were faced with a serious political problem: the absence of an obvious external enemy.

Mexico became that enemy through processes which made the Mexican War bitterly controversial. (It was condemned by opponents in terms similar to those used against the nation's next large-scale colonial war, the Spanish-American War, and later against the Vietnam War). It also was the first professional war and one of the most political wars in American history.

It was professional in the sense that more of the officers were career soldiers, the regular army sustained a disproportionate number of casualities, and 88 percent of the troops were regulars and national volunteers serving for at least 12 months. (By comparison, in the War of 1812, only 12 percent of the troops were "nationals," organized and supported by Congress.) However, desertions remained a serious problem (1700 deserted at the victory of Buena Vista, for example),[2] and political generals were common, with many congressmen serving as officers in a controversial dual status.

The war also was political because Democratic President Polk's two leading generals, Taylor and Winfield Scott, were prominent Whigs with presidential ambitions. When the war started Polk asked the nationally known Scott to take charge of the army. After a series of disputes, which culminated in a letter from Scott complaining that he had "a fire upon my rear, from Washington, and the fire, in front, from the Mexicans," Polk dismissed Scott[20]. Later reinstated as commanding general, Scott found himself surrounded by Democratic generals newly created to insure that war operations were consistent with administration plans. The Whig Congress censured the president for his conduct of the war, and after the war Polk returned the favor by forcing a military examination of Scott to bar him from obtaining the 1848 Whig presidential nomination (won instead by General Taylor). In all, Scott sought the presidency three times, *while commanding the army*.

Given the undisguised conflict between Polk and his generals, what kind of civilian control existed in this period? In the decades before the Civil War, the president could expect little assistance from a secretary of war, who had a few clerks but no assistant secretaries or administrative assistants. Between 1829 and 1861 there were only two commanding generals and twelve secretaries, with only one secretary serving for five years. The secretary and the commanding general often were at odds, and their relationship at best was

---

[2] General Zachary Taylor lost 40 percent of his army because their service time had expired. "The men marched home, leaving the general besieging a city where his remaining troops were greatly outnumbered" [3, p. 4]. Similar incidents occurred early in the Civil War. It should be noted that desertion, in the nineteenth century, was high in peacetime [5].

ambiguous; the relative permanence of the commander and the heads of bureaus gave them an enormous advantage in expertise and political contacts.

Military contracting became a larger business in this period, leading to a prohibition in 1838 against army officers engaging "in the services of an incorporated company"[17, p. 312]. However, the program most important to private industry was the naval shipbuilding program of the 1840s-1850s. Civilian shipbuilders often were appointed as secretary of the navy during the nineteenth and early twentieth centuries. The iron and coal industries and the New England shipping, commercial, and port interests were especially active in supporting the navy.

FROM CIVIL WAR TO WORLD WAR I

At the time of the Civil War many more West Point graduates were railroad presidents and university presidents than generals. The West Point curriculum still emphasized engineering, tactics, and routine administration over strategy. Despite the Mexican War interlude, the small professional army had continued to be used primarily for internal development tasks, and as late as December 1860 the Senate had asked its military affairs committee whether war department expenses could not be further reduced. Although commercial and colonial aspirations permitted naval expansion, national policy still relied primarily on militias and volunteers rather than on the regular army.

The events of 1860-1861 offered Southern officers a choice between continuing their nonpartisan role or becoming adherents of a regional cause. Many Southerners chose the Union, but the number of officers supporting the Confederacy ensured that both sides had professional leadership—and the South made more prominent use of its professionals. Of the 60 biggest Civil War battles, West Pointers commanded *both* armies in 55.

The strategy taught at the Academy tended to separate "war" from "statecraft," and the Union's first generals took this seriously. To them "war was a business to be carried on by professionals without interference from civilians and without political objectives. ... War [was] a kind of game played by experts off in some private sphere..."[14, p. 97]. Despite President Lincoln's frequent requests for offensive action to inspire public opinion, his first commanding general, George McClellan, refused to move his troops for that purpose. While Lincoln feared that the public would become discouraged and abandon the war effort, McClellan was concerned about limiting casualties. He wanted more time and more soldiers.

One of the precedents established in the Civil War was that the president had enormous "emergency" powers. In addition to asserting vast presidential powers over civilians in wartime, Lincoln involved himself in strategy, tactics, and military administration—from mapping war plans to the famous case of pardoning a soldier who fell asleep on sentry duty. Generals were replaced often, although not always because of Lincoln's wishes, since the president had to cope with an active Joint Congressional Committee on the Conduct of the War. Louis Smith wrote of the committee:

Members . . . preferred Republican generals to Democratic ones, radicals to moderates, apostles of the attack to masters of maneuver, and conquerors of the South to mild discipliners of our erring brothers. They undermined General McClellan and ruined his standing with the people. They systematically discredited and drove from . . . command Generals Stone, Franklin, Meade, FitzJohn Porter, Burnside, Brown, and others too lukewarm for their purposes[18, pp. 202-203].

The committee combined investigative, advisory, and managerial functions; it had no hesitancy in overriding recommendations of professional officers, whose strategic and tactical competence usually enjoyed little respect. A second governmental precedent from this war was that Congress was thought to behave irresponsibly (and perhaps unconstitutionally) when it attempted to direct field operations through a committee. Senator Harry Truman, during World War II, sometimes quoted General Robert E. Lee's statement that the Committee on the Conduct of the War was "worth two divisions" to the Confederacy [15].

Lincoln finally found two "modern" generals, Grant and Sherman. They were modern in the sense that they understood the close relationship between war and politics. The Civil War was modern also in its dependence on technological innovation (e.g., mass production of weapons and the use of railroads for troop movements), in its close military-civilian interchange (involving such groups as businessmen and the Pinkerton detectives used by the Union for espionage), and in its reliance on the country's first national conscription (conducted by the military itself, in house-to-house canvasses). When provisions were implemented to allow men to avoid service through the payment of $300 or by providing a substitute, draft riots broke out in several cities. In 1863, 1000 were killed in five days of rioting in New York City. (Lincoln's call for volunteers had gone largely unheeded.) The war also had much in common with previous wars: The unpreparedness of military forces in 1861 led to the customary opening-day massacre (Bull Run, where Union troops fled with less than 3 percent casualties) and later to massive desertions during the war (more than 200,000 Union soldiers deserted). In the face of continued disagreement with Lincoln and the Radical Republicans, culminating twice in his dismissal, General McClellan had talked openly in 1862 of marching on Washington but had been dissuaded from doing so by the lack of enthusiasm shown by his officers. In 1864 he opposed his former commander-in-chief as the Democratic presidential nominee and lost. After the war General Grant was twice elected president and served with little recognized distinction, while his colleague Sherman refused all nominations by the powerful Republican-associated veterans group, the Grand Army of the Republic. "I will not run if nominated, or serve if elected," Sherman said, and although army chief of staff for 15 years, he sought to inculcate apolitical values in his service.[3] The army was entering a period of isolation from civilian society and accelerated professional development. After the military governments in the South were removed, army units were scattered on remote posts in the West, where they launched 12 major campaigns against the Indians between 1865-1898. Garrisons were characterized as "monasteries" cut off from civilian society, intent only upon "ritual and rectitude"[9]. The late nineteenth-century officer corps adopted the customs of social and business elites, and an officer's social origins became more important, especially in the navy. The typical turn-of-the-century general was of an old American family of British ancestry from the rural or small-town Northeast. He was the high-school educated, Episcopalian son of a professional man from a politically influential family.

Isolation of the military from civilian society often had been a stated goal of American policy-makers; Jefferson's colleague, Albert Gallatin, said, "I never want to see the face of [a military man] in our cities and intermixed with the people,"[14, p. 68] and for the most of the nineteenth century his wish was honored. As late as 1904 certain states specifically denied the vote to "idiots, paupers, Indians, soldiers, and sailors"[4, p. 44] because of the prevailing image that enlisted men were ne'er-do-wells, adventurers, or bums. The phrase "soldiering on the job" meant loafing. And in 1911 a federal law had to be enacted to prevent public places of entertainment from refusing to serve uniformed military personnel.

There were countertrends. The military was used in the labor-management disputes of the late nineteenth century. The National Guard was established after the strikes and labor violence of 1877, and the army itself was used in strikebreaking more than 300 times between 1886-1895. Military training was introduced into land-grant colleges through a Civil War law. Military spending also was affecting more businesses on a continuing basis, although this did not lead to increased prestige for the military among businessmen or society generally. The first "battleship bill" for the navy was passed in 1890, and naval expansion continued in the first decade of the twentieth century, with the steel trust playing a significant part in congressional deliberations on the subject. At the same time President Theodore Roosevelt was prevented from keeping American naval vessels together as a permanent single fleet (after the 1908 world cruise), because local business interests insisted that the vessels be returned to their home naval yards where local economies could benefit from equipment repairs and naval payrolls[6, pp. 8-9]. In 1894, faced with serious domestic problems, President Cleveland apparently considered cutting army munitions spending. He was convinced not to do so by the argument that it would cause serious unemployment among munitions workers[10, p. 165]—an earlier national priorities choice. The primary economic beneficiaries of army spending continued to be mer-

---

[3] Sherman moved the headquarters of the army from Washington to St. Louis, to keep it out of politics and to move it closer to the Indian campaigns.

chants near posts (who resisted efforts by President Taft to consolidate scattered posts), and communities prospering from Corps of Engineers projects.

The Roosevelt administration is commonly seen as the beginning of America's self-consciousness as a "world power," the end of the isolation symbolized by the immovable, defensive seacoast gun. The new role was based on a first-rate navy, as advocated by the naval publicist Captain Alfred T. Mahan a decade earlier. The 1898 war with Spain, which had expanded America's international involvement, also led to a so-called managerial revolution within the war department during the Roosevelt years.

The Spanish territories had been won more because of Spain's weakness than because of efficient American military planning. Part of the expeditionary force was sent to Cuba in winter woolens, and military waste and lack of coordination were widespread. In both services, independent technical bureaus received direct appropriations from Congress, had close ties to influential congressmen, and thereby were beyond the control of the secretaries and commanding officers. President Roosevelt's Secretary of War Elihu Root wanted civilian control to be exercised through a single military expert of high rank, surrounded by a professional staff. This chief of staff was to be the "directing brain" of the army, as well as the secretary's adviser and loyal executor of policies made by the president and the secretary. This was Root's solution to the continuing problem of reconciling the need for civilian control with the need for military efficiency. In theory the secretary then could control the war department through the budget and by holding the chief of staff responsible for carrying out his policies[6, pp. 10-24]. Root's approach was opposed by different groups on different grounds. Congressmen feared it would reduce their influence over military appropriations and policy by cutting their relationships with the bureaus. Some within the military traced the beginning of civilian control *within* the defense establishment to Root's reforms; the commanding general earlier had enjoyed direct access to the president as commander-in-chief, but now a layer of civilian supervision was being imposed. (The chain of command has never been entirely clear, since the president is both a political and military figure, whereas the secretaries are political figures.) Jonathan Daniels, Wilson's secretary of the navy, was critical of Root's approach because he feared that centralization would strengthen the military. As late as 1885 the secretary of the navy had one stenographer, one clerk, three messengers, and no professional staff to control the military; just as congressmen favored calculated dispersal of military decision-making processes, so Daniels feared centralization and "efficiency." Such plans, he said, would "place the secretary of the navy on the Washington Monument and not give him a telephone, so that he will not know anything that is going on, but will just 'sign here' "[18, p. 126]. The general-staff concept continued to be a sensitive matter well past the middle of the twentieth century because of the belief that such a staff would lead to greater military influence within the government.

Root proposed other changes toward the goal of a single profession designed to wage war. Rotation between line and staff positions was introduced to end the technical bureaus' power, and selective promotion based on merit (rather than seniority alone) was proposed. Most of Root's reforms were adopted despite congressional and military opposition. Military power became increasingly centralized: (1) It was under federal control rather than state, including partial control of the militia in 1903; and (2) it was in the hands of executive department civilian and military leaders rather than Congress and the bureaus.

A Joint Army-Navy Board also was established for liaison after the lack of coordination in the Spanish-American War. The postwar occupation and administration of overseas territories provided military officers with new political experiences. Despite the new international involvement, however, officers felt the country was unprepared for the Great War which was to break out in Europe in 1914. In 1913 the cost of the military establishment to Americans was a mere $2.25 per person.

WORLD WAR I AND AFTER

Against President Wilson's stated wishes, Army Chief of Staff Leonard Wood began to appeal for public support for his "Great Preparedness Campaign." Not only would preparedness help in case of American involvement in the war, its advocates claimed, but it would boost industry, build a more prestigious military, and spur feelings of patriotism and sacrifice among the populace. Since there was no conscription, the lead in setting up voluntary "Plattsburg" training camps was taken by universities and by private patriotic associations funded by businessmen. Organized labor abandoned its anti-military position and supported job-producing preparedness moves. Chasing bandit-caudillo Pancho Villa back into Mexico in 1916 required a reserve call-up, and Congress then assumed the costs of the training camps. With the strong support of the military, a selective conscription act (to be administered by civilians) was passed in 1917.

No military contingency planning for war involvement was permitted by Wilson. There was little that could be called strategic thought, and defense plans rarely included industrial mobilization, foreign policy considerations, and allied relations. Military leaders maintained that military decisions were framed on their merits without any relation to national or international politics. When war came, however, military officers were involved in civil government, and "they established important relationships with business, industry, and educational organizations" through such groups as the War Industries Board [4, p. 51].

Wilson did not intervene in military affairs in the way Lincoln had and Franklin Roosevelt would do in the future. He approved selection of Expeditionary Force Commanding General John J. Pershing and insisted that American troops fight as organized units in Europe. Otherwise, he left war-waging to Pershing. This was easier than it would have been in World War II; since America became involved at a late stage of the war against only one major enemy, there were no grand strategic questions. Professional officers did not have to cope with political generals raising their own units; former Spanish-American War "Rough Rider" Theodore Roosevelt was refused a line command by Wilson. Pershing and Secretary of War Newton Baker, entrusted with running the mobilization programs, reported directly (and separately) to Wilson on their aspects of the war. Despite the Root reforms, centralized control by either civilian or military leaders still was not possible.

Many of the 116 congressional postmortem investigations of World War I focused on civilian-run procurement and supply programs. "Sliding-profit" contracts and business involvement in "propagandizing" America into the war were the subjects of investigations; the most famous were the Gerald Nye hearings of the 1930s directed against the "merchants of death" and "patriots for profit" (munitions makers and bankers with business interests in Allied nations).

No American war, except perhaps the Spanish-American, can be said to have been a "popular" war—and the Great War was no exception. Ninety-two percent of the married men who registered for the draft claimed exemption, and more than a third of a million men were classified as military deserters by the end of the war. It took some years for the reaction against business to set in, but the postwar reaction against the military occurred sooner. After efforts to sell a peacetime universal military training program failed, the army was cut back in size, and for a few years (except for ROTC programs), soldiers returned to their garrison isolation. For the first third of the century the Marine Corps—which the president could use as an international police force, without specific Congressional approval—was used widely to protect American economic interests in Latin American "banana wars." But it was not visible at home. Naval strength was curtailed only modestly by agreements made at disarmament conferences of the 1920s, but its personnel also were rarely seen. Journalist Hanson Baldwin recalled that in the interwar period his naval officer's uniform "was mistaken often for that of a railroad gateman, a bus conductor, or a messenger boy"[1, p. 98].

In 1935 *Fortune* characterized the "military mind" as a "queer mixture of the clergy, the college professor, and the small boy playing Indian." The soldier was widely viewed as an economic parasite, shielded from the financial responsibilities of civilian society, but also as "the people's poor relation" [21, p. 39]. The army's 1935 force of about 125,000 men was only the eighteenth largest army in the world. (At the beginning of World War II, it was the nineteenth largest, behind Greece, Belgium, and Portugal, but ahead of Bulgaria; the United States ranked forty-fifth in the world in percentage of population under arms.) The army's funds were so tight that target practice had to be curtailed at one point for lack of ammunition. It was equipped with 1918 weapons and 20,000 horses and mules, including 2000 polo ponies,

TABLE TWO

Occupational Groupings Within Army Enlisted Personnel

Occupational grouping	Civil War	Spanish-American War	World War I	World War II
Technician and scientific	0.2%	0.5%	3.7%	10.1%
Administrative and clerical	0.7	3.1	8.0	14.6
Mechanics and repairmen	0.6	1.1	21.5	15.8
Military-type occupations	93.2	86.6	34.1	36.2
Other	5.3	8.7	32.7	23.3
	100.0%	100.0%	100.0%	100.0%

Source: Report on Conditions of Military Service for the President's Commission on Veteran's Pensions, Question IV, December 1955 [8, p. 65].

which preserved the officer's gentlemanly image and life style. (The horse cavalry was not replaced by tanks until 1938.) The promotion "hump" caused by large numbers of officers commissioned during the war made seniority-based promotion prospects bleak; Dwight D. Eisenhower, for example, remained a major for 16 years. "One reaches the top in the Army," *Fortune* quipped, "by avoiding syphillis and reckless taxi drivers, also by refraining from murder, rape, and peculation" [21, p. 39].

World War I had seen a dramatic change in the job composition of the military, as Table Two shows. Peculiarly "military-type" occupations were declining, and the technical and mechanical jobs which would later become so critical were beginning to increase.

Despite closer military-industrial cooperation during World War I and 1930s contacts through the Army-Navy Munitions Board, a strong private arms industry had not yet developed. "No civilian arms manufacturer was able to produce a good semiautomatic rifle for a modest price," *Fortune* pointed out, because there was "no mass market" [21, p. 135]. Rapid technological obsolescence had not yet become an inevitable and profitable part of military weaponry. (In recent years it has served the same purpose for defense contracting as destruction of weapons in wartime.) Inventor Thomas Edison believed that only a "war-mad Nation could foot the bills" for replacing obsolescent weapons, so "we should make our war machines, store them, and when the next war comes, take them out and use them"[21, p. 130]. In large part that is what was done with World War I equipment.

A development which would open the way to more extensive defense contracting—airpower—was being debated in the 1920s. General Billy Mitchell took his campaign for strategic use of the new aircraft—as contrasted to tactical support for ground forces—to the press and people, as General Wood had done on preparedness. However, the strong resistance of senior army officers led to Mitchell's courtmartial and expulsion from the army for public insubordination. A semiautonomous Army Air Corps was established in 1926, and airpower in the 1940s was to become the core issue in interservice rivalry.

The Depression of the 1930s led to the involvement of the military in new domestic tasks. Although most officers disliked the police function, the army continued to be used to maintain order in labor disputes. On the liberal side army officers played a major role in organizing and operating the Civilian Conservation Corps (CCC) and Works Progress Administration (WPA), New Deal agencies concerned with providing employment.

WORLD WAR II

Today's armed forces were formed by World War II and the cold war which followed.

Like World War I, the second war has been subjected to theories of causation, including malevolence, incompetence, national interests, Great Men, and inertia. Few have suggested, however, that military men played a key role in American involvement. In fact, as with other major wars up to this time, military leaders were conspicuous prewar governmental advocates of caution and nonprovocation. Even if they had wanted to urge war, no officers other than General Douglas MacArthur had any congressional or public following in the 1930s, and few had strong executive support.

The Japanese attack on the fleet at Pearl Harbor in December 1941—an intelligence disaster implicating civilian and military personnel—propelled America into the war. Historians have noted a disillusionment following previous American wars, but in this case the war *began* with a relative lack of either a crusading spirit or pacifist sentiment. Despite strong congressional opposition to conscription up to Pearl Harbor, there was less public resistance to Selective Service after its 1940 adoption than there had been in earlier wars. Those who served in the military were not smitten by martial enthusiasm, however; for example, studies showed that less than one-fourth of the ground troops fired their weapons in battle. Public opinion at home was more supportive than in the Korean and Vietnam wars, but a substantial minority was unsure of what the war was "all about," and 15-20 percent would have accepted a stalemate settlement in 1944-1945[13].

Despite their general interwar isolation, military officers had been present at many of the international conferences, and some had had "innovative" international and domestic political experiences[8]. In 1937 the director of naval plans was sent to London to confer with British naval authorities, breaking a tradition of unilateral military planning and beginning the close cooperation between American and Allied officers.

The military ran the war because civilian leaders wanted them to run the war. The Joint Chiefs of Staff was formed for Allied cooperation and for joint planning and operations among the American services. On strategic matters the only civilian control was the president's. President Franklin D.

Roosevelt did not even have a civilian strategic planning staff other than his confidant Harry Hopkins. Civilian supremacy again became presidential supremacy, as the Joint Chiefs were given direct access to Roosevelt. The secretaries of state, war, and navy were not consulted nor sometimes even informed in advance on important strategic and diplomatic policies.

The president was convinced he could handle the generals through his usual method of winning "his way by quiet pressure and maneuver" and avoiding showdowns[2, p. 491]. He claimed never to have overruled a Joint Chiefs' decision, and probably no more than four nonunanimous Joint Chiefs recommendations ever had to be taken to Roosevelt for decision. The military did not propose plans which Roosevelt would have to veto flatly; with the assistance of Roosevelt's personal representatives (Hopkins and military adviser and "opinion collector" Admiral William Leahy), the Joint Chiefs learned what the president wanted and avoided open clashes. For example, military leaders had misgivings about the unconditional surrender doctrine, but Roosevelt was adamant, so contrary views were not pushed. The president did overrule military advice on the invasion of Africa and involved himself in several more technical navy decisions (e.g., the relative merits of several destroyers or one heavy cruiser in protecting carriers). But, in most cases, "even when the president felt strongly about an issue for political reasons, he was reluctant to overrule the military"[2, p. 491]. Thus, he avoided intervening on General George Patton's behalf when the general was transferred after slapping an enlisted man, and he did not press for a military commission for popular politician Fiorello LaGuardia. He also showed restraint in influencing the selection of generals and in replacing them. Roosevelt tried to work cooperatively with his military leaders and expected them to do the same by considering other than narrow military matters. Differences arose, in Burns's view, "not because he was following political objectives and they were pursuing military ones, but because of differing views as to correct military policy"[2, p. 494].[4]

Preparations for the inter-Allied war conferences were made by Roosevelt and his military leaders, not the civilian secretaries, and it was the military leaders who accompanied Roosevelt to the conferences.[5] Officers sat on subcommittees of the State-War-Navy Coordinating Committee. Field commanders also were given wide discretion in diplomacy and politics; of the Allied commanders, only they were supreme in their theater of war.

---

[4] On the other hand, Huntington felt both Roosevelt and the military were too concerned with immediate political objectives.

[5] By the time of the Potsdam conference in 1945 the War Department General Staff's operations division was preparing papers on political topics such as Soviet expansion intentions, U.S. policy toward Indochina, and the terms of a Japanese surrender. Less than half of the 86 Potsdam papers were concerned primarily with military operations.

"Military necessity" was used to justify a wide range of policies at home and abroad, including the relocation into detention camps by the army of more than 100,000 Japanese-Americans on the Pacific Coast. Some military leaders insisted that other foreign policy goals be subordinated to the immediate needs of the armed forces in every sector; there was little civilian resistance to this policy. Even so critical a decision as the one to permit Soviet troops to capture Berlin in 1945 was made by General Eisenhower alone as a military matter, rather than reflecting expectations about postwar international relations.

Industrial projects (some economically dubious) and military "discipline" of the economy also were justified on the grounds of military necessity. In the economic mobilization program civilian groups outside the White House did play important parts; where there was relative calm in civil-military relations on international affairs, there was continual conflict on economic matters. The Truman Committee of the Senate was concerned about military waste—they were accused of throwing away money with a scoop shovel—and the War Production Board (WPB) and other civilian agencies were concerned about military claims for an absolute priority in using productive capacity. The Truman Committee usually sided with the WPB, and the military often appealed over WPB Director Donald Nelson's head, to the president. Because his relations with the military had become so poor, Nelson, still charging that the military wanted to control the entire economy, was removed in 1944. But conflicts over economic demobilization continued.

Private industry was intimately involved in the war effort. The World War I law declaring that weapons should be procured through government arsenals was set aside in 1941 for the duration of the emergency and never reimposed. Military and industrial leaders said the arsenals had not been able to produce weapons which met performance specifications, but the motivations for abandoning the arsenals included corporate profits as well as how well the torpedoes worked.

CONCLUSION

A World War II general, Eisenhower, became president soon after the war—the tenth general to be elected, a figure which may not seem to be congruent with the view that Americans have been hostile to the military. Certainly, military service has been an important prerequisite for presidential candidates; two-thirds of the presidents served in the armed services at least briefly, and in addition to the 10 generals and Colonel Theodore Roosevelt, two presidents served as military governors. Five generals (including three professionals) have been defeated for the presidency, and at least five other generals and one admiral were seriously considered but never nominated.[6]

[6] Support for the only navy man, Spanish-American War hero George Dewey, is said to have declined after he stated that his years as a military man would be beneficial in the White House because they had taught him how to obey orders.

Most of the general-presidents, however, were in the citizen-soldier mold, serving only during war or the threat of war. Jackson and William Henry Harrison, the hero of Tippecanoe, had been militia generals. Except for Grant, the Civil War general-presidents had been instant political generals. Zachary Taylor (called "Old Rough and Ready" because of his unkempt appearance and rough manners) was the first career officer to be elected president, and only Grant and Eisenhower were West Pointers. Active-duty professionals such as General Scott and his namesake General Winfield Scott Hancock, nominated in 1880, were defeated by nonprofessional ex-officers. Louis Smith pointed out that military men usually have been elected for what they did in the past, not because of expectations that they would bring military discipline and approaches to the presidency[18, p. 39]. They have carried a strong belief in civilian supremacy into the White House. Except for the last months of the Korean War, no general has been president *during* a war.

Since the Spanish-American War probably saw the last citizen-generals, more recent presidential candidates have been able to offer three types of military experience: (1) a professional career, e.g., Eisenhower; (2) routine, lower-rank military experience, such as most candidates offer; and (3) lower-rank heroic experience, e.g., former PT-boat commander John F. Kennedy.

Legislation was passed in 1870 to prevent active-duty officers from holding elective or appointive public office, except with specific congressional approval; since then, military participation in partisan activities has been curtailed considerably and politics, in the smoke-filled-room sense, has come to be regarded as "dirty." Active-duty officers had served as secretary of war several times before 1870, but none served in the Cabinet again until 1947, when Congress authorized General Marshall to be secretary of state, then secretary of defense.

In addition to different forms of political involvement, we have surveyed in this chapter the growth of the military-industrial relationship, the cyclical prestige of the military arts, the place of the military in executive-congressional and federal-state conflicts, and the varying meanings of civilian control over war-making and military administration. In the following chapters we will discuss civil-military relations as they evolved after World War II.

REFERENCES

1. Baldwin, Hanson W., "When the Big Guns Speak," in Lester Markel, ed., *Public Opinion and Foreign Policy* (New York: Harper & Row, 1949), pp. 97-120.
2. Burns, James MacGregor, *Roosevelt: The Soldier of Freedom* (New York: Harcourt Brace Jovanovich, 1970).
3. Childs, E. Kitch, "Careers in the Military Service," Military Manpower Survey Working Paper No. 4, National Opinion Research Center (Chicago: May, 1966).

4. Coates, Charles H., and Pellegrin, Roland J., *Military Sociology* (University Park, Md.: Social Science Press, 1965).
5. Foner, Jack D., *The United States Between Two Wars* (New York: Humanities Press, 1970).
6. Hammond, Paul Y., *Organizing for Defense* (Princeton, N.J.: Princeton University Press, 1961).
7. Huntington, Samuel P., *The Soldier and the State* (Cambridge, Mass.: Harvard University Press, 1957).
8. Janowitz, Morris, *The Professional Soldier* (New York: Free Press, 1960).
9. Masland, John W., and Radway, Laurence I., *Soldiers and Scholars* (Princeton, N.J.: Princeton University Press, 1957), p. 4.
10. Millis, Walter, ed., *American Military Thought* (Indianapolis: Bobbs-Merrill, 1966), p. 71.
11. Millis, Walter, *Arms and Men* (New York: Putnam, 1956).
12. Mills, C. Wright, *The Power Elite* (New York: Oxford University Press, 1956).
13. Mueller, John E., "Trends in Popular Support for the Wars in Korea and Vietnam," *American Political Science Review*, 65 (June 1971), pp. 358-375.
14. O.Connor, Raymond G., ed., *American Defense Policy in Perspective* (New York: Wiley, 1965).
15. Riddle, Donald H., *The Truman Committee* (New Brunswick, N.J.: Rutgers University Press, 1964), p. 26.
16. Riker, William, *Federalism* (Boston: Little, Brown, 1964), pp. 17-20.
17. Smith, Dale O., *The Eagle's Talons* (Washington: Spartan Books, 1966).
18. Smith, Louis *American Democracy and Military Power* (Chicago: University of Chicago Press, 1951).
19. Smith, Robert B., "Disaffection, Delegitimation, and Consequences: Aggregate Trends for World War II, Korea and Vietnam" in *Public Opinion and the Military Establishment*, Charles C. Moskos, Jr., Ed., (Beverly Hills, Calif.: Sage Publications, 1971), p. 221-251.
20. Stone, Irving, *They Also Ran* (Garden City, N.Y.: Doubleday, 1943), p. 131.
21. "Why an Army?," *Fortune*, 12 (September 1935), pp. 39-41, 130-136.

CHAPTER THREE

The Military Profession and Society

Military service has never been more than moderately appealing to most Americans, as we have seen. As in most modern nations, conscription has been required to fill the military's ranks during wars and national emergencies. A military career has not attracted the sons of the nation's wealthiest and best-educated families; again, that has been true of most nations in the postaristocratic era.

What place does the military occupy in American society? What is the nature of the profession? Who is in the military and how do they get there? What is its status, and how have general societal problems been reflected in the armed forces? In this chapter we will look at some of the ways that ordinary civilians and soldiers interact.

THE MILITARY PROFESSIONAL

The military in recent years has been made up of 2.5 to 3.5 million men and women, many of whom do not serve voluntarily; the Defense Department employs many civilians, and the reserves (on paper) are one of the world's six largest armed forces. The direction for the American military, however, comes from a small number of civilians and military men in Washington and from the professional members of the active-duty officer corps.[1]

The military officer meets what Huntington believed were the criteria of professionalism: (1) expertise, (2) social responsibility, and (3) corporate-

---

[1] The career noncommissioned officer (NCO) plays a central role in the daily operations of the armed forces, but discussion here will be restricted to the officer corps, because of its command function. Reserve officers and officers such as physicians, who are unlikely to consider themselves *military* professionals, can be differentiated from professional officers in terms of dedication to the military.

ness[20, pp. 7-18]. The officer's expertise is what Harold Lasswell called "the management of violence" or more delicately, "the ordered application of force to the resolution of a social problem"[7]. It is an intellectual skill requiring study and training, not a craft nor an art, nor is it the act of violence itself. Others, pointing to the increased transferability of skills between the military and civilians, believe that the military man is expected to possess multiple skills to do whatever the state requires of him[7, pp. 60-62].

The officer's responsibility is the military security of the state. The profession is a purely public one, monopolized by the state. The subjective dimension of professionalism may be seen as an "unlimited liability clause" [7, p. 62] or unconditional commitment to serve the lawful government. Journalist Ward Just put it menacingly: "The Army is seen as the agent of the state. . . . The one *is* the other. . . . Identifying the Army with the society can, with brisk logic, become the vice versa"[23, p. 60]. The soldier's job, in any case, is to worry about national security, for as Lord Salisbury's dictum implies: "If you believe the doctors, nothing is wholesome; if you believe the theologians, nothing is innocent; if you believe the soldiers, nothing is safe"[4, p. 59].

The military is corporate in several senses. It regulates its own affairs through a system of internal administration which formalizes and enforces the standards of professional entrance, performance, and advancement. It has a body of ethics and a solidarity and cohesion based on the vestiges of the gentleman officer's code and the management of a large proportion of the officer's activities by the profession itself. The uniform and a shared sense of group identity help to distinguish the military man from the civilian.

Within the military there is stratification by rank (usually controlled by the officer corps) and stratification by office or position (over which civilian leadership has more influence). Rank determines eligibility for office, and the precisely calibrated rank structure sets the military apart from other complex organizations.

Janowitz proposed three ideal types of the military professional: (1) the traditional heroic leader, the fighter and descendent of the warrior type; (2) the military manager; and (3) a type not yet fully accepted at higher echelons, the military technologist[21, pp. 151-165]. Despite "civilianization," the military remains a distinctive organization because of its relation to combat preparedness. For this reason it must retain the traditional values of heroism and military honor in the midst of technological and organizational change and nonheroic job assignments. The ideal leader, in Janowitz's view, is the strategic commander who combines heroic and managerial skills with the capability to organize technical skills.

Of what does the military career consist? The aim of strongly bureaucratic, prescribed, or standardized career patterns is to develop an officer who has had experience in a wide variety of command and staff positions, and one who is familiar with problems arising in many segments of the service. Rotation of duty is designed to create a single profession with officers who have somewhat interchangeable skills and outlooks and an ability to master many roles. It prevents officers from thinking of themselves as uniformed members of various predominantly civilian skill groups (e.g., teachers). An officer might spend a third of his career in command (although usually in training situations rather than in combat), a third in staff work, and a third as a teacher and student in military schools. Rapid rotation is thought to form a generalist; it is "the theory of the utility infielder" who, in army language, has "gotten all his tickets punched"[23, p. 90]. Specialists increasingly are recognized as necessary to a technologically sophisticated military, but they are unlikely to become generals.

Promotion politics are complex; formal efficiency reports and proper career experiences help a man to advance, but so do informal contacts which sometimes become elaborate personal alliances. Critics charge that promotion depends on "not making waves" and avoiding bad reports, thus insuring that only the careful and the bland make it to the top. On the other hand, Janowitz found that leading officers in 1960 had had "unconventional" and "adaptive" experiences at earlier stages of their careers (e.g., language training before it became routine)[21, pp. 165-171]. Captain Pete Dawkins[12], a West Point football hero, wrote a widely quoted article asking that young officers be permitted "the freedom to fail" without destroying their careers. As in most bureaucracies, the most respected jobs have been those closest to the bureaucracy's major function: in this case, combat and combat-training operations. By the 1970s, however, perception of ideal career patterns were somewhat less clear, because some officers believed the military would have to take on new tasks to justify its existence in a post-Vietnam setting.

Many officers, for most of their careers, are bureaucrats in uniform, managers without the profit criterion of success. The management style of the military has become increasingly participatory, involving subordinates in the rationale for decisions and seeking to gain obedience through persuasion rather than by traditional disciplinary methods. There has been, Janowitz said, a continuing shift "from authoritarian dominance to greater reliance on manipulation, persuasion, and group consensus"[21, p. 58]. The sheer size of the military and its newer tasks require that it have more political skills, better coordination, higher morale, and greater initiative. Junior officers and NCOs are expected to exercise initiative; this trend probably was accelerated by Vietnam's "total war at the company level," where young company commanders, subject only to a colonel in a hovering helicopter above, were running their own wars.

Motivations for military service are complex. Studies have shown that many officers are "careerist" in motivation, that is, primarily interested in security, pay, perquisites, and retirement—the welfare state provisions. Career commitment now must be reaffirmed by officers who may have saleable civilian skills. In interviews conducted at several schools in 1971, the author and Guy Peters found that army officers most often gave "greater responsibility" and "variety, generalist orientation" as the distinguishing features of a military career[9]. Many officers say they are motivated by a "sense of mission" that is sometimes compared to the total commitment of the ministry. Journalist Lewis Lapham compared the army to the "medieval church, preserving what every good officer believes to be 'the true American virtues' in the midst of a decadent temporal society riven by disillusionment and despair"[24, p. 73]. Some officers point to the differences between the military, which values patriotism, discipline, and sacrifice, and the indulgent civilian society "outside," which is dominated by such commercial values as making money and "saving your own skin." Just wrote "Society's distrust of soldiers is equaled only by the distrust of soldiers for society. . . . The thing that binds military men together in 1970 is the belief that the country is falling to pieces, and the military the only place where duty, honor, country is put above self"[23, p. 60].

THE MILITARY MIND

The military officer has been accused of having, in effect, a crew-cut mind which is narrow, oriented toward rules, heavy on discipline and doctrine but light on independence and imagination. Self-assurance and a sense of purpose-fulness is thought to flow from this narrow acceptance of ways prescribed by doctrine, however.

Like the "authoritarian personality" with which it is often compared, the "military mind" has become a term of abuse rather than of analysis. Nevertheless, there are characteristics of military thinking which originate from the nature of the bureaucracy itself, its goals, and its professional education. "The education of an Army officer does not admit of doubt," Lapham said, "and theirs is not an existential habit of mind"[24, p. 73]. In an officer's education, facts are more important than questions. Officers usually call themselves "doers," not "thinkers." The proper orientation is "can do"; no situation is hopeless. It was an American general, after all, who coined the World War II slogan: "The difficult we do immediately; the impossible takes a little longer"[34, p. 105].

Huntington called the military mind one of "conservative realism":

The military ethic emphasizes the permanence, irrationality, weakness, and evil in human nature. It stresses the supremacy of society over the individual . . . the importance of order . . . [and] the continuity . . . of history. It accepts the nation state as the highest form of political organization and recognizes the continuing likelihood of wars among nation states. It emphasizes the importance of power (and national interest) in international relations. . . . It holds that the security of the state depends upon . . . strong military forces. . . . It urges the restriction of extensive commitments, and the undesirability of bellicose or adventurous policies. It holds that war is the instrument of politics . . . and that civilian control is essential to military professionalism. It exalts obedience as the highest virtue of military men. The military ethic is thus pessimistic, collectivist, historically inclined, power-oriented, nationalistic, militaristic, pacifist, and instrumentalist. . . . [20, p. 79].

Critics maintain this pessimistic orientation is self-serving, but concede that U.S. military men are more enthusiastic about preparedness than they are about war. Some officers refuse to accept this Hobbesian definition and point to liberals within the military; others see aspects of idealism and romanticism in the officer corps. Certainly, military education is optimistic in its tacit assumption that all problems have solutions. Military education also rewards diligence and accuracy rather than insight[28, p. 244]. Professional education and organization necessarily encourage certain ways of thinking (here, for example, collectivist as contrasted to individualistic thinking), but outstanding officers, like the leaders of most bureaucracies, rise above the emphasis on conformity. The military contains men with a wide range of attitudes and social dispositions, as can be found in their pluralistic nation.

SOCIAL ORIGINS, PUBLIC PRESTIGE, AND SELF-ESTEEM

"It is open season on the armed forces," President Nixon told Air Force Academy cadets in 1969. "The military profession is derided in some of the best circles. Patriotism is considered by some to be a backward, unfashionable fetish of the uneducated and unsophisticated"[22, p. 291]. For what groups is the military a "fetish"?

Studies of retired officers and military cadets show that their social origins have been predominantly working, lower-middle, and middle class, as compared to the middle- and upper-class origins of business executives and civilian federal executives. Not surprisingly, rank is associated with social class.[2] Higher-ranking officers have been of higher than average social background. Officers come from higher socioeconomic classes than do enlisted men, and enlisted men from rural and lower-status backgrounds react more favorably to the military than those from higher strata and urban areas. Officers, who were traditionally rural in origin, had predominantly urban backgrounds in the 1960s and were becoming more heterogeneous in religious

[2] Mills believed it was easier to rise above one's social origins in the military than in the other professions and in commercial business[29, p. 192]; certainly, the military claims to place little importance on social origins in promotion—in contrast to the importance of social pedigree at the turn of the century. Coates and Pellegrin concluded from data showing that officers outclimbed their fathers socially that "the military profession appears to afford an excellent avenue of vertical occupational and social mobility"[10, p. 281]. Cadets at the academies, however, have tended to come from families of moderately high social standing and have less room to climb.

background; most officers stress the social representativeness of the officer corps. Once in the military, social background becomes less important than professional experiences in determining the behavior of officers; their orientation becomes that of members of a common skill group, rather than as members of a certain social class.

"As long as the military was relatively insulated from civilian society," and was socially homogeneous, Janowitz noted, "what the public thought mattered less"[21, p. 226]. But as isolation declined, the officer's self-esteem became entangled with his societal esteem. According to opinion surveys cited below, the general public has neither a very good nor a very bad image of the military profession[8, pp. 123-126]. A national replication of relative occupational status was conducted by the National Opinion Research Center in March 1947 and June 1963. Of 90 occupations the "corporal in the regular army" tied for 64th place in prestige in 1947; 16 years later he was tied for 65th place. The "captain in the regular army" was tied for 31st place in 1947, and by 1963 had risen to 27th place. Although the captain ranked below such unmilitaristic occupations as novelist, symphony musician, accountant, sociologist, psychologist, and artist, less than 0.5 percent ranked the captain's prestige as "poor" (versus 2 percent who so ranked it in 1947), while 28 percent ranked it as "excellent"[18, p. 296]. R. W. Hodge, et al. noted that there had been few significant changes in occupational prestige dating back as far as 1925; the professional military had never been among the most prestigious occupations. And the cold-war period between 1947 and 1963 had no dramatically visible impact on military prestige. In a 1955 Gallup poll, adult civilians ranked the prestige of the officer below that of physician, scientist, college professor, lawyer, minister, and public school teacher, and above that of farm owner, carpenter, mail carrier, bookkeeper, and plumber. One of every two adults interviewed said he would be pleased if his son pursued a military career. The prestige of the enlisted man was ranked below that of garage mechanic and just above truck driver, barber, and salesclerk. Male teenagers held the military in slightly higher esteem. The Gallup study noted that "The civilian public bases its attitudes toward military service more on reports from people who have been in the service than on any other source of information. The next most often mentioned source is personal experience in the service"[21, pp. 227, 401].

In 1965 a national sample of the population was asked which of eight careers the respondents would like to have their children follow. Governmental official ranked seventh and a military career was eighth.

The status of higher-ranking military leaders has been studied even less rigorously, but it is likely that a higher rank leads to higher social esteem. In 1945 respondents in a national poll were asked to say "the first words that come to your mind to describe any man who is an admiral." Forty percent responded with favorable stereotypes: "courage," "intelligent," "smart guy," "leader," "big man," "man of character," "refined man," "straightforward," "honest," "strong and commanding," "he is tops." Sixteen percent chose less favorable stereotypes: "brass," "braid," "austere," "a little man," "bluff and blustery," "tough," "stern man," "scrambled eggs," "parade." (The navy traditionally has been believed to be the service having the highest prestige among civilians.) In 1966 a Gallup poll requested respondents in four countries to rank six leaders in terms of esteem. In the United States "military general" ranked fourth (accorded highest esteem by 10 percent), behind "high church authority," "president of a large business," and "professor," and ahead of "cabinet member" and "prince." In the other countries— Britain, West Germany, and Greece—a cabinet member was much more likely to be accorded high esteem. There the general was chosen by 5 percent, 3 percent, and less than 1 percent respectively.

One can make indirect inferences about the status of the profession from the benefits and drawbacks expected or reported from military service. After World War II, for example, 32 percent of veterans interviewed said their time in the armed forces had been a waste. The three reasons given most often for dissatisfaction were "regimentation, too many orders, discipline," "the caste system," and "officers." Samuel Stouffer's study showed widespread resentment of officers for allegedly abusing the privileges of their rank—but 80 percent of the officers were civilians in uniform, not regular or even reserve officers[37, pp. 364-379].[3] Reasons given for satisfaction with the military tended to be "civilian" reasons, such as education, training, and travel. The military, however has received widespread public support as an educational and character-building institution, as is noted in Chapter Six. In 1966, when a national poll offered the choices of having a son serve in the armed forces or in nonmilitary national service, 47 percent of respondents said they would choose the military and only 28 percent said they would choose the safer nonmilitary work.

To what extent do officers desire public appreciation? The majority of 150 army officers interviewed in 1971 said adequate public recognition was both necessary and lacking. A West Point study of academy graduates (classes of 1963-1967) showed that officers were most concerned about matters involving self-esteem and reputation[33, pp. 6-8]. Close association with civilians at the beginning of the seventies meant close association with an atmosphere perceived to be hostile to military service. To the extent that officers are integrated into the broader society and perceive an antimilitary

[3] Eighty-one percent of enlisted men interviewed by Stouffer did not think most officers put their men's welfare above their own, and there was widespread resentment of promotion procedures and "extra rights" enjoyed by officers. A 1946 national poll showed that 78 percent of veterans favored equalization of social privileges and perquisites for officers and men. On the resentment of the military caste system, Stouffer noted that "Civilians might complain that they cannot afford the Waldorf Astoria or abstain from going there because they would feel uncomfortable about their table manners, but they have the *right* to go there. (The same is not true of) enlisted men and officer's clubs"[37, p. 56].

bias there, their career commitment may be affected[27, pp. 137-144].
Reenlistment and attitudinal data for the 1960s suggests that career commitment is suffering. For the 1960-1965 period army resignations increased by
50 percent and air force resignations increased by more than 125 percent.
The resignation rates continued to climb after the Vietnam War escalated; by
1970, reenlistment rates (31 percent of all ranks and branches) were at their
lowest levels since 1955[19, p. 16]. Antimilitary feeling among civilians was
only one reason for this; low military pay often led to a perceived decline in
the standard of living, repeated Vietnam tours made some officers (and their
wives) dissatisfied, and higher force levels brought in a larger proportion of
unwilling soldiers. Some young officers criticized the rotation policy for
discouraging the use of their more specialized skills (including combat skills),
and some middle-level officers felt the organizational structure prevented
them from exercising meaningful responsibility. Studies showed that the
resigning officers included many scoring high in tests of desired officer traits.
It was widely reported in the services and academies that "some of the
best" were leaving or planning to leave—in part, a mark of the military's
successful integration into civilian society. "We are part of the same . . .
environment as the rest of our generation," one West Point cadet told Just.
"Now is not when MacArthur was here"[23, p. 67]. Returning to the old
garrison isolation was not feasible in the 1970s.

THE OFFICER CORPS AND ROTC

Civilian animosity, vaguely delineated in the society at large, was more
specific and intense on college campuses. And it was from Reserve Officer
Training Corps programs on these campuses that the army and air force
received the largest proportion of their officers.

In February 1970 the composition of the army officer corps, by
method of entry, was: West Point, 5 percent; other, 6 percent; direct
commission, 15 percent; Officer Candidate School, 33 percent; and ROTC,
41 percent. These figures may vary widely within a short time period, but
ROTC is always important. OCS was expanded for Vietnam and then virtually closed down by 1970 because of the proposed force level reductions.
The military disliked having to rely on "low-quality" OCS graduates; the
most celebrated OCS graduate that year was Lt. William Calley. West Point
usually produced no more than 1 to 2 percent of any year's officers, but they
were more likely to remain for a career and to dominate the higher echelons.
During World War II, for example, although West Pointers made up only 1
percent of the total army officer corps, by the close of the war they held
well over half of the divisional and higher combat commands. Annapolis
produced a higher percentage of naval officers and dominated the higher
ranks even more conspicuously. The academies set the standards for the

services and provided the basis of "old school tie" promotions and informal contacts. The most distinctive part of the academies' instruction is "character building," that is, inculcating the cadet with the virtues of loyalty, obedience, honor, and attachment to the profession[28, p. 198]. But the army obtained more than half of its officers between the Korean and Vietnam wars from ROTC and hoped to do the same after Vietnam.

During spring 1970 college demonstrations against the U.S. invasion of Cambodia, ROTC—the most visible manifestation of the military establishment on campuses and the one most amenable to college control—became the target of sometimes violent protests. Classrooms were occupied, offices sacked, and 30 ROTC buildings firebombed. Uniforms and equipment were damaged on some campuses, parades disrupted, and cadets harassed. Although 350 colleges continued to offer programs in 1970, and more officers (24,000) were produced, a dozen of the country's most prestigious universities dropped ROTC.

The arguments against ROTC (also see Chapter 5) included: (1) the allegedly nonacademic content of ROTC courses; (2) the alleged absence of normal faculty control; and, more broadly, (3) allegations that ROTC was a totalitarian Trojan horse within the open academic community, amounting to campus complicity with the "war machine." Just as some opponents of an all-volunteer army purported to see dangers of praetorianism, so ROTC supporters said the program prevented formation of a like-minded military officer caste through exclusive reliance on academy "factories." Defense Secretary Melvin Laird said in 1970 that he had been "continually mystified by those who on the one hand oppose the so-called militarization of our society and on the other hand seem determined to dry up an important source of civilian-trained officers of our armed forces"[32, p. 3-D]. Saying "We must resist any attempt to isolate or separate the defenders from the defended," President Nixon charged that "those who agitate for the removal of ROTC from college campuses only contribute to an unwanted militarism. ... Every man in uniform is a citizen first and a serviceman second"[22, p. 294]. The assumption here is that a liberal education will have a greater influence on the military than vice versa.

ROTC enlistment dropped more than 100,000 between 1968-1970 (to 109,000, the lowest level since 1947), with particularly sharp declines among freshmen. Fewer schools were requiring students to enroll in the ROTC program, and the lessening of draft pressures also affected enrollment. Some schools withdrew academic credit from ROTC courses and faculty rank from military instructors. Others asked the Pentagon to pay more of the program's costs, since ROTC was a relatively inexpensive method of officer production. The Defense Department rejected university suggestions to transfer ROTC training programs, especially the formerly ubiquitous drills, from the campus to summer encampments on military posts. "We have no intention of removing the exterior military signs (rifles, uniforms, and marching) from the campus," Assistant Secretary Roger T. Kelley said. "If you have to remove the signs, this is symptomatic of a much greater problem . . . and it might be better for ROTC to get out altogether."[13, p. 2].

VOLUNTEERS AND DRAFTEES

The military's Vietnam-period problems of finding officers were serious, but the problems of finding enlisted men were far more controversial. Early in the war the inequities of the Selective Service system, and later the idea of conscription itself, became increasingly unpopular. Like veterans group politics, draft politics sometimes does not directly involve the military; but, of course, what makes the draft so controversial is that the "little groups of (civilian) neighbors" are drafting young men for military service.

The system was criticized, especially in the late sixties, for permitting higher-income youths to escape service through educational and occupational deferments, medical exemptions, and more adept manipulation of the draft laws. In every state in 1970, the percentage of whites who failed medical examinations for induction was considerably higher than the percentage of blacks who failed; the percentage of whites failing the exam was highest in the northeastern states, the center of antiwar feelings; and examination failure rates went up in direct relation to the subjects' educational levels. The percentage of medical disqualifications rose steadily between 1966 and 1970.

Between 1965 and 1970 the number of draft evasion cases prosecuted by the government rose more than 12-fold. The most famous draft evader was black heavyweight champion Muhammad Ali (Cassius Clay), who pleaded exemption on the basis of his Muslim religious beliefs. When he refused to be inducted, he was stripped of his title and was not allowed to box for several years. In 1971 the U.S. Supreme Court overturned Ali's conviction, and some additional draft evasion defendants were equally successful.

James W. Davis and Kenneth Dolbeare maintained in 1968 that, although the qualified low-income registrant's chances of being inducted were 50 percent higher than the higher-income registrant's chances, the system worked most to the disadvantage of lower-middle-class high school graduates of average intelligence; they passed most of the tests and qualified for few of the deferments[11, p. 129]. The number of blacks and low-income whites in the military was increased by Defense Secretary Robert McNamara's "Project 100,000," designed to induct, educate, and train thousands of men who normally would fail the army's mental tests. (This was the kind of "social uplift" program which was unpopular with military officers who disliked being used as a welfare agency.) Although rejections of blacks declined sharply between 1965 and 1967, they were not grossly overrepresented in the military. In March 1969 blacks made up 9 percent of the armed forces, 11 percent of those serving in Southeast Asia and, since draftees were more likely to be placed in the casualty-heavy infantry, 12 percent of war deaths.

(The proportion of blacks in the army combat arms was rising in the early 1970s, however.)

A lottery system of random conscription was introduced in 1969, and most deferments were removed. But discussions of an all-volunteer army raised many of the same objections. Liberal Senator Edward Kennedy opposed a volunteer army because it would lure the poor, mostly blacks, with promises of "streets of gold" to fight for the rich. Military men disliked the idea of a "mercenary" army and did not want the military to be isolated from society. On the other hand, perhaps a volunteer army would relieve them of their reform school and welfare tasks and reduce internal dissent. They were skeptical of whether enough volunteers with technical skills could be attracted, and others were concerned about how much it would cost.[4] Before the draft law lapsed briefly in summer 1971, despite DOD warnings of serious personnel shortages, the latest time in which the United States was without conscription had been in 1948. The military then had numbered 1.5 million, which was below authorized strength, and the services claimed that troop quality was low. President Nixon vowed to institute an all-volunteer army by mid-1973; although the armed forces were to be cut by one million between 1969 and 1973, they would remain almost a million larger than 1948. The army estimated that for an all-volunteer force of 900,000, a number equivalent to three-fourths of its strength in late 1970, reenlistment and true volunteer rates would have to be doubled. If, as the military maintained, 50 percent of the army's volunteers, 30 to 40 percent of the other services' volunteers, and 70 percent of reserve enlistees were draft-induced, then radical changes would have to be made in the nature of military life [39, p. 17-B].

"TODAY'S ARMY WANTS TO JOIN YOU"

Plans to stimulate the volunteer rate to the point where the draft could be abolished meant a new, appealing military image. Instead of "The Army Wants You," one public relations theme became "Today's Army Wants to Join You." In 1970-1971 the services rushed to eliminate the "irritants" and to "humanize" military life. (A conspicuous exception was the Marine Corps, which vowed to continue to take the hard line. Heads were still shaved like cue balls.) Experimental casualties at various bases included reveille, Saturday duty, kitchen police (KP) duty, unnecessary inspections, demeaning or make-work "policing" assignments, passes and restrictions on travel, bed checks, "hurry up and wait" lines and formations, restrictions on long hair and off-duty dress, and other so-called Mickey Mouse regulations. Partitions were

---

[4] Conservative economist Milton Friedman, however, maintained that the hidden costs of conscription (e.g., loss of productivity and salaries of skilled civilian workers who were drafted and costs of training short-term draftees) exceeded the costs of a volunteer army [14, p. 100].

put in barracks to make semiprivate rooms, and beer machines were installed, an innovation later dropped by the army. Trial visits to bases by prospective recruits were initiated. "Action line" procedures for enlisted men's complaints were instituted, greater effort was purportedly placed on matching skills and interests to jobs, and the words "communication" and "listening" became fashionable. At several test bases, reenlistment rates rose and AWOL rates declined. "The Army was never like this . . ." newspaper headlines read. Army recruiters offered guaranteed service in Europe and billed the army as "the largest campus in the world" with 200,000 men in general education programs and tens of thousands more in training and correspondence courses. An experimental 13-week 1971 advertising campaign, devised by Madison Avenue, brought in 4100 additional recruits at $2600 apiece, the army said. Changes in the style of the enlisted man's life and the salary increases passed by Congress in 1970-1971[5] probably would encourage more volunteers, but the services were left with serious internal problems which could not be solved by their advocating longer hair and beer in the barracks. Civilian animosity toward the military persisted, leading the services in several places to permit their personnel to come to work in civilian attire to avoid harassment. The military was a chunk of America and reflected America's problems—race, drugs, political dissent, and the associated deterioration of discipline and professional standards. Because of the tensions related to the war, the military faced these problems on a grander scale.[6]

The army was one of the first large institutions to be integrated; the first black general was appointed in 1940, and eight years later the services were ordered desegregated. But in 1969 98 percent of army officers and 99.5 percent of navy officers were white. Black soldiers complained of racial discrimination in promotion, unfair work assignments, inadequate representation in the military police, prohibition of overt expressions of black pride (e.g., black power salute), and off-duty segregation. Nine black soldiers were charged with attempted murder and related crimes in the grenading of an army mess hall in West Germany in 1970, and a Pentagon task force claimed

[5] The National Council on Hunger and Malnutrition reported in 1970 that 200,000 military families were eligible for welfare food stamps, and commissaries began accepting stamps. The Defense Department found that at least 12,000 military families were on welfare but maintained that "abnormal family situations," not low military compensation, were responsible[35, p. 13].

[6] Large-scale corruption is a part of all wars, but in the Vietnam War it has been especially conspicuous, which does little to boost military morale or prestige. The army post exchanges and clubs in Vietnam were the center of congressional and federal grand jury invistigations for kickbacks, bribery, and fraud. Charged were former Sergeant Major of the Army William Wooldridge, the service's highest ranking enlisted man, and seven other NCOs involved in running the clubs. A brigadier general in charge of service clubs also was implicated by Senate witnesses, demoted by the army and retired. (In the United States, the army's former "number one policeman," a major general, was sentenced to 3 years in prison for soliciting firearms from a police department for his own use and for future sale.)

to have averted an "ugly situation" by calming black troops on "the verge of violent action" in Germany. "We did not anticipate finding such acute frustration and such volatile anger as we found among blacks," the task force reported; it blamed poor leadership for some of the problems[16, p. 12-A].[7] Verbalized hatred of the army as a white-directed instrument of oppression was restricted to a small minority, but discipline of black soldiers was a common command problem at U.S. bases throughout the world.

Military estimates of drug usage among American soldiers in Vietnam ranged from 30 to 60 percent. Boredom, homesickness, combat fears, and breakdown of communication with officers and NCOs were given as reasons for drug use in Vietnam, where hard and soft drugs were easily available, strong, and cheap. A congressional subcommittee reported in 1971 that up to 60 percent of all U.S. servicemen had tried drugs (principally marihuana) and that about 20 percent of them might be regular users[15, p. 25-A]. The military estimated that 5 to 10 percent of the GIs in Vietnam had taken heroin; drugs in the war zone became a problem in terms of hospital admissions and lowered military effectiveness. The military's traditional method of dealing with drug addicts was to give them a dishonorable discharge. As the drug problem spread, several bases in the United States and Vietnam began offering voluntary, "compassionate," and nonpunitive treatment.[8]

Drugs and racial tensions had implications not only for the kind of veterans being returned to civilian life, but for the amount of control officers were able to exercise over their men. A Pentagon task force report undertaken at the direction of Vice Adm. William P. Mack blamed permissiveness toward narcotics for deteriorating discipline that extended from squads to company commands. Some officers interviewed by the task force felt that "such permissiveness emanates from the Washington, D.C. level down to the lowest unit," and urged that existing punishments (such as bad conduct discharges) be used more often, even though that is what some drug-users were said to desire. The report also noted that: "Many military officers were concerned about the amount of interest that certain politicians exhibit

[7] The deputy assistant secretary of defense for civil rights reported in 1969 that racial unrest was "a pervasive problem throughout the armed forces. . . . In World War II and Korea we had racial problems after the war came to an end. . . . Here, sometimes, we're faced with a problem at the height of enemy hostilities"[4].

[8] Beginning in 1971 a urinalysis test was administered to all servicemen returning from Vietnam, to determine which of them had used heroin recently. By the end of the year the Pentagon claimed a "unique triumph," a reversal of a heroin epidemic, and planned to extend the urinalysis test to other American bases. Although drug-related deaths declined and urinalysis data showed lowered drug addiction, the test was not foolproof and 2000 men a month were still being referred to rehabilitation centers. The navy and Marine Corps were reluctant to offer amnesty or rehabilitation, and continued to administer discipline or summary discharges for drug usage until they were ordered to conform to Defense Department policy. Some outside the military felt that rehabilitation was incompatible with the mission of the military.

regarding the use of drugs in the military. They feel that if the military is not careful, it will become the scapegoat for the domestic drug problem"[3].

INTERNAL DISSENT AND DISOBEDIENCE

Not only were the society's racial and drug problems reflected in the military, but so were its antiwar protests and other forms of dissent. Some of the Vietnam War's critics were drafted into service, and still others became war opponents while in service. Lack of respect for authority, which military men saw in civilian society, now appeared more militantly in their ranks. The military's "fifth column" problems began in isolated incidents but soon extended to most bases, and even to the Vietnam battlefield itself.

Several active officers and military cadets fought through the courts for discharge because of their opposition to the war, but the most celebrated cases of conscience involved orders disobeyed. Capt. Howard Levy, an army dermatologist at Fort Jackson, South Carolina, was court-martialed in 1967 for refusing to train Green Berets for service in Vietnam. Efforts by his attorneys to justify Levy's insubordination by Nuremberg war crimes precedents were unsuccessful, and Levy was found guilty and sentenced to 3 years at hard labor.

To meet their war-time quotas, draft boards were forced to induct some men who found it as difficult to cope with military life as with civilian society. The second longest court-martial in American military history involved 27 of these societal marginals. The 27 enlisted men had "mutinied," that is, conducted a sit-in in October 1968 at the Presidio, California, stockade to protest alleged overcrowding, lack of adequate medical treatment, and brutal guards. The trials, Robert Sherrill charged, showed that "military justice is to justice as military music is to music"[36]. Stiff sentences against the Presidio soldiers were reduced by military superiors with unaccustomed haste, however; a civilian commission subsequently recommended reforms in the army confinement system to upgrade stockades and to remove their control from local post commanders.

Levy and the Presidio were tokens of what was to come; by 1970-1971 enlisted men's protests often were organized and explicitly political and antiwar, and it was this kind of protest which most disturbed senior officers. GI coffeehouses appeared near most American bases, and more than 50 GI "underground" newspapers were published. Founded in 1967, the several thousand-member American Serviceman's Union demanded such changes as bargaining rights for enlisted men, popular election of officers, and abolition of the salute. None of the groups such as ASU could claim the support of a significant number of servicemen, however.[9]

[9] Resistance Inside the Army, GIs United Against the War in Indochina, and Reserve GI Associations assured soldiers that they were not alone in resisting "arbitrary" treatment and in demanding unfettered exercise of political rights. Members of the

In 1969 the army laid down guidelines on dissent wich required officers to impose only such minimum restraints as were deemed necessary to enable the army to perform its mission. Commanders were cautioned not to move too hard against possession and distribution of political materials, coffee-houses, servicemen's unions, underground newspapers, and demonstrations. Commanders were told not to prohibit activities just because they were political or because the commander disapproved of them, but the guidelines were not always followed.

Increased AWOL and desertion rates also reflected growing antiwar feeling within the military, despite the 1-year limit on Vietnam tour of duty for morale purposes. In Korea desertions ran at an average of 20 per 1000 troops. (To be classified as a deserter, a soldier has to be absent without leave for 30 days.) Army desertion rates in Vietnam rose from 21.4 per 1000 in fiscal 1967, to 29.1 in 1968, and to 42.4 per 1000 in fiscal 1969, while marine desertion rates also rose. In 1970 the army reported 65,643 deserters, four times the 1966 rate. However, air force and navy rates were much lower, and army desertion rates remained below the levels recorded toward the end of World War II, when the army (including the air force) showed 63 deser-tions per thousand in 1944 and 45.2 per 1000 in 1945. AWOL rates sometimes rose higher (e.g., up to 150 per 1000 for the 197th Infantry Brigade in 1970) in stateside units suffering from drug-related crimes and tensions among Vietnam veterans. Not even the crossing of international boundaries was uniquely frequent during the Vietnam War; between 1966 and 1969, at least 1400 GIs crossed international boundaries to desert to foreign countries, and in 1970 there were more than 1000 deserters in Canada and Sweden. During the American Civil War, about 15,000 army deserters, known as "Skedaddlers," crossed into Canada; most returned in 1865 when amnesty was granted.

Battlefield insubordination presented commanders with a distressing problem. Something resembling "situational" or "structural" ethics had come to the battlefield. In "The World of Charlie Company" (1970), for example, CBS-TV followed an army company in Vietnam for several months. Camera-men were there when a platoon commander ordered his men down a jungle

---

Concerned Officers Movement said they refused to be "unquestioning agents" of national policies. The U.S. Court of Military Appeals was besieged by servicemen's demands for rights, political and otherwise. Although base regulations often prohibited enlisted men from associating with peace organizations, after 1968 some antiwar groups within the military cooperated with the civilian antiwar movement and even with antiwar groups in foreign countries. Editors of underground papers, pamphleteers, demonstrators, and coffeehouse operators in some cases were transferred, refused passes, or given stiff punishment for various civil and military offenses (e.g., Article 134, undermining discipline and loyalty). When newsmen for the American Forces Viet Nam Network and other military media complained of censorship of the news given to servicemen, several were disciplined.

trail. They refused to move, saying the trail was made to order for a Viet Cong ambush. Orders and persuasion having failed, the officer gave up trying. No punishment was meted out to any of the platoon members, and the brigade officers later praised the men for showing common sense and also for having the ability to think for themselves. Other senior officers were not so sure.

Unspoken negotiated battlefield settlements between officers, NCOs, and their men became common; many commanders, to avoid the blemish on their records from a combat refusal by their unit, apparently chose to give orders that would be obeyed. Combat refusals, such as that of Charlie Company, were still rare in 1971, but officers found it necessary to explain and justify orders in ways that had not been necessary 3 or 4 years earlier. *Newsweek* reported that soldiers commonly thwarted the "green machine" simply by failing to carry out orders, by engaging in "search and evade" tactics to avoid contact with the enemy [38, p. 30]. Field discipline became lax, and injuries by accidents increased. As national policy shifted to disengagement and "Vietnamization" of the war, American units' involvement in combat declined significantly; for the soldiers, few of whom shared the homefront hawks' enthusiasm for the war, the sentiment was to survive 12 months, to get the "freedom bird" home[31, pp. 148-150; 38, p. 37]. "You owe it to yourself" became a familiar GI expression.

Practices of awarding combat medals were criticized widely by enlisted men and younger officers, who felt they were doled out to unheroic higher-ranking officers. Enlisted men's resentment toward "lifers," i.e., career officers and NCOs, was reported to be high, and there was much talk of "fragging" (enlisted men throwing fragmentation grenades at officers and NCOs who tried to enforce unpopular orders). The Pentagon reported 209 fragging incidents in 1970, more than double the previous year's total. The extent of fragging probably was exaggerated by the antiwar press, and in any case, was not peculiar to Vietnam. However, the widespread talk of such incidents—highlighted by alleged placement of cash bounties on the heads of unpopular officers—probably encouraged officers to adapt to the new mood. Costly "Hamburger Hill" charges were no longer possible, officers told newsmen in 1971; what was different was this adaptation.

The military organization was under severe stress. The White House dispatched a general to Vietnam in 1970 to study declining morale, and some military leaders were reported to be worried about the potential disintegration of the army in Vietnam as an effective fighting force. *Newsweek* maintained that it was "one of the most deeply troubled undefeated armies in military history," and that managing a strategic retreat from an unpopular war would raise the question of whether an army "can just wilt a little"[38, pp. 29, 37]. Some conservative military men feared that liberalizing efforts, combined with the officers' difficulties in controlling their men because of racial tensions, drug use, and dissent, would lead to a long-term erosion in discipline. Military historian S. L. A. Marshall warned: "Once you deviate from the sanctity of an order, you're in trouble. And we are right on the ragged edge of reducing discipline to the point of danger"[19, p. 22].[10] Liberal military leaders sought to avoid what some believed could become an "open revolt" by explaining why orders were given. But they agreed that one could go too far in this direction and were no more anxious than Marshall was to repeat the example of the French army—defeated, divided, and politically involved. That the U.S. military, through 1971, had *not* collapsed under these pressures was a tribute to its organizational strength. But General Westmoreland warned: "An Army without discipline, morale, and pride is a menace to the country that it is sworn to defend"[38, p. 37].

Other observers were more sanguine. Moskos predicted:

The probability of sustained internal agitation or even questioning of the military system is unlikely once the war in Southeast Asia ends. With the advent of a curtailed draft or an all-volunteer force, the military will find its membership more acquiescent to established procedures and organizational goals. Without broadly based civilian representation, the leavening effect of recalcitrant servicemen—drafted enlisted men and ROTC officers—will be no more. It appears that while our civilian institutions are heading toward more participative . . . control, the post-Vietnam military will follow a more conventional and authoritarian social organization[31, p. 292].

Battlefield tensions, the sanctity of orders, civilian attitudes toward the military, and more were wrapped up in the court-martial of a first lieutenant. . . .

MY LAI

On September 5, 1969 a public information officer at Fort Benning, Georgia released an announcement that Lt. William L. Calley, Jr. was to be charged with murder. What was not announced for several months was that Calley was to be charged with murdering 109 (later 102) unarmed and unresisting Vietnamese old men, women, and children. It was to be the longest court-

___

[10]One of the army's most celebrated officers retiring in 1971 was Col. David H. Hackworth, holder of 10 silver stars. He said, "The army seems thunderstruck by it all and is openly looking outside the institution to fix the blame. The draftee soldier of today . . . will not become a dedicated, Spartan trooper by drinking beer in the barracks or wearing sideburns to his knees or never pulling another day of K.P. Give this soldier a leader that he respects and the U.S. Army will once again be proud and strong." Retired Gen. Hamilton H. Howze said the military faces "a disciplinary situation, which if not already critical, is at least one of rapidly growing proportions. Should senior commanders not be able to reverse the trend . . . this country will, not long from now, lose its status as the world's first power"[2, p. 8-A].

martial in American history and the most controversial war crimes trial of many years. Unlike the Nuremberg trials of German leaders or the trial of Japanese general Tomoyuki Yamashita after World War II, this time America was trying its own soldiers. And this was not a barroom brawl; it involved a company of soldiers in the field, and left dead 350 South Vietnamese civilians (give or take 100) in the My Lai village. What had Vietnam service done to citizen-soldiers, and what did My Lai mean to the American public and to the military profession?

Psychiatrists Robert Jay Lifton and Peter G. Bourne have pointed to the insecurities of fighting a guerrilla war such as the one in Vietnam [25, p. 1; 6, pp. 1-2]. It was impossible to distinguish enemies from allies, soldiers kept repeating. Lifton and Bourne said all civilians came to be seen as the enemy, a judgment abetted by pervasive racism among American soldiers, which lumped all Vietnamese together as "dinks," "gooks," or "slopes." Thus, atrocities involving prisoners and noncombatants were widespread. Every brigade has its My Lai hidden some place, charged My Lai's Col. Oran K. Henderson. It was because the phantom Vietcong could not be forced to "stand still and fight," and civilians *could* be located, Lifton maintained, that civilians sometimes would be killed to "pay back" the Vietcong for their attacks on American soldiers. This permitted the Americans the "momentary illusion . . . that they were finally involved in a genuine 'military action' " [25, p. 2]. Given the unreliability of American reports of either enemy or civilian casualties, it is impossible to know how accurate this analysis is, but the My Lai trials offered some support for Lifton's thesis.

Capt. Ernest Medina's company had suffered losses from booby traps and mines in the My Lai area in early 1968. On the night of March 15, Medina gathered his company together and gave what many later described as an "inflammatory" briefing about their casualties and what he wanted his men to do the next day to the enemy, who supposedly were elements of a tough Vietcong battalion. Innocent civilians would be gone from the village, he said. Whether he ordered his men to destroy everything in the village became a matter of controversy, but certainly the "enemy" was to be "wasted," that is, killed. It was a unit of "grunts," foot soldiers "who understood they were to take orders, not question them," journalist Seymour Hersh believed [17, p. 57]. The story is complex, but in short, intelligence reports were wrong, the Vietcong were elsewhere, and Lieutenant Calley's troops were not met by so much as a sniper shot or a grenade when they entered the village. But the lieutenant had received his orders.

In his 1970-1971 trial, Calley's attorneys offered mitigating factors for his behavior: anger because of the unit's losses and Vietcong atrocities; hatred and fear of the Vietnamese people, as being responsible for so many American casualties (Calley stated, "There was never any word of exactly who the enemy was, but to suspect everyone, that men and women were equally dangerous and because of the unsuspectedness of children they were even more dangerous"); he felt frustration that his troops had been mauled by "an enemy I couldn't see, I couldn't feel, I couldn't touch—that nobody in the military system ever described ... as anything but Communists. I had an inside feeling to destroy the enemy, but I never met the enemy. We never killed him"[1, March 14, 1971, p. 2-A]. But the defense assertions that "war is hell", that Calley was "a perfectly normal American soldier" mentally incapable of committing premeditated murder, and that false intelligence and adrenalin were to blame, were mere corollaries to the central defense claim: Calley was acting under Medina's orders to "waste" everything in the village. Killing of civilians was so common, Calley said, that he never considered disobeying; 3 years later he still refused to testify against Medina or to criticize him.

Calley admitted to some of the slayings. He said he and his troops fired into a ditch full of "the enemy." He did not see women or children, he told the prosecutor; "I imagine they were, sir. ... I wasn't discriminating. . . . They were all the enemy. They were all to be destroyed, sir." He did not report the civilian deaths in detail, he said, because "it wasn't any big deal"[1, March 14, 1971; p. 2-A].

In addition to Medina, Calley, and the intelligence officer, 20 enlisted men were charged with criminal acts. Two enlisted men were tried and acquitted, and charges were dropped against the other 18. For them the defense of following superior orders was successful. But Calley was an officer, and the prosecution maintained he should have been able to tell that killing an entire village of unresisting civilians was a patently illegal order, even if it had been given. Further, Medina denied giving such an order and maintained he told Calley to make sure no innocent civilians were killed. After 4½ months and 104 witnesses, Calley was found guilty of the premeditated murder of at least 22 civilians and was sentenced to life imprisonment. As this book was being written, the sentence had been reduced to 20 years and his case was still under review. Captain Medina, who was charged with failing to stop the massacre but not with ordering it, was acquitted.[11]

Within the public, both those who had favored and those who had opposed the war criticized the Calley verdict for making the lieutenant a scapegoat; the former said no one should be punished, and the latter felt higher civilian and military leadership should be punished for My Lai and the "war crimes" of "body counts," "search and destroy" missions, "free fire zones," and napalm raids. The army higher command was charged by some with covering up the massacre, and by others with using "command influ-

---

[11] To some observers, this resembled the case of Yamashita, executed after World War II for failing to control his men in regard to war atrocities against Allied prisoners. The Supreme Court upheld Yamashita's conviction, but a dissenting justice warned that the case would come back to haunt future presidents and military chiefs.

ence" to put the blame on lower-ranking officers. What *was* the involvement of Calley's superiors?

Initially, My Lai was reported as a costly defeat for Vietcong troops by Captain Medina, who admitted trying to cover up the evidence: "No. 1, I realized exactly the disgrace that we brought upon the Army uniform that I am very proud to wear. No. 2, I also realized the repercussions that it would have against the United States of America. Three, my family, and No. 4, lastly, myself, sir"[1, March 11, 1971; p. 1-A]. Although Medina urged his men to keep quiet about the killings, word spread to other units in Vietnam. More ridicule than disapproval was directed at Medina's company. "If they had been Americans, I might have felt different," one company member said. "I never really understood those people"[17, p. 75]. Colonel Henderson, who had been in a helicopter 1500 feet above the village, was later charged with failing to conduct a thorough investigation and was acquitted. Reports that war crimes had been committed, despite Pentagon directives to the contrary, did not get past the division commander, Gen. Samuel Koster.

The incident did not come to public attention for 20 months. A former enlisted man started writing letters to Congress, and House Armed Services Committee Chairman Mendel Rivers and several others called on the army to investigate. The army promised a full-scale inquiry. Soon, army investigators came to feel that someone would have to be charged before the news leaked. Results of the investigation were sent to the president in late August 1969. Delay in hearing from the White House nearly caused a staff revolt among young legal officers at Fort Benning, where Calley was stationed. One of them, Capt. William R. Hill, said they "became a little frustrated because we felt the incident had become politically oriented. We feared that he might not be charged because of the political repercussions"[1, February 11, 1970; p. 6-A]. But under the military code of justice, the army had the right to disregard the White House and to ask for a court-martial anyway. Two days before Calley was to be released from the army, the Pentagon told the Benning officers they would receive no instructions but that they were free to file charges if they were so determined. Within a week of the Calley verdict, President Nixon announced he would review the final military judgment personally, to bring in other than "stark legal issues." Capt. Aubrey Daniel, the Calley case prosecutor, said Nixon's intervention, "in the midst of public clamor," opened the military justice system to charges "that it is subject to political influence"[1, April 7, 1971; p. 1-A]. The White House maintained that Nixon was merely exercising the powers of commander in chief.

An army panel, investigating the alleged cover up, recommended non-criminal charges against 14 officers, including Major General Koster who, at the time of the charges, was the West Point commandant. Charges were dropped against all but Colonel Henderson, although Koster and a brigadier general were demoted one rank and reprimanded. Later, a new secretary of the army ordered that five of the officers be censured and that four enlisted men be discharged in connection with My Lai.[12]

"THE BATTLE HYMN"

Before the guilty verdict was pronounced on a Monday, only a few copies of the song, "The Battle Hymn of Lieutenant Calley," had been sold. On Tuesday orders were received for 10,000 copies. On Wednesday 40,000. And on Thursday more than 150,000. Set to the music of "Battle Hymn of the Republic," it portrayed Calley as a folk hero: "My name is William Calley, I'm a soldier of this land,/I've vowed to do my duty and to gain the upper hand./But they've made me out a villain, they have stamped me with a brand,/As we go marching on"[1, April 4, 1971; p. 8-A]. Calley was described as the ideal antihero for a war without glory or nobility. Calley was one of us and he had killed some of them. Perhaps it was that simple.

Reaction cut across attitudes toward the war, and in the first week of emotional catharsis, opinions seemed almost unanimous: Calley was a scapegoat. If the government and army which had trained him to kill would not stand behind him, who would? Letters, telegrams, petitions, and telephone calls were directed at the media and governmental offices. Mail to politicians tends to represent the "antis" disproportionately, but few could remember such unanimity: White House mail ran 100 to 1 against the decision, and only 27 of 11,500 letters received in the first few days by Georgia congressmen favored the verdict. (Four Georgia congressmen protested by voting against the draft and for a stop-the-war-amendment—the first time any of them had so voted.) Not since the firing of MacArthur had there been such an outburst of sympathy for an American soldier. "Rally for Calley" protest marches and "Fighting Men Days" were held. Resolutions condemning the verdict came from state legislatures and city councils, and flags were flown at half-mast in some places. Vice President Spiro Agnew deplored "prosecuting to the fullest" a soldier who may have made a mistake in combat. And a New Mexico woman asked, "How can I explain to my son the difference between the good guys and the bad guys?"[1, April 4, 1971; p. 8-A].

State veterans organizations raised money for Calley's defense. Selective Service board members quit in droves, especially in the South, or said they would refuse to draft any more men; how could they draft men to serve in

---

[12]In 1971 a much-decorated brigadier general became the first U.S. general accused of war crimes (murder) since 1901, in regard to separate incidents, but charges later were dismissed. Efforts by a civilian attorney for an enlisted man charged with My Lai murders to bring war crimes charges against his commanding generals were unsuccessful.

the army, if the army in turn would convict them of murder? However, the passage of a month's time cooled tempers considerably; draft boards continued to order inductions, even in Alabama, where Governor George Wallace had threatened to halt the draft.

Some went beyond labeling Calley a scapegoat and proposed him for the Medal of Honor for "doing his job." A more typical reaction, from 65 percent of those polled in December 1969, was that "incidents such as this are bound to happen in a war"; 22 percent disagreed.[13] Sixty-five percent also disagreed that My Lai proved that American involvement in the war had been morally wrong all along (Louis Harris, in 40, pp. 10-11). A national Harris poll before the verdict found that 55 percent believed Calley was "being made a scapegoat by the government"[1, October 11, 1970; p. 1-C]. In a Gallup poll after the verdict, 79 percent of those questioned disapproved of the verdict, and only 9 percent supported it. Of those who disapproved, 20 percent said they felt the events at My Lai were not a crime, and 71 percent said they believed that many others besides Calley shared the blame[1, April 4, 1971; p. 9-A].

How much the Calley verdict hurt army morale is more difficult to measure. Although veterans groups, enlisted men, and noncareer officers supported Calley, professional officers tended to endorse the guilty verdict. They did not want to be part of a profession that condoned the massacre of unresisting women and children; to them, the Calley defense claim that My Lai was what the army trained its men to do was a terrible slander. Army doctrine continued to deal with the need to "win the hearts and minds of the people," and practical instruction to new troops in handling civilians was not changed by My Lai; to senior officers, especially, My Lai was an aberration. Some officers felt that by "cleaning its own house" the army system had been vindicated. To prosecutor Daniel, the Calley jury was the army's conscience. But the chief defense attorney felt the verdict would pull the army apart from within; soldiers would be more likely to question battlefield orders. Even some who supported the verdict admitted they resented the fact that the civilian leaders who had sent Calley to Vietnam were, in the words of a Fort Benning lieutenant, "no doubt drinking brandy and smoking cigars while Calley is in the stockade"[1, March 31, 1971; p. 1-A].

REFERENCES

1. *The Atlanta Constitution* and *The Atlanta Journal-Constitution*, on the Calley case, February 11, 1970, p. 6-A; October 11, 1970, pp. 1-C, 4-C;

[13]A later survey by the Roper organization asked a national sample "what would most people do if ordered to shoot all inhabitants of a Vietnamese village suspected of aiding the enemy, including old men, women and children." Sixty-seven percent said most people would "follow orders and shoot," and 19 percent chose the "refuse to shoot them" answer [1, December 28, 1971, p. 11-A].

March 11, 1971, p. 1-A; March 14, 1971, p. 2-A; March 31, 1971, pp. 1-A, 10-A; April 4, 1971, pp. 8-A, 9-A; April 7, 1971, pp. 1-A, 23-A; December 28, 1971, p. 11-A.

2. Ayres, B. Drummond, Jr., "Morale Problem Puts Army Into Toughest Fight," *The Atlanta Journal-Constitution*, September 5, 1971, p. 8-A.

3. Belair, Felix, Jr., "Military Stymied in Fight on Drugs," *The Atlanta Constitution,* January 4, 1971, p. 15-A.

4. Blumenthal, Ralph, "Racial Unrest Grips Forces," *The Atlanta Constitution*, November 29, 1969, p. 2-A.

5. Bourne, Peter G., *Men, Stress and Vietnam* (Boston: Little, Brown, 1970).

6. Bourne, Peter G., "The Psychological Effects of the Viet Nam War," unpublished paper, 1970.

7. Bradford, Zeb B., Jr., and Murphy, James R., "A New Look at the Military Profession," *Army*, 19 (February 1969), pp. 58-64.

8. Clotfelter, James, "The American Military and the Garrison State," unpublished Ph.D. dissertation, University of North Carolina at Chapel Hill, 1969.

9. Clotfelter, James, and B. Guy Peters, unpublished research, Emory University.

10. Coates, Charles H., and Roland T. Pellegrin, *Military Sociology* (University Park, Md.: Social Science Press, 1965).

11. Davis, James W., Jr., and Kenneth M. Dolbeare, *Little Groups of Neighbors: The Selective Service System* (Chicago: Markham, 1968).

12. Dawkins, Peter M., "Freedom to Fail," *Infantry*, 55 (September-October 1965), pp. 8-10.

13. DeLong, Edward K., "No Change in ROTC—Pentagon," *The Atlanta Constitution*, September 17, 1970, p. 2-A.

14. Friedman, Milton, "On a Volunteer Army," *Newsweek*, 68 (December 19, 1966), p. 100.

15. Gailey, Phil, "Army Battling Drugs, Alcoholism," *The Atlanta Journal-Constitution,* May 16, 1971, pp. 1-A, 25-A.

16. Garwood, Darrell, "Must End Bias, Pentagon Tells Armed Forces," *The Atlanta Constitution*, December 18, 1970, p. 12-A.

17. Hersh, Seymour M., "My Lai 4," *Harper's*, 240 (May, 1970), pp. 53-84.

18. Hodge, Robert W., Paul M. Siegel, and Peter H. Rossi, "Occupational Prestige in the United States, 1925-1963," *American Journal of Sociology*, 70 (1964), pp. 286-302.

19. "Humanizing the U.S. Military," *Time*, 96 (December 21, 1970), pp. 16-22.

20. Huntington, Samuel P., *The Soldier and the State* (Cambridge, Mass.: Harvard University Press, 1957).

21. Janowitz, Morris, *The Professional Soldier* (New York: Free Press, 1960).

22. Joint Economic Committee of the U.S. Congress, Hearings before the

Subcommittee on Economy in Government, "The Military Budget and National Economic Priorities," (Washington: Government Printing Office, 1969).

23. Just, Ward, "Soldiers," *Atlantic*, 226 (October 1970), pp. 59-90.

24. Lapham, Lewis H., "Military Theology," *Harper's*, 243 (July 1971), pp. 73-85.

25. Lifton, Robert Jay, "Have Americans Become Murderers?" Promoting Enduring Peace pamphlet, 1970.

26. Lovell, John P., "The Professional Socialization of the West Point Cadet," in *The New Military*, Morris Janowitz, ed. (New York: Russell Sage Foundation, 1964), pp. 119-157.

27. Lucas, William A., "The American Lieutenant," unpublished Ph.D. dissertation, University of North Carolina at Chapel Hill, 1966.

28. Masland, John W., and Laurence I. Radway, *Soldiers and Scholars* (Princeton: Princeton University Press, 1957).

29. Mills, C. Wright, *The Power Elite* (New York: Oxford University Press, 1956).

30. Moskos, Charles C., Jr., *The American Enlisted Man* (New York: Russell Sage Foundation, 1970).

31. Moskos, Charles C., Jr., "The New Estrangement: Armed Forces and American Society," in *Public Opinion and the Military Establishment*, Charles C. Moskos, Jr., ed. (Beverly Hills, Calif.: Sage Publications, 1971), pp. 271-294.

32. Nelson, Warren L., "ROTC Getting Roughed Up," *The Atlanta Journal-Constitution*, May 31, 1970, p. 3-D.

33. Office of Institutional Research, U.S. Military Academy, *Perceived Importance of Various Job Characteristics by West Point Graduates* (West Point, N.Y.: U.S. Military Academy, 1971).

34. Riddle, Donald H., *The Truman Committee* (New Brunswick, N.J.: Rutgers University Press, 1964).

35. "Service Families on Welfare Lists," *The New York Times*, February 7, 1970, p. 13.

36. Sherrill, Robert, *Military Justice Is to Justice as Military Music is to Music* (New York: Harper & Row, 1970).

37. Stouffer, Samuel A., Edward A. Suchman, Leland C. DeVinney, Shirley A. Star, and Robin M. Williams, Jr., *The American Soldier*, vol. I (Princeton: Princeton University Press, 1949).

38. "Troubled U.S. Army in Vietnam," *Newsweek*, 77 (January 11, 1971), pp. 29-37.

39. "Volunteers Adequate, Anti-Draft Senators Say," *The Atlanta Constitution*, June 3, 1971, p. 17-B.

40. "The War: New Support for Nixon," *Time*, 95 (January 12, 1970), pp. 10-11.

CHAPTER FOUR

The "Complex":
The Military, Business,
and the
Economy

So long as there have been wars and preparation for wars, there have been "merchants of death," and in a capitalist economy, these weapons producers are likely to be found in private industry. What sets apart the post-World War II period is the *permanence* of the American defense industry and its *size*. No longer were military goods produced in hastily converted plants, but in plants built especially for weapons production; workers were hired not from among the unemployed or from appliance assembly lines but were especially educated and trained for the technical, managerial, and scientific needs of defense industry. The cold war, the speed and destructiveness of modern weapons, and the rapid rate of weapons obsolescence meant that standing armed forces and a permanent defense industry were necessary. The technological arms race of the quarter century after World War II led to the development of countless new weapons with long lead times; some were deployed, most were discarded, but all cost unprecedented amounts of money. Contractors were in the defense business to stay because, as a General Dynamics vice-president said in 1969, "One must believe in the long-term threat"[34, p. A-1].

Joint Economic Committee (JEC) economist Richard F. Kaufman said the danger of the military-industrial complex "lies in its scale. Reasonable men will tolerate a war machine as a necessary evil. It is the size of the machine, its claim on national resources and individual lives and (its growth) that is at issue"[25, p. 71]. Critics of the complex—so named in President

Eisenhower's often-quoted farewell address in 1961—pointed to its economic bulk, and the influence brought by its size. The Defense Department was the primary employer, contractor, purchaser, owner, and spender in the nation. At various times during the 1960s, the Pentagon owned from 27 million to 32 million acres of land in the United States (plus 10 million acres placed under army civil works control); thousands of bases, camps, installations, and arsenals; and several hundred thousand buildings of consequence. In 1969 the value of military property was conservatively estimated at $202 billion. Its true wealth was $300 to $400 billion. Despite efforts by the McNamara administration to unload much of this property, along with base closings and ship mothballings to cut costs in 1969-1971, the economic holdings were enormous by any measure. More important than assets, of course, was the continuing dependence of communities, workers, and companies on $70 to $80 billion a year in defense spending, ranging from 7.5 to 10 percent of the Gross National Product in recent years, and representing services and millions of procurement items. Defense spending is so distributed among industries, and has such a multiplier effect, that its economic impact may be even greater than GNP figures would indicate.

More politically meaningful, defense spending has represented 50 to 65 percent of the "controllable" federal budget (after deducting trust funds); more if veterans' pensions and debt costs of past wars are included. And the Pentagon has said military spending will have to be high after Vietnam, for expensive new strategic weapons. That it is an economic juggernaut is impossible to deny; but does economic bulk give the Pentagon and its allies commensurate political power? Do they exercise public power while making private profit?

In this chapter we will discover: (1) What is at stake in controversies surrounding the complex; and (2) what is the nature of the relationship between the defense establishment and civilian beneficiaries of defense spending. The basically quantitative question of what is at stake involves data on profitability and irreplaceability for corporations; concentration by localities; and employment impact. In examining the relationship, we want to know how the complex does business, how procurement occurs, who initiates the various steps in the process, and who benefits. We also will investigate the nature of contacts between corporate and defense establishments and their members, and the ways in which economic power can or cannot be brought to bear in defense decision-making. In what sense are "free enterprise" contractors separate from the Defense Department?

WHAT IS AT STAKE?

At stake are profits for defense companies, jobs, prosperity for communities, and a developmental stimulus for the economy.

Profits

At the beginning of the Korean War 74 percent of the military budget was set aside for personnel, operations, and maintenance. A wide range of civilian businesses benefit from the spending of defense employees' salaries. Maintenance spending is often for standard commercial items, such as petroleum, spare parts, medical equipment, and office supplies. Many businesses also are interested in this relatively stable market which has a low rate of product obsolescence [45, p. 68]. Military construction benefits local construction companies.

But the growth factors in the defense budget have been the procurement and research and development categories. DOD expenditures rose from $20 billion in fiscal 1951, to $43 billion in fiscal 1961, to $70 billion in fiscal 1971, a growth rate in excess of most areas of the economy. By 1970 procurement and research and development (R & D) accounted for more than half of this enlarged budget. In all, half of the defense funds went to private industry through contracts and this is the core of the complex.

At the end of the 1960s the Pentagon annually signed agreements with about 22,000 prime contractors and 100,000 subcontractors, although the top 100 companies accounted for about two-thirds of the prime contractors' funds. Seventy-six industries, from aircraft to x-ray apparatus, were classed as defense-oriented, with some, aircraft manufacturers and shipbuilders, deriving more than half their income from defense contracts. More than half of the R & D funds spent in three leading growth industries, i.e., electrical equipment and electronics, communications equipment, and aircraft, came from the Pentagon. Military contracts and profits increasingly have gone to newer industries rather than to the automobile, shipbuilding, steel, and oil industries, which traditionally supplied the services' needs. Although contract spending touches much of industrial America in every region, increasingly the companies holding defense contracts have been firms which have little that they can sell in competitive, open, commercial markets. Military production in World War II and the Korean War was centered in Detroit. But contracting has shifted from firms such as General Motors (which was the largest military contractor, during the Korean War, but down to 20th place by 1960) to companies such as General Dynamics and other defense-specialized, defense-dependent, medium-sized firms (i.e., those with $250 million to $1 billion assets). From 1961-1967 10 of the top 15 defense contractors received more than half of their total sales from defense contracts, and some major firms received more than 80 percent. Vietnam temporarily brought old-line, broadly based firms (e.g., General Motors, and textile, rubber, and chemical companies) back into the defense business, often to operate munitions plants and to supply maintenance goods and less sophisticated hardware. But the end of the war likely will see a return to dominance by the aerospace and electronics firms.

Clearly the defense budget provides a high volume of sales to contractors. But what about profits?[1] Are there "synergistic" payoffs in commercial business from military research and development? Is defense business irreplaceable, or has diversification been possible? How much, in other words, does the defense industry stand to lose if defense spending is reduced, if the complex's ways of operating are altered, or if a more drastic dismantling of the complex occurs through disarmament?

The Proxmire subcommittee of the JEC was shocked in 1969 to learn that neither the Defense Department nor the General Accounting Office really knew what defense profits were, and did not require the kind of records and accounting which would have permitted determination of actual profit levels. Without such uniform accounting standards, Adm. Hyman Rickover and the GAO agreed, it was impossible to determine what profit rate was reflected in a given set of cost records.

Defenders of the complex usually refer to profit on costs or sales,[2] while their critics refer to profit on capital investment.[3] Because of high capital turnover ratios attributable to accessibility of *government* property, equipment and financing, contractors usually are allowed a lower-than-average return on the sales dollar, but may make a higher-than-average return on their stockholders' investment.

Murray L. Weidenbaum, later assistant secretary of the treasury in the Nixon administration and a leading academic specialist on military spending, compared a sample of earnings from large defense contractors doing at least three-fourths of their business with the government with the earnings from similar-sized firms whose business was primarily commercial. For the

[1] In defense contracting, Seymour Melman (p. 180) believed, "profits are, in effect, grants of capital from the top management (DOD) to the sub-managements—(contractors) —reflecting decisions to differentially enlarge or support subdivisions of the empire."

[2] A Defense Department-commissioned study, released in 1969, showed that the average pretax profit margin for all U.S. industry was 8.7 percent (8.3 percent for 1967) whereas defense work showed an average profit margin of only 4.2 percent (4.4 percent for 1967) on sales. Using profit as percentage of total (equity plus debt) capital investment, the study reported that a selection of hard goods commercial manufacturers earned 18.2 percent in 1967, while defense contractors earned only 13.0 percent, and that the rate of defense return had been declining for a decade[22, pp. 530-531]. The DOD also showed that excess profit determinations as a percentage of renegotiable sales before the government Renegotiation Board in 1965-1967 were less than 0.1 percent. However, the board had warned that its work could not be used as a basis for generalizations about profitability. The DOD-commissioned study included firms for which defense business was a small portion of their total sales; it also was characterized by technical weaknesses, as well as being greeted with some congressional suspicion because of its origin. Furthermore, other studies (likewise incomplete) showed a much different picture.

[3] In an extreme example, an air force contract with North American Aviation provided for profits of 8 percent of costs, but the tax court found the contracts returned 612 percent and 802 percent profits on the contractor's investment in two succeeding years.

1962-1965 period the defense companies' profit as a percentage of stock-holders' investment was 17.5 percent, compared with 10.6 percent realized by commercial firms, and the difference had widened since 1952-1955. [21, p. 58]. "The large companies," Weidenbaum said, "have done a very good job of adjusting to the so-called McNamara reforms. . . . The smaller, less specialized defense companies (included in the DOD study) that cannot afford to devote as much . . . staff resources . . . have not done as well in adjusting"[21, p. 62].

The GAO pointed to a 26-percent increase in profit rate (as percentage of costs) comparing the 1959-1963 rate with the average rate negotiated during the last 6 months of 1966, although the Pentagon said that realized ("going-out") profits had not increased in this period. For 1964-1968 *Forbes* [1, p. 138] ranked the aerospace and defense industry first in earnings growth of all industrial groups, with McDonnell Douglas and Rohr Aircraft increasing their earnings more than 20 percent a year. In 1967 the RAND Corporation found that, even when adjusted for risk factors, the aerospace industry's rate of return on investment was exceeded only by that of the drug industry. A study by a Budget Bureau official not only purported to show that aerospace firms consistently earned more (on capital investment) than industry as a whole,[4] and especially between 1959-1966, but that the highest profits went to the companies whose weapons had the *poorest* technical performance records.[5] On a sample of negotiated military contracts in 1971 contractors had reported profits on equity investment of 21.1 percent (with larger firms earning a higher rate). But an independent analysis by the GAO found pretax profit on equity to be 56.1 percent (28.3 percent on total investment, and 6.9 percent on costs). The highest profit rate reported on total investment was 240 percent, and the largest loss was 75 percent. The GAO later recommended that capital investment be made a factor in deter-mining how much profit contractors would be permitted to make.

The late 1960s and early 1970s were rough on defense contractors, however; Vietnam was more burdensome than bountiful, leading to financial

[4] Studies of specific weapons or types of contracts also uncovered high profits. Col. (Ret.) A. W. Buesking reported that the prime contractor's pretax profits as a return on investment in the $8 billion Minuteman missile program (1958-1966) were 43 percent or almost double the average rate, although the return on sales was only 9.7 percent. Admiral Rickover reported that naval suppliers were making higher profits, compared with the early 1960s[21, p. 214, and Part II, p. 8].

[5] Richard A. Stubbing found that although the technical performance of sophis-ticated weapons systems manufactured in the fifties was bad, that of those produced in the sixties was worse. Of the electronics systems for 13 major aircraft and missile programs, only four performed at more than 75 percent of specifications. Five broke down 25 percent more often than promised, or worse, and two others had to be dropped within 3 years due to their unreliability. The remaining two programs were canceled. Thus, despite cost overruns of 200 to 300 percent, and schedule delays running to 2 years, less than 40 percent of the systems had acceptable electronic performance[22, pp. 96-98].

and program disruptions. Sales of aircraft, missiles, and spaceships increased by 10 percent annually through the sixties, but costs got out of hand. For 1965-1969 the industry ranked eighth among 25 industrial groups in return on equity, but in 1969 it ranked 15th and in 1971 18th. The industry is highly cyclical, and the cycles were running more closely together. Defense Undersecretary David Packard warned in 1969 of "tough days ahead," and earnings did plummet in 1969-1971 for most aerospace firms.

The industry is profitable, or rather, it can be so, given favorable politico-economic settings. Which period is chosen for study is important. During World War II return on investment far exceeded the prewar rate, despite the Renegotiation Board's success in recovering a fourth of pretax war profits. The defense industry prospered during the Korean War, which combined a hot war with the beginning of heavy cold war spending on strategic weapons. International crises still were a boon to the stock market in 1958-1961; stocks fell when Khrushchev visited America, and rose when the "spirit of Camp David" was broken by the collapse of the Paris summit conference. The Berlin crisis of 1961 led to a "Berlin bounce" in the market. But the Vietnam War occurred during a time of domestic prosperity and high employment (rather than during unemployment as was the case preceding World War II), when political and economic leaders believed the country could have "guns and butter." Inflation was stimulated, particularly within the defense industry where skilled labor already was in tight supply. Contracts for technologically sophisticated strategic weaponry often were postponed, reduced, or canceled, and production stretch-outs were common. "Few industries," *The Value Line Investment Survey* [44, p. 102] reported, "have been hurt more by the Vietnam War than aerospace." Although defense spending on manufacturing rose 55.3 percent between 1965-1967, spending on the biggest manufacturing items (aircraft and parts, and communication equipment) rose by lesser rates—39 percent and 23.4 percent respectively. The 39-percent rate included more sales of helicopters and tactical support aircraft for Vietnam, and curtailed missile and long-range bomber sales. However, it was inflation, schedule disruptions, and extensive overtime caused by heavy commercial and military sales in 1965-1966, which was to blame initially for lower profits in the aerospace industry. The impact of uncertain strategic weaponry sales began to be felt in the next few years. The war temporarily helped diversified firms[6] and it also helped firms such as Norris Industries, which sold bomb casings and other unsophisticated hardware, ranking 13th among the 650 largest companies in per-share earnings growth between 1965-1969. But for the specialized defense giants, the war was a mixed blessing, which later became a disaster. These firms must have

[6] By 1968 it was clear that the war was severely damaging the American economy and most businesses. Peace rumors sent the stock market upward, and the Cambodian invasion of 1970 helped to send it to its bear-market low.

come to feel that their prosperity was dependent not on wars, but on preparation for wars that never came.

Distinctions must be made between return on sales and on net worth, and between profits from hot and cold wars. Rapid technological obsolescence has given cold wars the financial advantage of hot wars—old weapons cannot be stored in the barn, as Edison suggested—without the disruptions of hot wars. The kind of weaponry produced for cold wars costs more per item, permits more technological "gold-plating," and requires much lower personnel costs to operate, thus saving a bigger share of the defense budget for procurement and R & D.

Risks

Higher defense profits sometimes are justified on the basis of the greater risks entailed. In what sense is defense-contracting risky? What kind of risks are faced by whom? Commercial projects can fail to gain customer acceptance and collapse after a company has invested millions of dollars; in defense, no weapons are built until the customer has contracted to buy a given quantity. The risks for defense firms are more likely to be those involved in contracting to invent something: How do you cost out technical problems which you do not yet know you have to worry about? These are what the industry calls the "Unk Unks," the unknown unknowns, and even with weapons that do not carry the state of the art into exotic new areas, they can appear with their attendant cost and scheduling problems.

The financial community views the defense industry as both profitable and risky. According to *Moody's Stock Survey* [32, p. 616] aerospace stocks performed better than industrials as a whole in 1954-1955; did substantially worse between 1958-1963 (reflecting the Eisenhower administration's budget stringency and the market's slowness to respond to the Kennedy buildup); performed better than other stocks in 1964-1966 (as space and Vietnam spending prospects sent some stocks almost straight up); and dipped much lower than other stocks in 1968-1969. For the 15-year period aerospace stocks and Moody's industrials performed about equally well.[7]

The business is regarded as one of feast-and-famine, *particularly for individual companies.* Even when total industry sales remain steady, prospects for individual contractors may be less certain. There is only one customer, and relatively few large-dollar-amount contracts to go around. Thus, most defense stocks have sold at low price-to-earnings multiples, reflecting the companies' cyclical fortunes.

[7] The Value Line Investment Survey (p. 102) indicator of relative strength (with 1.0 representing exact comparability) between defense stocks and the overall stock index moved from 1.0 at the beginning of 1965 to 1.6 in fall 1967 and to below 1.0 by mid-1969, where it remained for several years.

Part of the risk in defense contracting involves public relations. The Dow Chemical Company, for example, was the target of an attempted product boycott following unusually virulent protests on college campuses in 1966-1967. Less than 0.50 percent of the company's sales were of napalm (a controversial jelly-like inflammable material widely used in Vietnam), but because of protests directed at Dow recruiters, the company became as well known for napalm as for its Saran Wrap. Dow's board of directors decided to continue napalm sales to the government and their 1966 policy statement read, "Our position on the manufacture of napalm is that we are a supplier of goods to the Defense Department and not a policy-maker. We do not and should not try to decide military strategy or policy. Simple good citizenship requires that we supply our government and our military with those goods which they feel they need whenever we have the technology and capability . . ." [16, p. 19]. There were protests at stockholder meetings of several other defense contractors in 1968-1971, and several mutual funds were organized to invest in "peace" portfolios. The National Council of Churches in 1972 criticized churches for holding considerable stock in defense contractors in their investment portfolios.

More commonly, however, risks involve keeping up with technological changes, so as to maintain one's defense market. Four companies have been among the top 10 contractors since 1940, and 18 of the top 25 in 1967 also had been there in 1958.

Firms have lost out in technological shifts (e.g., from aircraft to missiles); Curtiss-Wright was the largest aircraft producer during World War II, and had dropped to 45th place in defense-contracting by 1960. Individual company fortunes rise and fall, but does the company lose money? The most conspicuous loss by a major contractor which the air force reported to the Proxmire subcommittee in 1969 was from a prospective $30-million subcontractor loss on the F-111. The Pentagon pointed out that $350 million was lost in 36 programs in 1967. Of the submittals to the Renegotiation Board in 1969, 16 percent of the firms (676) reported losses totaling $215 million, although the Pentagon conceded that the rate of loss was lower than the national average. Undeterred by such figures, 15 Democratic Senators and Alabama governor George Wallace, separately, called for an excess profits tax to eliminate Vietnam War profiteering.

Earlier in the decade the Defense Department sought to increase contract profits to draw more competent firms into bidding, while the GAO sought to reduce profits. The intent of McNamara's weighted guidelines for determining profits had been to serve as an incentive and reward for risk-taking; good firms would do well, and poor firms would do less well. But since the profit spread among contractors had not changed with the implementation of these policies (and their accompanying higher profits), it seemed unlikely that the risk-rewarding purpose had been achieved as yet. Theoretically, the Total Package Procurement Concept (TPPC) held the possibility of higher earnings for contractors *if* they delivered a product on schedule and within cost targets. But it also was intended to increase the contractor's responsibilities and, thus, his risk. The contracts did not prove profitable because targets were not met. In addition to the F-111 avionics losses and General Dynamics' marine losses, Lockheed Aircraft faced a potentially disastrous loss on its TPPC-contracted C-5A cargo plane.

The extent to which there are risks in defense-contracting, for which firms should be rewarded, may be seen in a closer examination of General Dynamics; 1969's leading contractor has faced problems in both civilian and defense sectors. Within a decade it moved from (1) prosperity (1958-1959, airplanes, nuclear submarines, and missiles); to (2) the brink of bankruptcy (1960-1961, due to its commercial venture, the Convair 880-990); to (3) new prosperity and a bright outlook (1962, with the F-111 contract); through (4) years of political controversy; and (5) in 1968-1969 to a $120 million after-tax loss and drastically decreased working capital attributable to navy shipbuilding problems and cancellations and cutbacks in the F-111. The company attempted several commercial diversifications but at the end of the decade 83 percent of its sales still came from the government. The natural areas for diversification, commercial aviation and electronics, already were crowded with companies, many of them also defense contractors. Its 1960 commercial aviation project sent the company back to the more familiar territory of defense. (Its two presidents in this period were a former secretary of the army and a former assistant secretary of the air force, and it employed the largest number of retired military men of any firm.)

Critics charge that the F-111 contract was awarded to General Dynamics less because of its superior technological strength (many military and civilian experts had favored a Boeing proposal) than because of the firm's weakness and vulnerability. It needed a major contract to maintain high employment in the Fort Worth, Texas area. Originally the contract could have led to production of 2400 planes at less than $4 million a plane. By the end of the decade estimates were that production would be less than a third of that number, and costs had escalated to $12.5 million per plane. Related to costs were severe and persistent technical problems: Sixteen F-111s had crashed by 1970. The U.S. Navy and the British canceled orders, and employment had to be cut by more than 20,000 in 1970 alone. But whereas General Dynamics had lost $425 million on its commercial Convair 880-990, it still was expected eventually to make a modest profit on the F-111. (In 1969, design changes made the air force contract basically a cost-plus-incentive-fee,[8] rather than a fixed-price contract. General Dynamics maintained that it was "still operating on the price of the original contract," but

[8] Some cost-plus contracts involve very little risk to companies; rather, they are open-ended commitments by the government. Brown and Root, for example, said it participated in a combine which constructed over a billion dollars worth of bases in Vietnam "mainly for patriotic reasons." With a negotiated profit rate of 1.7 percent to 3 percent of estimated costs, the firm insisted it would rather be where the profit rate was higher, although here the rate was assured[46, p. 62].

that changes had boosted the price.) The company's record looked so bad, however, that it lost out on several other defense contracts "even," *Business Week* noted, "in such a customer-forgiving industry as defense" [14, p. 49].

Defense contracting traditionally has been a situation of more opportunity than risk. Packard, for example, pyramided a several thousand-dollar investment into a several hundred million-dollar personal fortune through defense contracts. Nieburg's [pp. 200-217] story of the founding of TRW, Inc. shows how opportunities can be exploited. An air force consulting firm, started by two obscure scientists with a $13,000 investment and an air force commitment of future contracts, became one of the 50 leading defense contractors and one of the country's 100 leading firms in profits and revenues. Simon Ramo and Dean Wooldridge participated in a technical recommendation study for the ICBM program, then got the contract for consulting and designing the hardware, a practice later prohibited. Their privileged position within the Pentagon's decision-making councils led other aerospace firms to complain, but Ramo-Wooldridge, after absorbing a going concern into their "high-level recruiting agency," continued to receive contracts for which Nieburg said it had no prior competence. The firm was permitted to claim a number of government-subsidized patents, according to the GAO (which recommended futilely that economic sanctions be imposed), and Ramo and Wooldridge within 4 years, "with no known dishonesty," had become multimillionaires.

Diversification

Defense profits and risks are important, as are jobs and impact on communities, because of the behavior which can be inferred from them. If profits are high and jobs plentiful, and *if neither can be easily replaced*, then companies and workers have a great deal at stake in the preservation of a large military-industrial establishment; and, therefore, they can be expected to resist efforts to alter or curtail it. Below we will discuss data regarding defense workers seeking new jobs. What has been the experience of defense firms looking for new markets?

After World War II most aerospace firms sought to diversify and most were unsuccessful except on a small scale. One study showed that in 12 cases of defense industry diversification, all had had some failures. Of 23 internal diversifications examined, nine were profitable, but only after 3 to 7 years [26, p. 43]. Electronics and commercial engine efforts were successful in several cases, and aerospace firms dominated the government's space program. But the only large-scale commercial effort utilizing existing capabilities was passenger and cargo aircraft. Even here firms such as General Dynamics, Lockheed, and Fairchild Hiller suffered stiff losses, and Boeing moved heavily into commercial production partly because of its sustained inability to win defense contracts. Several conglomerate aerospace firms diversified into unrelated businesses.

The defense industry possesses business practices which might prove, and in some cases have almost proved fatal if applied in commercial fields. Industry spokesmen admit that technical performance considerations weigh more heavily than costs. Cost controls would be vital in a volume-based commercial business. Companies are heavy on engineering skills and weak on marketing and distribution capabilities, and it is the latter which separates profitable from less profitable commercial firms. Defense firms, in short, have been accustomed to the adaptive environment discussed below, which shields them from many of the risks of commercial business.

In the early 1970s the commercial dreams of aerospace companies focused on oceanography, pollution control, rapid (ground) transit, educational hardware, and housing, but most firms were reluctant to make the leap without the assurance of the same kind of governmental funding and cooperation with which they were familiar in defense. There was much talk of "synergism," i.e., applying the technology or methods of one field (say, the systems analysis common to large-scale defense projects) to another field (say, law enforcement in urban areas); this was attempted by firms producing machine tools and in commercial shipbuilding. To the extent that obtaining military R & D contracts helps to prepare firms for profitable commercial business, defense contracting might be perceived as essential, but this is not often the case. Most spinoff involved commercial aircraft. Lockheed, for example, hoped the C-5A contract would cover most development costs for a profitable new commercial cargo plane. But defense work usually is so exotic that it has little spinoff value even for commercial aviation. Scientist W. E. H. Panofsky summarized the R & D situation: "If you want the by-product, you should develop the by-product"[33, p. 78].

Defense work for most firms cannot be easily replaced in the immediate future. Further, some defense firms in the mid-1960s indicated that Pentagon procurement personnel were not encouraging diversification efforts. DOD apparently preferred continued company dependence on defense contracting, and the companies were not disposed to offend their major customer. So long as no major arms control or disarmament agreements appeared imminent, several studies showed that defense firms felt little pressure to diversify. Even if arms control became a reality, a Battelle Memorial Institute study said, "most (companies) are certain that the federal government would divert large sums of money into other contracts to provide markets for them"[26, p. 43].

Jobs

Also at stake, even after the 1969-1970 personnel cuts, were jobs: There were 2.5 million to 3 million men in uniform; more than one million civilian DOD employees; and defense-related employment of at least 2.4 million. Not counting the multiplier effect, direct defense-related industrial employment hit a peak of 2,972,000 in 1967. Employment in the aerospace industry alone was 1.4 million. With a few exceptions, labor union leaders were outspoken in their support for large military budgets, by the beginning of the 1970s more so than most businessmen. "Suppose last night," Joseph Beirne, president of the half-million-member Communications Workers of America said in May, 1970,

instead of escalating into Cambodia, President Nixon said we are pulling every man out in the quickest manner. . . . This morning the Pentagon would have notified thousands of corporations and said "your contract is canceled"; by tomorrow millions would be laid off. The effect of our war . . . is to keep an economic pipeline loaded with a turnover of dollars because people are employed in manufacturing the things of war. If you ended that, tomorrow those same people wouldn't start making houses[9] [41, p.8] .

The United Auto Workers' late Walter Reuther tried to convince UAW members that the country would be better off if plants could be converted to production for domestic needs, but at the time he was moving against the tide. The Vietnam War buildup, according to the Department of Labor, added more than one million jobs in 1965-1967, or 23 percent of the total increase in civilian jobs during this period. In all, the Indochina war accounted for 1.5 million industrial jobs. Many of these new jobs were in highly skilled and highly paid positions: 141,000 were in aerospace, 74,000 in transportation, 30,000 in iron and steel, 30,000 in clothing. By the end of the decade, defense accounted for 5 percent of civilian employment, and about one-tenth of the total labor force. (The Pentagon estimated that five persons were affected for every person employed in defense work.) Galbraith noted that "once war involved the conscription of a large mass of low-wage participants on whom the dangers and discomforts of the battlefield fell with particular weight . . (and thus) encountered, although by no means universally, the opposition of the working masses. The Cold War arouses no such antipathy, nor has the modern union energy to spare for . . . a purely intellectual reaction against immediate interest"[13, p. 330] .

But 1969 saw the first post-buildup budget cuts and job layoffs in the defense industry, with several hundred thousand jobs being abolished; estimates for 1969-1971 cuts exceeded one million jobs. Armed forces and civilian Defense Department personnel (total direct DOD payroll: $18.7 billion) also were reduced by several hundred thousand, with cutbacks at several hundred installations in more than 40 states. Small-town government arsenals, activated for Vietnam production, were closed one by one. By August 1971 the number of servicemen, civil service employees, and defense-contract workers had been reduced by 2.3 million.

Particularly hard hit were minority group members only recently hired, and physicists, engineers, and skilled technicians. Half of Lockheed's unem-

---

[9] By 1971 Beirne and his union had turned against the Vietnam War. The AFL-CIO that year did not pass a resolution of support for the administration's war policy.

ployed, for example, were white-collar workers; in an industry prone to white-collar featherbedding (or, more politely, hoarding skilled personnel for future work), an unusually large number of professionals had to be laid off, and some had to be retrained.[10] Since the Korean War aerospace work has required a decreasing percentage of industrial workers, and more managerial and technical personnel. Whether unemployed defense workers can find work elsewhere is important for the political meaning of defense unemployment. Contract cancellation or bidding failure by defense contractors usually has led to intense lobbying in Washington by local officials for compensatory contracts to maintain employment.[11]

What happens if new contracts are not forthcoming? Seattle, home of Boeing's main plant, has seen several employment disasters. After the Dyna-Soar contract cancellation in the early 1960s employment fell by more than 15,000. Within six months 78 percent of the men and 41 percent of the women had found new jobs, a study found, but most took pay cuts, and some had to move to find work; Seattle's unemployment of 1969-1971 proved more intractable, as Boeing alone cut its payroll by more than 50,000.

The National Planning Commission estimated that reallocation of $20 billion from defense to specified domestic purposes would net 325,000 *more* industrial jobs (not counting decreased DOD employment). However, the skills required would be different: engineers and semiskilled operatives would lose jobs to craftsmen and service workers.

A recession and high unemployment in 1970-1971 made "jobs" a potent issue in the congressional debate on military spending. The politically dangerous end of the military-industrial complex always has been industrial employment, and unemployment in defense-dependent areas had hurt the Republicans in the 1970 elections.

Communities: From Prunes to Polaris

What is at stake for the communities with defense plants and installations? Local defense jobs mean sales for retailers and realtors and congregations for clergymen. They usually mean active involvement in community affairs, although defense contractors may bring in "outsiders" with new perspectives and policies (e.g., unionism and minority group employment in the South). On the other hand, contracts and installations mean increasing burdens on

[10] An earlier New York State study found defense-production workers to be more vulnerable than nonproduction workers: of 455 production job types, 210 were closely defense-oriented, and 85 of those were relatively unique to defense work; only 10 of 700 nonproduction job types were closely defense-oriented[26, p. 41].

[11] Galbraith noted that the "new economics" favored by Democrats in the 1950s and 1960s sought to use military spending to sustain high employment and for its general stabilizing effect. Liberals fought for a larger federal budget, he said, not for the things it bought but for the unemployment it prevented[22, p. 6].

schools and other tax-supported community services. There were charges from communities that defense projects keep other businesses out and (e.g., by high wages) make conditions rough for local businesses.

Since 1953 California has been the nation's leading defense contracting state. Its Santa Clara Valley used to be known as "the prune capital of the world." Since the Korean War the Valley city of Sunnyvale has become "the Polaris-Poseidon capital of the world." From a 1940 population of 4373 Sunnyvale had grown to 95,000 three decades later and had become almost totally dependent on military spending for the continued prosperity of its highly mobile, predominantly white, working middle-class families with an average annual income of $11,000. One defense firm alone had a weekly payroll of $6 million. City leaders hoped for an early end to the Vietnam War, with expectations that it would loosen funds for spending on more sophisticated weaponry, but not end international arms competition[12] [31, p. 77]. Dependency is a double-edged sword, and in 1970 aerospace industry engineers, technicians, and executives accounted for more than a third of the county's unemployed.

Although about 5300 American communities had at least one defense plant or company with defense contracts in 1968 and hundreds more had military installations, defense spending is concentrated by geographic region, no less than it is by industry and company. In the mid-1960s Newport News-Hampton, Virginia received almost $900 per capita in unclassified prime military contracts, and Bridgeport, Connecticut got over $750 per capita. South Bend, Indiana received $700 per capita, while in the same state the Gary-Hammond-East Chicago area received $4.12 per capita in defense contracts[20, pp. 10-12]. Those with economic stakes in defense decision-making, therefore, are concentrated in certain states and congressional districts. Concentrated interest groups are believed to have more leverage in Congress and other political arenas because (1) representation and electoral voting is on a geographic basis, and (2) groups can be more easily mobilized, with fewer counterpressures, when supporters are close to each other. In

[12] Smaller-scale dependency could be found in Hermiston, Oregon, where in 1969, 750 people in a town of 5000 were employed by an army depot which stored poison gas. Although state officials opposed the army's plans to ship more poison gas from Okinawa to Hermiston, local citizens supported the army. When a nerve-gas accident at Dugway Proving Grounds in defense-dependent Utah killed 6400 sheep in 1968, state officials were no more anxious than the army to dramatize the incident. Other communities have responded differently. In 1969 Libertyville, Illinois (a Chicago suburb) was not anxious to receive an ABM site, for example, and some Wisconsin residents were not sanguine about the navy "Sanguine" program there. One of the most heated community controversies occured in 1960, when Tucson, Arizona was to be ringed by Titan missiles; despite scientists' warnings about how the wind might carry nuclear fallout, the dominant sentiment there was to welcome the defense money.

1960 presidential candidate Richard Nixon was reported to have persuaded President Eisenhower to authorize additional funds for the B-70, being built in vote-heavy California, and in 1968 Nixon made a strong pledge to support the F-111 project in similarly crucial Texas. Other candidates have done the same.

California receives almost $7 billion in procurement funds annually, and more in DOD payroll. In the 1950s defense-spending accelerated California's industrial and population expansion, as New York business and political leaders expressed concern about their state's loss of preeminence. California firms have held 17 to 24 percent of production awards, and sometimes more than 40 percent of defense R & D contracts. California's rise was associated with (1) the shift to procurement (from 20 percent of the total defense budget in fiscal 1951 to 35.4 percent in fiscal 1960) and R & D (from 3.8 percent to 8 percent); and (2) the shift within procurement and R & D from conventional land and sea weapons to aircraft and later missiles, both requiring sophisticated electronic equipment. The shift from aircraft to missiles temporarily threw 60,000 people out of work in California, but the state soon became the missile leader as well. Bigness, it is said, leads to further bigness, and the giant aircraft companies created by World War II were believed to be most capable of taking responsibility for the overall development of complex weapons systems. By 1970 Los Angeles County alone received more defense contracts than many of the midwestern and northeastern states which once had played important roles. The decline of military orders to the midwestern automobile industry was most notable, e.g., defense employment in Michigan falling from a high of 220,000 during the Korean War to 40,000 in 1960, while the state's share of contracts was cut from 9.5 percent to less than 3 percent [45, p. 79]. Texas became the second-ranking defense state with contracts up from $1 billion in 1962 to $3.5 to $4.1 billion in the late 1960s.

Less wealthy areas of the country were even more dependent on defense spending—states such as Utah and New Mexico in the west and Georgia and Virginia in the south, and cities such as Wichita. A study of potential defense cutbacks in Baltimore showed there would be relatively little impact; a study of New Mexico in the mid-sixties, however, showed that over half of the state's revenue was derived from military activities[26, p. 43]. Several far-western states experienced declining military-stimulated employment even during the Vietnam War, as missile orders declined, and the 1969-1970 defense budget cuts brought further job losses. In at least half a dozen states the defense industry accounted for more than 20 percent of all manufacturing jobs and for 6 percent of the total labor force. Nine states in 1968 had over $200 per capita in prime military contracts, and subcontracting did not significantly alter this pattern of concentration; 13 states received more than double their "fair share" (based on state income) of direct military payrolls.[13] The Council of Economic Advisers in 1969 conceded that no governmental studies had been conducted on the regional impact of defense spending and employment, so we are left with data on its percentage contribution to local economies, rather than causation information.

Georgia is an example of the intimate relationship between political, military, and economic factors. The presence until 1964 of Richard Russell and Carl Vinson, two Georgians, as chairmen of Senate and House Armed Services committees probably was not unrelated to (1) the location in Georgia of 13 major military installations; and (2) the increase in procurement contracts for its one-company aerospace industry, Lockheed, which in 1969 was the largest industrial organization and the largest employer in the southeast. Georgia was one of the few states to rank among the top ten in prime-contract awards, civilian defense payroll, military payroll, and increased employment from the Vietnam War. About 15 percent of the state's gross annual product came from defense.

In the late 1960s private industry and research institutions in Georgia were awarded between $950 and $1150 million a year in military contracts. Salaries of military men and civilians employed at installations amounted to nearly $1 billion, and was a more stable factor despite significant 1969-1970 payroll reductions at most bases. The bases spent $150 million a year on local procurement, and more money for construction.[14] Among the 11,000 Georgia firms classified as defense contractors were companies providing rocket boosters, armored vehicles, ammunition components, practice bombs and ammo boxes, plastic sandbags, electrical items, chemicals, military photo supplies, tropical combat boots, and rabies vaccine for the K-9 Corps. The state ranked third in the nation in production of textiles and clothing for the military, and even supplied several thousand dollars worth of peanut butter[47, pp. 63, 65]. But the bulk of its defense business (about $750 million a year) went to Lockheed-Georgia for air frames, assemblies, and

---

[13] In the fifties and sixties, congressmen from economically depressed areas often asked for defense contracts to boost local economies. The Labor Department supplied DOD with a list of several hundred areas of high unemployment, and some contracts were set aside for them. In 1971 Congress voted to make areas hit by high unemployment, including such aerospace cities as Seattle, eligible for the same type of disaster assistance available to areas hit by hurricanes or floods. (Limited federal conversion assistance had been available to communities previously.)

[14] For the full economic impact, funds from the reserve programs, Atomic Energy Commission, Army Corps of Engineers, retired military careerists (20,000 in Georgia), and the Veterans Administration ($280 million in annual benefits for Georgia) should be included. Georgia suffered more than any other state when lower draft calls and reduced manpower led to cutbacks in 1968-1970 in base employment and military payrolls (35,000 jobs in 2 years, or a 23-percent decline).

The Army Corps of Engineers, with its river and harbor programs, has had the longest impact on most communities, but it is separately administered for civil purposes.

spare parts. The county where Lockheed's partially government-owned Air Force Plant No. 6 is located was among the five most dependent counties in the nation. Lockheed employees came from and spent their $6 million weekly payroll in more than 80 Georgia counties, and tens of millions of dollars were subcontracted to Georgia firms. Between 1961-1968 the county's total wages rose from $33 million to $85 million a quarter, as plant employment rose from 13,000 to 30,000. The county's retail sales almost tripled, population increased almost 60 percent, the price per acre of land doubled, and unemployment dropped to less than 1 percent. The company paid nearly $1 million a year in local taxes and brought in additional federal "impacted area" school funds.

When Bell Aircraft stopped making B-29s at the government plant after World War II and 32,000 people lost their jobs, Marietta Mayor L. Howard Atherton said, "it felt like the end of the world, but it wasn't so bad." Atherton said the Bell employees were transients. When they left Marietta became a ghost town until Lockheed moved in. "Now it's different, Lockheed people are much more solid, they pay their bills, participate in the community life. They couldn't just move away"[2, p. 28]. Lockheed's capital investment had increased over the years, and the futures of the company and the community were intertwined. They shared concern about where the next defense contract was coming from.

In the early 1960s they had worried about what would take the place of the C-141 when that contract ended. Lockheed and Boeing were in competition for the C-5A cargo plane contract, and Senator Russell's intervention (upon constituent urging) was thought to have played a key role in getting Lockheed the contract (see Chapter 7). Similarly, local officials responded with lobbying efforts when the air force announced in 1969 that it would halt C-5A procurement at less than the original contract had called for. Employment at Lockheed was cut back sharply, since half of its workers were involved in C-5A production. If Lockheed were to shut down, officials estimated the county's economy would be cut by at least 50 percent. A local union official said, "I guess it would be like the 1930s again"[29, p.33].

IN SEARCH OF CONSPIRACIES AND PUPPETS

Which comes first—the corporation's need to sell a weapon or the perceived strategic need for the weapon? Are we dealing with an industrial-military or a military-industrial or simply an industrial-political establishment? And who benefits?

In this section we will examine the nature of the relationship whereby military "needs" are translated into forces-in-being. Is the defense industry really a Frankenstein's monster threatening to swallow up the government departments which brought it into being? Or have defense corporations been turned into regulated utilities? Has private enterprise been lured and coerced into a Contract State, where the lines between private and public industry have disappeared so that everyone works for the good of the state bureaucracy? Are business and its civilian and military customers in some kind of symbiotic conspiracy to defraud the American people? Or are they patriotically bringing together their technical expertise, management capabilities, and productive facilities?

We are now entering, in the words of critic Reuther, a "complex maze of rituals and procedures whereby weapons systems are born and die, or so frequently prolong their existence in a stretched-out limbo of half-life, acquiring new names and numbers"[22, p. 425]. This is the key point at which the complex does business: the $35 to $45 billion worth of annual procurement decisions. It is a world in which cost overruns are "cost growth" over extended "time frames," in which "progress payments" are unrelated to developmental progress, and in which "competitive" bidding (prior to 1967) could involve only one bidder and rarely involved advertising. Problems created by excessive costs are called "funding problems." It is a world of "fixed-price-plus-incentive-fee," "probable costing" and "should costing," "undefinitized contracts," "contract incentives" and "contract nourishment," "tracking system," "buy-in," "thresholds," "procurement career development programs," "fat," "state of the art procurement," "gold plating," "MTBF" (Mean Time Between Failure), "going-in" versus "going-out" profits, "cure notice," and "get well." It is a world in which contractors seek to be long-term, "sole-source suppliers" in a "cost-plus environment."

The nature of the complex brings sharp disagreement: Critics find it threatening; defenders say it does not exist and, even if it does, it is necessary. "There may be a military-industrial complex," William W. Kaufmann noted, "but no one has yet found its address and telephone number"[22, p. 167]. And Chairman of the Joint Chiefs of Staff Gen. Earle G. Wheeler agreed in 1969, "If I'm in a conspiracy, I have yet to meet my fellow conspirators." Anyway, he said, the complex is not a "malignant, semiautonomous, conspiratorial grouping dedicated to foisting off unneeded weapons on our fellow countrymen," but a group of patriots doing their job[36, p. 20].

Most critics agree that the complex is not a conspiracy in the consciously malevolent style of cabalistic "merchants of death" wearing diamond tiepins.[15] Rather, it is conceived of as an open conspiracy of integrated institutions with parallel goals. The most charitable criticism would be that events combine to bring about a preponderant allocation of resources to defense. There are examples of conflicts of interest and illicit collusion in the cause of weapons or profits, although businessmen maintain this is rare because of competitive pressures. Most critics, while avoiding the scandal-

---

[15] Military supporter Rep. F. Edward Hébert dismissed the complex notion as "an idiot's delight—the idea of scurvy figures running around trying to promote wars"[9, p. 54].

mongering approach to the complex, could not agree that it just grew, like Topsy, from the momentum of faceless events. "The problem," Galbraith[13, p. 30] said, "is not conspiracy or corruption but unchecked rule." Rather than search for bad men, these critics urged bringing the system of relationships under control by undermining the military-industrial coincidence of bureaucratic and pecuniary interests.

Men are involved: usually well-intentioned, moral men, who "conspire," i.e., cooperate and plan, constantly and often openly because that is their job. Like other men, those working for contractors and military departments are committed to the goals of their organizations; because the goals tend to be complementary, they also are committed to the goals of most of the other organizations in the weapons "team": what's good for General Dynamics is good for the air force is good for America. ... Each component of the complex, by protecting its own interests, maximizes the collective power of the complex.

To determine which part of the complex controls the others, we need to know which is the initiator and which benefits the most. "In the conspiratorial view," Galbraith[12, pp. 23, 27] said, "the ... goal is mutual enrichment (of generals and conniving industrialists). ... The industrialists are the *deus ex machina*; their agents make their way around Washington arranging the payoff." Thus, conspiracy theories focus on the role of industrialists. "Since they are the people who make the most money, they are assumed to be the men who ... pull the strings. The armed forces are assumed to be in some measure their puppets."

With the dismantling of government "in-house" capabilities to design weapons (and the leasing to corporations of many government plants in the 1940s and 1950s), the Pentagon became dependent on the defense industry for weapons innovation as well as for production. Without service arsenal and shipyard weapons-development capabilities, there is no "cost yardstick" other than that provided by contractors themselves[33, p. 218]. The military is partly dependent on business for political defense of service missions. Control of contractors also may be weakened by long lead-time procurement contracts. The C-5A contract ran more than three times the term of a congressman and more than twice the tour of duty of almost everyone in the Pentagon.

Business leaders scoffed at the notion that they could control the Pentagon. "I don't see anything improper in the relationship between the military and industry," General Dynamics President Roger Lewis said:

Any analogy between this country and prewar Germany or Japan simply won't stand up. We do not have a strongly centralized government as they did and further, there are some 40,000 companies doing defense work. ... There are the numerous echelons of authority both within the executive branch and within the Congress. ... and lastly, the whole procurement operation is done through a free enterprise system. The competition is more severe, the risks are usually greater, and the profits are lower . . . than in commercial business [19, p. 9].[16]

Defense Department officials, with the exception of an occasional skeptic such as Gen. James Gavin who was R & D chief in the fifties, have expressed confidence in their ability to check pressures from their industrial partners. Former Air Force Secretary Eugene M. Zuckert said, "Sure, there's a chance of abuse in any large power concentration, but . . . you've got to consider what the 'complex' does for you. Without it, how can you get the weapons we need. . . . I think an alert public opinion and strong civilian control of the President will guard satisfactorily against the dangers of abuse" [9, p. 54]. Secretary of Defense Clark Clifford told a contractors' association in 1968 that he was sure the dangers President Eisenhower had warned against "were real dangers. But I am also convinced that they have been avoided through the checks and balances of our governmental system." His predecessor, McNamara, was under heavy corporate and military pressure for specific weapons systems. He claimed to have "lost" only 2 percent of his battles with the complex, and these because his case was not presented well enough. Asked if he shared Eisenhower's concern, he said in 1968: "I don't, as long as the Secretary of Defense operates as he should, examines all factors of a problem and makes decisions on his own analysis, regardless of the pressures applied to him" [42, p. 5]. Those, however, are big "ifs."

● ● ●

Most industry and DOD officials would moot the question of who benefits from the complex by maintaining that the country does, that only through close cooperation could weapons be produced successfully. But let us pursue the beneficiary question further.

Seymour Melman has pointed to two main theories of American civil-military and defense-business relations. The first, said to be espoused by the DOD and most political scientists and political spokesmen, is that "the military establishment is nothing more than the traditional, constitutionally ordained, military arm of the civil state. The fact that it is larger and more powerful than in the past is blamed . . . on external events. . . ." The Marxist theory, on the other hand, sees the military establishment serving two purposes. "The first is the aggressive promotion of the interests of the capitalist order against the revolutionary forces . . . of the third world. The second is the creation, with the implicit blessing of the business community, of an area of production that is totally noncompetitive with the normal economy, allowing capitalism to find an expansive salient without which the system would suffer from glut, falling profits, and inner crises" [17, p. 6].

[16] On the other hand, economist Robert Heilbroner (p. 6) compared the U.S. complex to "the ambiguous relationships between the chieftains of big business and the fascist movements in Italy and Germany—relationships in which business at first welcomed but then lived to regret fascist power, which took over in its own right."

Both theories "assert the predominance of the civilian interests over the military." It is the "people" or the "capitalists" who command, and the military who obeys.

Melman suggested a third theory, "that the military establishment has constituted itself as a self-contained entity, capable of . . . imposing its will not only on the civil establishment to which it pays a ritual obeisance, but over a section of the economy in which the language of private enterprise is merely a fiction to hide its absolute authority"[17, p. 6]. (Here Melman speaks of the military establishment as including all DOD leaders.)

Barnet wrote:

The defense contract is much like the royal franchise under which the King[17] used to give private interests the right to make money from colonies while at the same time advancing the interests of the Crown. Much of the power of the Pentagon, like that of the King, derives from its broad discretion to make private fortunes for its clients. But, . . . as Melman has noted, it is the Pentagon and not the clients whose interests are paramount. In the DOD the leading defense contractors are regarded as subsidiaries that must be protected for the benefit of the whole system[3, p. 120].

These critics justifiably would waste little sympathy on McNamara and Laird, because they believe it is the Defense Department which dominates the complex. They see the complex working toward the maintenance and expansion of bureaucratic empires, not businesses. DOD is more necessary to defense firms than vice versa; it can decide whether they profit or even survive. The concentration of power in the Pentagon can be matched by no combination of defense firms. The contractors, in this view, are kept in existence only because they serve the Pentagon's interests. Where the interests of the two appear to diverge, the Defense Department, with the ultimate decision on funds allocation, and several contractors from which to choose, has the upper hand. Individual company fortunes rise and fall. And large contractors cannot prevent the Pentagon from awarding desired contracts to competitors, canceling them (e.g., Lockheed's Cheyenne helicopter for which the army refused to ease specifications or to stretch out schedules, at least in 1969), or joining in government action against business decisions (e.g., moves against steel, aluminum, and copper price hikes in the 1960s). But the interests of DOD and industry do not often diverge.

[17] The king analogy has been popular. Newsweek[31, p.80] compared the complex to "a King bestowing favors on the ministers and knights in his court. The King needs the support of all against some future war or emergency. He dips into his treasury . . . to bestow boons upon them . . . for good service." Translated, that becomes: the government fears that in an emergency, sufficient military strength cannot be amassed unless there is a defense industrial "base in being," and is willing to assure economic security in return for this base. Or, in Heilbroner's (p. 5) analogy, the king "takes care to shore up the weaker members [vassals] lest by their disappearance the boundaries of the inner state shrink."

PROCUREMENT RELATIONSHIPS: THE CHICKEN AND THE EGG

The parameters of the Defense Department procurement bureaucracy are variously set to include 5,500, 40,000, and 55,000 people to arrange terms of contracts; to administer, oversee, and carry out contractual arrangements; and to provide supporting services. Final decisions on major weapons during the 1960s were made by "teams" (a key word[18]) of about 200 scientists, military men, and bureaucrats, although many civilians and military men further down the line also were empowered to make significant procurement decisions. To run the military business takes 15 million purchasing decisions each year, and many more administrative decisions[17, p. 5].

Who takes the first step? Do new weapons originate in the design shops of contractors to be "sold" to the Pentagon, or do corporations respond to itemized requests from the Pentagon? The elements of the teams have become so cooperative so early in the procurement process that it becomes difficult to determine who initiates the hardware proposals and who responds to them. "The day is past," the president of the Air Force Association (a corporate executive) noted in 1959:

when the military requirement for a major weapons system is set by the military and passed on to industry to build the hardware. Today it is more likely that the military requirement is the result of joint participation of military and industrial personnel, and it is not unusual for industry's contribution to be a key factor. Indeed, there are highly placed military men who sincerely feel that industry currently is setting the pace in the research and development of new weapons systems[9, p. 57].

A decade later a North American Rockwell executive said: "A new system usually starts with a couple of military and industry people getting together to discuss common problems. . . . It isn't a case of industry here and government here. They are interacting continuously at the engineering level." Industry tries to "foresee the requirements the military is going to have three years off," another corporation executive said in 1969. "We work with their requirements people and therefore get new business"[34, p. A-18].

Before World War II selling weapons was more difficult. Military or arsenal engineers usually decided what improvements or innovations were needed, designed and developed the weapons, and then called on industry to produce the hardware in quantity. But in a period of a little over a year in the late 1950s, for example, the navy alone received 486 unsolicited bids for new weapons systems plus other, more serious informal contacts. The navy had designed its own vessels for almost two centuries until the 1960s when the FDL cargo and LHA assault ships were contracted out. In 1969 the navy, for

[18] There are DOD-industry teams and there are managerial-technical teams within companies; both types are seen by DOD as national assets to be preserved through adversity.

the first time, gave up design of a major combat ship (the new class of destroyers, DD-963) to private industry.

The building of the Polaris missile, plotted out at a 1955 secret session with scientists and contractors, and eventually involving 20,000 subcontractors and suppliers, is pointed to as an example of the complex at its most efficient[31, p. 79]. Despite the enormous risks of concurrent development and production, a successful weapon was created. In procurement decisions there has to be a lot of faith and trust on both sides, contractors and Pentagon officials say. Since weapons technology has become more complex, it has become almost impossible for a company to produce a reasonably accurate cost estimate on a new system. So the Pentagon may be reduced to saying: this firm has built good weapons before, we have to trust them to do it again. Faith and trust are not all that are involved; the "pity curve" influences contractor selection, as described by journalist John F. Lawrence:

No self-respecting U.S. businessmen like to go around poor-mouthing to obtain business. Yet that's precisely what's required of defense contractors. . . . [The pity curve] is the chart that shows how your employment and sales and everything else are falling off and how badly you need new business to keep all those poor souls employed. It's one of those things politicians listen to. . . . A pity curve shows just how much available capability a company has to handle a new project. That's a polite way of putting it, anyway[27, p. 17-B].

A General Dynamics official in 1969 maintained that the initiative on weapons development lay with the military. "Things are too systematized at the Pentagon for us to invent weapons systems and sell them on a need," he said[34, p. A-18]. Although ideas usually come from the military, industry "strategic systems salesmen" and engineers are called in at early stages. Not only does industry participate in the technical design, but Galbraith[13, p. 311] noted that a firm developing a new plane "can have something to say on the mission for which it is adapted, the number of planes required, their deployment, and by implication, on the choice of the enemy toward which it is directed." Some critics maintain that contractors sell not only threat-ameliorators (weapons) but threats themselves—through their ability to identify threats in think-tank studies and informal interchange with the military.

• • •

The Armed Services Procurement Act provided for contracts to be let through written competitive bids obtained by formal advertising. However, almost 90 percent of contract awards have been negotiated under 17 exceptions to that act, with 55 to 60 percent of contracts being single-source negotiated arrangements: one company makes a bid, gets the contract, and delivers the goods. Although the Pentagon conceded that formal advertising reduces costs 25 percent or more, the percentage of formal advertising declined by one-third between 1957-1968, mostly during the Vietnam buildup.[19] The government said negotiated arrangements were necessary because so few firms were able to deal with technologically complex, security-related weapons; the real competition, the Pentagon and defense firms agreed, came in technical and completion-date competition, not in pricing. (Galbraith conceded that one "cannot let out the MIRV to competitive bidding in the manner of mules or muskets"[22, p. 5].) Kaufman, a critic, said[25, pp. 68-69] negotiation "permits subjective decision-making" on firm selection and price setting, and leads to loss of "control over the costs, quality and time of production, insofar as they resulted from competition. ... If one (contractor) later complains that he had promised to provide a weapon at a lower price than the contractor who obtained the award, the Pentagon can respond by asserting that the price was not the major factor, that the Government simply had more faith in the contractor who won." This "faith" variable often is important to services which have long-standing sole-source relationships with suppliers; it was the Pentagon's response to the Maremont Corporation's challenge of a contract award to General Motors for the controversial M-16 rifle, and to the controversy over the ammunition supplier for the rifle. The army used a powder produced by Olin Mathieson, the sole source of army ball propellant since 1941, rather than powder from the originally intended source; an extensive jamming problem in Vietnam was attributed in part by congressional investigators to the Olin powder. The navy's objection to a joint air force-navy F-111 was based in part on reluctance to deal with "outside" contractors (e.g., General Dynamics) and its preference for contractors geared mainly to navy work. Bidders for the contract for the successor plane to the cancelled F-111b all had close ties to the navy. Corporations usually refrain from complaining about favoritism if they lose out on a contract, because there is no other buyer and, in any case, they are likely to be compensated with a later contract.

The concentrated nature of defense markets helps to make negotiated contracts controversial. Although the top 25 contractors received 45 percent of all defense contracts at the end of the 1960s, compared to 55 percent at the beginning (despite conglomerate mergers), the business remained highly concentrated. Because of (1) technological requirements, (2) service tendencies to favor firms they have dealt with before, and (3) contractors' lack of success in diversification, there have been substantial barriers to entry into and exit from the major weapons markets. To the extent that there is turnover in major contractors, it has been due to changing product mix (technology) rather than to heightened product competition. Aggregate sales figures underestimate the concentration, because specialized markets often are duo-polies or trio-polies. Two firms controlled 65 percent of the aircraft engine market in 1966, and 12 of 17 major air force product categories were

[19] The percentage of contract dollars awarded on what the Defense Department called a price-competitive basis, however, rose during the 1960s from 32.5 percent to 37.7 percent.

classified as "heavily" or "moderately" concentrated[21, pp. 55-57]. However, a similar concentration can be found in many commercial businesses. Small business was reserved a share of defense work, especially in subcontracts.

PROCUREMENT PERSONNEL

Some critics have blamed ineffective cost-control practices and the sympathetically adaptive process within the Defense Department on the close personal ties between and interchangeability of DOD procurement officers and industry officials. The former may be employees of defense contractors on leave for a few years to work in high-level policy or technical positions at the Pentagon, who plan to return to their old firm or to another defense firm with which they have worked while at DOD. They may be military officers who anticipate working for industry when they retire. Some officers have taken jobs with the same defense firms whose work they supervised while in uniform, to deal with their old service friends and former subordinates (whom they may have promoted); sometimes they have worked on the same weapon systems for which they were responsible while in the Pentagon. After retirement they assume the role of "seller" rather than "buyer," causing critics to maintain that the distinction in defense procurement is blurred.

Here we will examine the personnel crossover controversy (whose importance may have been exaggerated by critics), and the larger question of whether there is a procontractor and anti-cost-control "attitude problem" among procurement personnel.

Two air force plant representatives and a project officer for North American's Minuteman II missile guidance system, who had been stationed as "watchdogs" at the contractor's plant to ensure that delays and overruns were avoided and that contract specifications were fulfilled, retired from the military in 1969 and joined North American's Autonetics division in managerial positions. The general who had been chief of the air force division handling the contract became a North American vice president, and his chief procurement officer also joined the company.[20] A general directly involved in procurement of the M-16 rifle, after retirement from the army, worked for

---

[20] Critic A. Ernest Fitzgerald had complained in 1967 about the "mass migration of Air Force officers into the management ranks of contractors with whom they have dealt" on Minuteman and the avionics system for the F-111. He told the air force:

The Air Force plant representative who revoked our clearance at Autonetics is now a division manager at Autonetics. His predecessor, equally protective of the contractor's interests, is also now employed by North American Aviation. The procurement officer who blocked access by the Minuteman program control office to Autonetics contract negotiation records is now employed by North American Aviation. The immediate superior of the project officer who was excluded from Autonetics plant is now employed by Autonetics. The officer cited to me as responsible for killing the cost reduction project I contracted to perform at Autonetics is now employed by North American Aviation[22, pp. 759-760].

the firm which had the original sole-source contract for the rifle. On almost every major weapons contract, similar examples can be found.

Military men are not the only ones who leave the government to take jobs with defense contractors. Interlocking roles may be more easily assumed by civilians with broad political and financial contacts.[21] Compilations by the Brookings Institution and critic Barnet[pp. 88-89] showed that more than 75 percent of the top-level civilian defense decision-makers were from business, finance, or business-oriented legal firms in the three decades before 1967.

The business practice of hiring retired military men began after World War II. Some, like Gen. Brehon Somervell, had been businessmen in uniform, and were hired for their administrative abilities, to direct companies with diversified markets. Others, such as Gen. Douglas MacArthur, were hired for symbolic purposes. Some were hired for their technical experience. Others were hired by defense contractors for what they knew of military procedures and plans and for whom they knew in the Pentagon. Since World War II the firms hiring military men have tended to be defense contractors.

The military is widely seen by officers and civilians as a profession incompatible with monetary self-interest. Officers were never meant to be adjuncts of Lockheed Aircraft, they say. "We think it unethical and unconscionable," a House Armed Services subcommittee reported in 1959, "for a person to have anything to do in private life with a subject with which he was directly concerned while in public employment"[6, p. 305]. DOD regulations prohibited some kinds of military-industrial fraternizing while the officer was in service, and a 1966 executive order prohibited retired officers from "selling" or negotiating contracts with the Defense Department for 3 years after retirement (and for life, with their former services). However, Congres-

---

Fitzgerald said he was sure that many had no plans to go to work for North American "at the time they were so vigorously protecting the interests of that company vis-a-vis the Government." Despite the retired officers on its payroll, Autonetics saw the order for its cost-spiraling avionics system reduced by the air force in 1969.

[21] Former Assistant Secretary of Defense for Installations and Logistics Thomas D. Morris, for example, went directly from the Pentagon to Litton Industries, whose defense contracts had grown by 150 percent during Morris's last year as procurement chief. (Morris, however, was given a vice presidency in a Litton division with little defense business, and said the job offer came after he left the Pentagon.)

Personnel crossover from or to government is not even peculiar to defense. It is "part of the American tradition," Barnet (p. 111) said. "The successful tax lawyer learns the ropes in the IRS. The good broadcasting industry lawyer may have spent time at the FCC." Senator Goldwater said he was just as concerned about government-to-business crossovers from civilian agencies. Officials of the Office of Education and other Health, Education, and Welfare agencies are likely to have come from the publishing, academic, and foundation fields which often have monetary interests in HEW decisions. RAND's Charles Wolf, Jr.[48, pp. 21-22] pointed to the existence of powerful nonmilitary "complexes" in the fields of health and education.

sional Quarterly Service[9, p. 55] reported that "at least 90 percent of the retired officers hired for top-level positions by the defense contractors ignore that regulation." Military men scorn most civilian "selling" jobs, and do not like to think of themselves as weapons salesmen; "I studiously avoid even being in the room when anybody talks about a contract," a retired chief of naval operations serving as a self-identified "glorified messenger boy" for General Electric told Congress in 1956[43, p. 107]. Retired officers help the company's salesmen find their way around; they provide access to the customer.

Senator and Reserve Air Force Maj. Gen. Barry Goldwater dismissed the importance of the military "old school tie" problem in contracting. Although he knew many retired high-ranking officers, he said he never had been approached by one of them on a procurement matter, and at least one assistant secretary of defense said the same thing. But Goldwater added: "Frankly, if I were in the defense business, and wanted the weapons know-how I don't know where else I would go but to a retired general or colonel or admiral"[22, p. 485]. Retired officers in industry, former Air Force Secretary Dudley C. Sharp said, "contribute a great deal to the defense of their country because of the knowledge that they can offer industry." He said the Pentagon was not pressured by such officers[38, p. 60]. Others defended officers' records of honesty and disinterested service. Even critics acknowledged that proof of influence-peddling by ex-officers was lacking. Borklund[7, p. 236] believed there were too many bureaucratic decision-making levels prior to a final decision, for personal contacts at any single level to be decisive. "The large numbers of persons involved in major procurement decisions," he said, "make it unlikely that even the largest defense manufacturers could ever 'buy' their military customers' loyalties to themselves." General Wheeler said in 1969: "I think there are very few indeed who try to take advantage of their former positions in the military to sell us defense products." During his 5 years as Joint Chiefs chairman and 2 years as army chief of staff, he said only once had a retired officer come in to talk about "anything to do with business. He told me he was having trouble getting a yes-or-no response from the Army and asked me to give him the name of somebody to contact. I gave him a name, and that was that. Most officers are not salesmen. A friend of mine who retired and went into industry told me, 'The idea of my going back and trying to peddle products on the basis of my military friendships is so repulsive to me that I would rather starve to death.' And so would I"[36, p. 21].

Although the meaning of crossover is open to question, its extent has been measured. A 1959 congressional investigation found that 721 retired officers of the rank of colonel (navy captain) or higher (including 261 of general or flag rank) were employed by the leading 100 defense contractors. This was 4.1 percent of the retired officers. Those companies with the largest number also received the largest share of contracts. By February 1969, 2124 retired regular colonels and above (5.6 percent of total) worked for the 100 largest contractors, with the top ten firms employing more than half[37, pp. 153, 167]. The Senate voted 89 to 0 that year to require more complete disclosure of DOD-industrial personnel connections and crossover.

The danger, as seen by critics, is twofold: retired officers may be using their influence at the Pentagon, the "rainmaking" problem; or active officers involved in procurement decisions may be influenced by the prospect of jobs with companies they are buying from or whose work they are supervising. This second, less dramatic, influence may be more important. If the only important economic reward for a military career is the possibility of post-career recruitment by weapons contractors, procurement officers' conception of their relationship to contractors must be affected.

● ● ●

Even if military procurement officers are not being influenced by the prospects of industry jobs, are they properly trained? "Their upbringing," navy procurement control director Gordon W. Rule[22, p. 515] said, "is antithetic . . . to what we are supposed to do in prudent procurement. . . . The average military man is trained to get hardware to the fleet, tanks to the Army, et cetera, just as soon as possible. And if they had their way . . . they would go to a sole-source producer, where they knew they could get a good plane or a good engine, and they wouldn't care what it cost."

The GAO has criticized military rotation for preventing development of technical specialization. Rotation assures that project and contract officers will be dependent on contractors for information vital to negotiating with and supervising the contractor. The lack of experience of officers in the field, Fitzgerald[22, p. 831] maintained, leads many "to assume that the large contractors must know best, and that they must be efficient, otherwise they wouldn't be so rich. The military officers in particular . . . are ill equipped to cope . . . with the top management people in the contractor companies." Even a member of the complex, Grumman President Llewellyn J. Evans charged that Pentagon procurement decision-makers—the colonels or navy captains— were "not too bound up with what they're doing" because they put in only "two- or three-year tours at the Pentagon, where you can't make rank like you do in the field." Since "they frequently lack expertise to evaluate complex engineering systems . . . they fall back on procedure, they pass the buck"[40, p. 46].

Much of their adult life must be devoted to the more purely military aspects of their profession which are increasingly complex. They are also faced with the necessary up-or-out policy of the services, which results in many capable officers being forced to retire during their most productive years . . . (and) when their family expenses are typically at a peak. . . . Between these two limitations on their acquisition career span, most officers simply do not have the time to become as skilled in business as their contractor counterparts[22, p. 606].

DOD tacitly conceded that military-procurement personnel did not have the technical training or status of their industrial counterparts, and during the 1960s expanded programs designed to build a corps of procurement experts who would know what they were buying. Only one service academy had a course in business administration or accounting in 1969, although weapons design and production were studied. The training that officers received at the Industrial College of the Armed Forces, whose motto is "Industry and Defense are Inseparable," reinforced conservative, pro-business attitudes. "The college's roots have long been nourished by large industry, and a close tie is maintained with such organizations as the American Ordnance Association" [28, p. 404].

Critics pointed to personnel "attitude problems" at the top of the procurement apparatus and in the field. Most officers feel that technical performance ("effectiveness") is more important than costs ("efficiency"). Military men had rather be on the safe side in adding technical capabilities, so they contract for more weapons that can do more. And their careers benefit from identification with a militarily successful weapon, not from cost-consciousness.[22] Critics charged that procurement officials sometimes told contractors not to worry about excessive costs. On the C-5A, the Pentagon was charged with suppressing data on cost overruns to protect Lockheed's stock market position. On the other hand, Pentagon officials complained that contractors have withheld cost problems from *them* until it was too late to do anything. If the air force had known the true scope of Lockheed's financial problems, deputy air force chief of staff for research and development Lt. Gen. Otto J. Glasser told Congress in 1970, the service would have "blown the whistle" and ended the contract without committing itself to buy the last 23 C-5As. Glasser charged Lockheed with concealing information; "the longer they can keep you involved," he said, "the more secure is their ultimate position" [18, pp. 1-A, 15-A]. In 1971 Deputy Secretary Packard was angry at Grumman and the navy for not warning him earlier that the F-14 fighter program was having severe cost problems.

Military project and contract officers also have been charged with being unduly tolerant of contractor costs. Cost controls can be affected at award time, or in the program's administration. At the later stage, military plant representatives control much of the information about a program. "Down where the work is being done," the navy's director of strategic systems said,

---

[22] A House Armed Services subcommittee reported in 1970:

. . . So much time and money had been spent in developing the Sheridan/Shillelagh (tank) system that the developers felt irrevocably committed to production. Under such circumstances the project manager became more a captive than a manager of his project, and might understandably feel that a failure of the project to reach fruition could be interpreted as demonstrating his own lack of managerial skills and thus affect his army career [24, p. 67].

"reputations rest on performance and schedule. . . . Almost never did you hear: 'Is it worth it?' " [39, p. 97] . Some procurement critics believed that the McNamara policies might have been successful in restraining costs and improving weapons quality if they had been enforced in the field. Studies simply were killed down the line, except for those with sustained high-level support. Packard's procurement policies in the Nixon administration included greater surveillance of changes approved by military program managers. Program officers and contractors, most critics felt, had a common stake in preventing "visibility" (that is, covering up production problems by altering internal reports) to prevent cancellation of troublesome weapons programs.[23]

If cost overruns on the C-5A and F-111 avionics were concealed from Pentagon leadership, as well as from Congress, then, in Parkinson's phrase, there was "dark at the top of the stairs." " 'Homefront' resistance" from within the government to enforcement of cost controls, the Navy's Gordon Rule said, "can be much more brutal than that from a contractor" [23, p. 28] .

THE ADAPTIVE PROCESS

The Defense Department claims it uses its tremendous economic bargaining power to reduce suppliers' profit margins, and that it does not delay in taking corrective action against contractors. Critics justly contend that contracting procedures and specific contracts are adapted to the financial needs of the contractors. Contracts are constantly renegotiated and restructured. What *is* the setting within which contractors work, and what kind of assistance do they receive from the government?

Under the last two Republican administrations—before and after Secre-

---

[23] Officers sometimes saw themselves as the company's allies against a common congressional enemy. Inspectors who sought to "tell the truth" about contractor failures or to make changes reportedly were disciplined, isolated from information, or removed from their jobs, and the government accepted either faulty products, paid unduly high costs, or both. Colonel Buesking and Admiral Rickover[23, p. 27] testified of such sanctions being imposed against the few officials who did not "hew to the party line" on cost controls. Given the existence of more than adequate funds, Fitzgerald claimed trying to cut costs was seen as "antisocial behavior" by service leaders and most officers in the field, whereas cost growth, in defense analyst Merton Tyrrell's view, was "socially acceptable" [22, p. 495] . More costs, and hence more funds meant increased personal security for all members of the procurement community, critics charged. Nieburg[33, p. 274] agreed but also asserted that project officers were made the "fall guys" by top military managers who refused to support lower-level cost-control efforts.

In 1965 the GAO in auditing 5 percent (in value) of defense contracts, found: (1) excessive prices and inadequate pricing data; (2) acceptance and payment by the government for defective equipment; (3) charges to the government for costs applicable to commercial work; (4) companies' use of government-owned facilities for commercial work for extended periods without payment of rent to the government; (5) duplicate billings to the government; (6) unreasonable costs; and (7) excessive progress payments without payment of interest. The GAO found little improvement in the early 1970s.

tary McNamara –contracts usually first were awarded for R & D[24]; often these involved a planned loss for the companies. Most R & D awards were negotiated (85 percent "pre-selected" and 60 percent sole-source in the mid-1960s). Profits were made in the production "follow-on" contracts for which the R & D contractor occupied a strategic position. Realizing that the government often got locked in with a particular contractor who "bought in" with a low design bid, McNamara instituted the TPPC, combining all phases of development, testing, and production, which was awarded on the basis of paper studies. Rather than five or six separately priced and administered contracts, there would be one contract for what was purported to be a single, fixed price. In 1961 46 percent of air force contracts were cost-plus-fixed-fee; this had dropped to 6 percent by the end of the Johnson administration. The TPPC *permitted* the government to hold contractors to fixed prices and specifications, and thus to transfer to them huge monetary risks. Of course, the government had to be willing to enforce the fixed prices. In an early test, that of the F-111 avionics, the contract provided for firm option prices for follow-on buying; however, the air force, because of large increases in actual costs, chose not to use the fixed prices. Efforts to allow for unidentified contingencies by *starting* with fatter cost estimates failed to stop overruns, because most contractors geared up to spend the contingency funds at the outset. TPPC also had the potential of reducing government involvement in contractors' operations, but it did not work out that way.

This industry claimed to be the only one that contracts to invent something, to produce an unknown for a known price. TPPC bidders were required to estimate direct and indirect costs and economic conditions for up to 8 years, with less opportunity for trade-offs (e.g., more performance for more costs). In the first big TPPC contract, that of the C-5A, Lockheed made commitments on technical performance, delivery schedule, and price prior to the start of engineering development; it also was responsible for total system integration. McNamara's insistence upon awarding contracts to the lowest bidder led to considerable "low-balling," i.e., bidding of unrealistically low prices or unrealistically high quality, with expectations that the contract would be amended later. McNamara's "success" in getting firm low bids may have been responsible for the embarrassing series of cost overruns that

[24] In the Nixon administration there were promises to employ contracts with prototype construction (fly-before-you-buy) more often. In August 1971 Deputy Secretary Packard announced a new program in which different industry design teams would be kept working on prototypes of experimental weapons systems. Production contracts would be negotiated only if a prototype tested well in competition with others.

The Nixon administration also sought to avoid the costs of "gold-plating," i.e., building unnecessarily expensive and delay-provoking technical sophistication into a weapon, as apparently happened with the M-16 and the F-111. Technical complexity too often led to technical problems. Official Pentagon policy became: "All military weapons of the early 1970s will be designed for minimum necessary performance"[39, p. 96].

followed his administration—embarrassments later exploited by his contractor critics to undo many of his "reforms." Overruns[25] during the 1950s had averaged at least twice as much, but many of them were never officially identified as such because of the flexibility of contract readjustment procedures. A "good" cost estimate then and now was one which came true, regardless of its size. The Nixon administration acknowledged the problem of "chronic optimism." It sought to deal with the problem by avoiding concurrent development and production, and by shifting away from fixed-price systems covering both stages and away from contracts for extended periods. Deputy Secretary Packard called for a "comprehensive assessment of risk" before undertaking new programs, and blamed industry and military overoptimism for much of the antidefense-spending sentiment of 1969-1971.

Packard's "milestone" formula provided for contracts to be let in at least two stages, rather than in a package. The first stage, that of development, would be cost-plus-incentive-fee, the most profitable kind of contract. Major components would have to reach certain technical milestones, and testing and prototype stages would have to be completed successfully before fixed-price production contracts would be let. Under a cost-plus-incentive-fee arrangement, the contractor was said to be motivated to hold down costs, because his fees would increase if actual costs proved less than target costs. At certain points target costs would be revised upwards, if actual experience warranted, but they could not go beyond specified ceilings. Thus cost increases, eventually, could bring a loss for the contractor. The fixed-cost ceiling also was intended to limit gold-plating and force performance trade-offs. This policy "will decrease contractor risk during the development phase when technical complications are greatest," according to *Business Week* [11, pp. 97-98], "and give the government more contractual flexibility." It also would increase contractor profits.

Contractor risk had not been a major problem for firms until recent years. When costs and prices rose, official reprimands followed, but chief

---

[25] Cost overruns played a major part in stimulating recent defense controversies. Every major weapon system suffered from cost growth, and cancellations or contract revisions of the Cheyenne, C-5A, F-111, and F-14 were attributed to costs. Official overrun estimates on major programs went as high as 395 percent for the Mark 48 torpedo and to 250 percent for the SRAM missile. The F-111 overrun was set at $4.5 billion. The much-discussed C-5A overrun was estimated at a mere $882 million to $2 billion. The Pentagon acknowledged in 1969 that projected overruns on 35 major programs then exceeded $20 billion or 27 percent. But it cautioned that overruns were "well within the control" of Congress and the administration and "should not be equated with wasted dollars." During the fifties and early sixties, the average unit cost of missiles was three times the original estimate, and manned aircraft overruns were not far behind. Estimates of funds expended on canceled weapons exceeded $11 billion. The Senate Armed Services Committee reported that the cost of tanks would increase fourfold between 1965-1975 and that fighter planes in 1971 cost five to six times what they did in 1960. The avionics package in some new aircraft cost over $1000 per pound, or twice the price of gold.

procurement officers sided with the company against strict-constructionist cost analysts. "There is a common belief," economist Frederic Scherer said, "that one should not rock the boat vigorously through criticism at the start of a program. The (belief) is that troubles can be pinpointed and corrected later on when the program has its momentum." Systems are accepted with serious technical defects. Because of technological uncertainty the military supports "a whole stable of programs, letting each get going on its highly optimistic bases," to provide a cushion for failure[22, pp. 379, 403]. Lockheed, while denying using a knowingly low bid to get the C-5A contract, admitted being optimistic in its cost and technical performance estimates. The optimism problem was cited by the navy's Rule, who told the Proxmire subcommittee that industry and the Pentagon "play games" with cost estimates: "We know that if we tell the DOD across the river how much something is really going to cost they may scrub it, and they know if they tell Congress how much it is really going to cost the Congress may scrub it. So you start in with both sides knowing that it is going to cost more." Rule declined to call this "lying"; I think it is wrong, but I think it would only be disingenuous"[22, pp. 510, 513]. The Nixon administration's response was simply not to attempt to hold the contractors and services to firm price estimates, on the assumption that it was impossible.

● ● ●

Nieburg[33, pp. 268-287] charged there were "multiple tiers of hidden profits" in the contracting, subcontracting, and patent-claims stages, and multiple overlays of administration and fringe benefits or "overhead on overhead." The contracts have been "sweetheart deals," permitting the government to reimburse companies for unanticipated costs, or to increase the final payment price by accepting gold-plated modifications, or to accept a profitable option, or to lower technical performance standards (the industry's pride) or a later delivery time. For example, ceiling-less escalation

---

Cost overruns occur in all executive agencies, Budget Director Robert Mayo said in 1969, but in defense the "surveillance problem" is more acute[22, p. 680]. Reasons given for overruns included: inflation; unanticipated technical problems; technical changes ordered by the military; program stretch-outs and order reductions that increase unit costs; deliberate or inadvertent underbidding by contractors, mixed with initial governmental overoptimism; and poor contractor performance. Going into production before development problems were solved ("concurrency") was cited as a key procurement weakness of the 1960s, despite business complaints that the Kennedy and Johnson administrations overstudied programs and postponed new production. Unanticipated technical problems led to what Fitzgerald[22, p. 596] called the "fail-spend cycle," the "assumption that the cure for poor quality is more money." He had "never heard a program manager propose cost reduction as a solution to a 'funding problem.' . . . Regardless of initial level of costs or of increases . . . a 'funding problem' does not exist if money is available to pay the bill." Problems are solved by adding more money to the program, cutting it back, or "stretching" it over a longer period.

clauses such as the C-5A "repricing formula" were designed to permit the company to make larger profits on the second run if actual costs on the first run were higher than anticipated. The official reason for such a formula was to reduce catastrophic losses to manageable proportions. This was what the Proxmire subcommittee labeled a "reverse incentive," inviting the contractor to increase costs, then tighten controls on the second run, a charge Lockheed felt was "highly theoretical." Or unprofitable or trouble-plagued contracts can be canceled, sometimes for the "convenience" of the government, to reduce losses.

Should he get into trouble with regard to any contract conditions, a contractor can expect that DOD will take care of him and get him well. Change notices may be used to amend unfavorable contract provisions, or in some cases, firms repropose terms essentially without regard to their original written agreements. Each of hundreds of changes made annually on each major program (e.g., more than 3000 changes on the C-5A by 1970) offers an opportunity to increase payment prices in line with actual and anticipated costs. It was not until 1970 that DOD insisted that all changes in weapons systems at least be priced and written into a contract before they were accepted. The 1969 contract for the DD-963 destroyer was hailed as a step forward, because use of performance specifications supposedly made design changes the contractor's problem, and because 90 percent of the equipment used would be supplied by the contractor. As Rule[22, p. 518] commented: "No matter how poor the quality, how late the product, and how high the costs, (companies) know nothing will happen to them. . . . You have never heard of a defense contractor going bankrupt because there is a philosophy (in the Pentagon) that they shouldn't lose money."

Senate critics sought unsuccessfully to deny Lockheed first a $200 million "contingency fund," and then a $250 million guarantee for loans, to set a precedent that bad management practices would be punished; Congress, however, accepted the view first that it would be a "startling waste" to let the C-5A program collapse, and later that letting Lockheed go bankrupt would hurt the economy. The 1971 "Lockheed lobby," including banks which had loaned the company money and machinists' unions with jobs at stake, managed a one-vote Senate victory by emphasizing the employment impact.[26] With rare exceptions, grudges are not held against firms that fail to

[26] In 1969-1970 Lockheed was faced with cancellation of its production contract for the Cheyenne helicopter (potentially worth nearly $1 billion), big cost runups on navy shipbuilding, technical and cost problems on its portion of the Short-Range Attack Missile (SRAM), and a reduction in the number of C-5As to be ordered. The air force estimated that Lockheed would lose a "catastrophic" $450-$671 million on the first shipment of C-5As, although much of that could be recouped on the second run through the repricing formula. Lockheed was caught in the corporate liquidity crisis of 1970, and announced that it would have to stop C-5A production unless it received emergency funding from the government for charges the government said it did not owe. These

perform well; instead, the adaptive process insures that their losses will be small or nonexistent. Contracts between company and government, then, can be seen as agreements between allies; "contract nourishment" is a natural response to an ally's difficulty in meeting obligations.

FREE ENTERPRISE OR MILITARY SOCIALISM?

The relationship between buyer and seller in defense contracting is cooperative, not adversary. They are partners, with much talk of esprit and teamwork. "The buyer (government) is as interested in the survival and well-being of the seller (company) as is the seller himself"[22, p. 51]. As with the regulatory agencies, the Defense Department is expected to protect the industries with which it does business. Senator Fulbright believed that the complex was a giant concentration of socialism in the midst of a free-enterprise system.[27] Others charged that companies doing most of their business with the military and space agencies were tokenly private enterprises.

The production and distribution system managed by the Pentagon is the largest planned economy outside the Soviet Union. The Pentagon is the complex's central planning agency which uses the military budget to stimulate overall economic growth, and to assist certain sectors. It plays an important role in the regulation of economic demand.

No one denies the existence of planning. But, more specifically, have defense relationships eroded the distinctions between buyer and seller, and

---

problems would be enough to make most corporations lose heart, but until Lockheed's commercial L-1011 ran into trouble the next year, the adaptive process promised to see it through.

Funds were supplied to meet part of Lockheed's unprecedented request for $641 million in "interim financing," pending settlement of contract disputes with the air force. Also a new C-5A contract was drawn up to remove the ceilings on Lockheed expenditures, and shift the contract from fixed-price to cost-plus. Lockheed agreed to accept a fixed loss of $200 million, after Packard said the government had no precedent for funding a contract during litigation. Lockheed initially rejected Packard's offer on the basis that the repricing formula was intended to protect it against large losses. However, Lockheed could not afford to wait for litigation, under which it risked a much larger loss anyway, and accepted the settlement. This loss of the $100 million already invested and $100 million that the company did not have to begin repaying the government until 1974, was part of $480 million in pretax losses for settlements on four defense contracts in 1970. The government accepted substantially increased costs through those settlements. Lockheed was relieved of some penalties for substandard performance and late delivery of the C-5A, and was partially relieved of its managerial responsibilities.

[27] Melman (pp. 176-177) said that "state-management" of the Pentagon has "all the main attributes of industrial capitalism (other than the profit calculation). . . . The state-management gets the effect of profit-accumulation and investment (i.e., enlarging its decision-power)without an intervening process of selling products and accumulating an actual money profit." This does not make the Pentagon "submanagements" capitalist enterprises in the usual sense of the term.

therefore the protections against misuse and concentration of power supposedly built into the market mechanism? In return for a favorable adaptive process, the Defense Department has taken over many management tasks normally included among the internal decision-making prerogatives of corporate management: Decisions (or review with veto powers) about sources of materials, e.g., "buy America" clauses which restrict the use of imported goods; wage scales and overtime; choices of subcontractors and decisions on what to subcontract; decisions about internal financial reporting, engineering, and planning systems; and even the imposition of Army Corps of Engineers' safety standards in factories. Internal operating decisions may be made by military contracting and surveillance officers. Procurement regulations state that the government does not expect to participate in every management decision, but it reserves the right to review the contractor's management efforts. Meanwhile, it imposes hundreds of formal management systems (estimated as high as 680 since World War II) on industry, and provides incentives for the continuance of the "arsenalization" of industry.

Contractor Lewis said "the so-called management limitations of the Department of Defense are only very tight *reporting* systems"[19, p. 9]. Weidenbaum disagreed, claiming long-term "loss of company initiative . . . entrepreneurship and risk bearing. . . . We seem to forget why . . . we prefer to use private enterprise rather than government arsenals. It is not because private corporations are better at following rules and regulations. . . . It is precisely for the opposite reason"[21, pp. 66-67]. To the extent that the government is taking on the traditional risk role of the private entrepreneur, the buyer is making the product decisions, with its risk being possible failure to recover its R & D investment. The companies come to resemble government arsenals or agencies, making decisions that the government itself should make. This is convergence. In an extension of "economic federalism," the government permits private corporations to act in a quasi-governmental role in regards to subcontractors and certain geographic areas, over which the "primes" have substantial power. Smaller subcontractors are vulnerable to having any cutbacks passed on to them. Defense firms are granted the ability to allocate state resources, to dispense jobs and financial patronage, to absorb other firms, and to dominate others through "interlocking directorships" as prevalent as they were before the 1914 Clayton Antitrust Act[33, p. 196]. But all this is done under guidelines set by the Pentagon.

• • •

Throughout the fifties and the sixties prime contractors were provided both liquid and fixed capital. They often operated in government-owned plants, paying nominal fees. At low prices they leased government equipment and machinery which was used for commercial as well as military work. Through progress payments the government provided interest-free working capital, saving the company the cost of raising capital through equity or debt issues. Eighty to ninety percent of the costs a contractor reports can be paid in regular installments (averaging one every 11 days); these payments were tied to companies' need for funds, not to progress on constructing the system.[28] In 1971 the Pentagon had over $9 billion out in progress payments, compared to less than $4 billion in 1964. Firms were not permitted to charge off interest on private borrowing as a business expense, although DOD in 1971 began forcing contractors to seek more private capital. Some defense firms have reported that government-supplied working capital exceeded their total book assets, and the same was true of government-supplied and company property. More than $13 billion worth of government property (plant, equipment, materials, office equipment) was in private contractors' hands in 1969.[29] Barnet (p. 120) remarked that "if LTV Aerospace did not exist, it would have to be invented"; and, in a sense, that is what happened. Only 1 percent of its 6.7 million square feet of office, plants, and laboratories were company-owned in 1970. Private R & D costs have been permitted as overhead on government contracts, as were salaries for "stockpiled" technical and proposal-writing personnel, although "independent" R & D grants were reduced in 1969. Patents developed by a contractor with DOD support have been retained free of charge by the company, subject only to royalty-free licensing to the government.

The belief that a "deep chasm" separates the state from private business, that "the first decides and commands, the second responds," is important to the autonomy of the business "technostructure." Galbraith[13, pp. 232, 310] also said: "The technostructure comes to see the same urgency in weapons development, the same security in technological pre-eminence, the same requirement for a particular weapons system, the same advantage in an enlarged mission for (a service), as does the particular service itself." The belief that signing contracts with private industry greatly reduces government responsibility persists. "It is not our proper role," Lockheed Board Chairman Daniel J. Houghton told Congress, "to decide about the need or the degree of need for the C-5" [35, p. 3]. But when the program got into trouble, the Pentagon believed it was *its* proper role to assume increased direct involvement in management of the project. When a congressman suggested to General Glasser that Congress was "bailing out" Lockheed with contingency funding, the general said no, "we are in the boat with them. So we are bailing us out" [18, p. 1-A].

Companies maintain that private enterprise has been preserved by the

[28] On the C-5A, for example, Lockheed received $1.207 billion in progress payments out of total costs through 1968 of $1.278 billion. According to the GAO, progress payments may increase profits by 20 percent.

[29] In 1966 40 percent of the shipbuilding industry was government-owned. In 1956 the government furnished 70 percent of all productive facilities in the aircraft industry, a percentage reduced in the early 1960s. When government property was sold to contractors, however, often it was for a fraction of its market value.

contracting system. They oppose nationalization of the defense industry on the grounds that government-operated industry would not only be less efficient but uncapitalistic. But one may not really need to nationalize what *already* is part of the government in all but name and formal control.[30]

CONCLUSION

In this chapter we have seen that much is at stake in the military-industrial complex, the largest economic activity in America, profitable and irreplaceable for companies, and valuable to labor and communities. The possibility that contractors could control the Pentagon, e.g., through retired officers on industry payrolls, seems unlikely. *There are no "puppets,"* only individuals working in different uniforms in different parts of the defense empire, clashing as allies - sometimes do in pursuit of parallel goals. The Nixon administration and some congressmen may have departed temporarily from one of the complex's articles of confederation set down by Charles E. Wilson in January 1944. The future defense secretary suggested creation of a business-military alliance in a "permanent war economy." "Industry's role in the program," Wilson said, "is to respond and cooperate . . . in the execution of the part allotted to it; industry must not be hampered by political witch-hunts, or thrown to the fanatical isolationist fringe tagged with a 'merchants of death' label"[10, pp. 66-67]. There is some justice to contractors' complaints that they have been made scapegoats in recent years, thrown to the antiwar and "new priorities" critics by their political allies. Also, little was done by Nixon for unemployed defense workers and communities suffering from defense unemployment, despite much talk about converting to a peacetime economy. But the relationship remained one of cooperative interdependence, albeit an uneasy interdependence.

The argument that defense contractors should be considered, analytically, as part of the military establishment is a convincing one. This establishment's success can be measured by the breadth of its decision-making power, from strategies to prosperity in Cobb County, Georgia, even after the Nixon administration's budgetary and personnel cuts.

REFERENCES

1. "Annual Report on American Industry," *Forbes*, 103 (January 1, 1969).
2. Astor, Gerald, "Defense Contract: The Money Web," *Look*, 33 (August 26, 1969), p. 28.
3. Barnet, Richard J., *The Economy of Death* (New York: Atheneum, 1969).

[30] Nieburg suggested that the return of government plants and equipment for in-house work, and rehiring researchers and engineers lured away from governmental and academic jobs would serve the same purpose as nationalization, since many defense firms were little more than collections of managerial and technical personnel.

4. Benoit, Emile, "Economic Adjustments to Disarmament," in *Disarmament and the Economy*, ed. Emile Benoit and Kenneth E. Boulding (New York: Harper & Row, 1963), pp. 271-300.

5. Benson, Robert S., "How the Pentagon Can Save $9,000,000,000," *The Washington Monthly*, 1 (March 1969), pp. 32-45.

6. Biderman, Albert D., "Sequels to a Military Career: The Retired Military Professional," in ed. Morris Janowitz, *The New Military* (New York: Russell Sage Foundation, 1964), pp. 287-336.

7. Borklund, C. W., *The Department of Defense* (New York: Praeger, 1968).

8. Clayton, James L., "Defense Spending: Key to California's Growth," *Western Political Quarterly*, XV (June 1962), pp. 280-293.

9. Congressional Quarterly Service, *Legislators and the Lobbyists*, 2nd ed., (Washington: CQ Service, 1968).

10. Cook, Fred J., *The Warfare State* (New York: Macmillan, 1962).

11. "The Dogfight Over the F-15," *Business Week*, no. 2132 (July 11, 1970), pp. 96-98.

12. Galbraith, John Kenneth, *How to Control the Military* (New York: Signet Books, 1969).

13. Galbraith, John Kenneth, *The New Industrial State* (Boston: Houghton Mifflin, 1967).

14. "General Dynamics: In Trouble Again," *Business Week*, no. 2092 (October 4, 1969), pp. 48-52.

15. Gilmore, John S. and Dean C. Coddington, *Defense Industry Diversification: An Analysis with 12 Case Studies*, U.S. Arms Control and Disarmament Agency Publication No. 30 (Washington: Government Printing Office, 1966).

16. Halverson, Guy, "Dow a Major War-Protest Target," *The Christian Science Monitor* (June 6, 1969), p. 19.

17. Heilbroner, Robert, "Military America," *The New York Review of Books*, vol. 14 (July 23, 1970), pp. 5-8.

18. Hurt, Bob, "Lockheed Hid Data, AF Says," *The Atlanta Constitution* (June 30, 1969), pp. 1-A, 15-A.

19. "Industry Defends the 'Complex'," *The Christian Science Monitor* (July 11, 1969), p. 9.

20. Isard, Walter and Gerald J. Karaska, *Unclassified Defense and Space Contracts: Awards by County, State and Metropolitan Area, United States, Fiscal Year 1964* (Philadelphia: World Friends Research Center, 1965).

21. Joint Economic Committee of the U.S. Congress, Hearings before the Subcommittee on Economy in Government, "Economics of Military Procurement," (Washington: Government Printing Office, 1968).

22. Joint Economic Committee of the U.S. Congress, Hearings before the Subcommittee on Economy in Government, "The Military Budget and

National Economic Priorities," (Washington: Government Printing Office, 1969).

23. Joint Economic Committee Report, *The Economics of Military Procurement,* (Washington: Government Printing Office, 1969).

24. Just, Ward, "Soldiers," Part II, *The Atlantic*, 226 (November 1970), pp. 59-90.

25. Kaufman, Richard F., " 'We Must Guard Against Unwarranted Influence by the Military-Industrial Complex', " *The New York Times Magazine* (June 22, 1969), pp. 10, 68-72.

26. Lall, Betty Goetz, "Arms Reduction Impact," *Bulletin of the Atomic Scientists*, 22 (September 1966), pp. 41-44.

27. Lawrence, John F., "$1.4 Billion Deal Just Starts Their Day," *The Atlanta Journal-Constitution* (January 11, 1970), p. 17-B.

28. Masland, John W., and Radway, Laurence I., *Soldiers and Scholars* (Princeton, N.J.: Princeton University Press, 1957).

29. McGaffin, William and Knoll, Erwin, "Making It in Marietta," *The Progressive*, 33 (November 1969), pp. 32-35.

30. Melman, Seymour, *Pentagon Capitalism* (New York: McGraw-Hill, 1970).

31. "The Military-Industrial Complex," *Newsweek*, 73 (June 9, 1969), pp. 74-87.

32. *Moody's Stock Survey*, May 19, 1969, p. 616.

33. Nieburg, H. L., *In the Name of Science* (Chicago: Quadrangle, 1966).

34. Nossiter, Bernard D., "Arms Firms See Post-war Spurt," *The Washington Post*, (December 8, 1968), pp. A-1, A-18.

35. *The Other Side of the C-5 Story* (Burbank, Calif.: Lockheed Aircraft Corp., 1969).

36. "The Power People," *Look*, 33 (August 26, 1969), pp. 20-27.

37. Proxmire, William, *Report from Wasteland* (New York: Praeger, 1970).

38. Raymond, Jack, "The Military-Industrial Complex," *Harvard Business Review*, 46 (May-June 1968), pp. 53-64.

39. "A Retreat From Gold-Plated Contracts," *Business Week*, no. 2132 (July 11, 1970), pp. 96-97.

40. "Shout Hallelujah!" *Forbes*, 106 (September 1, 1970), p. 46.

41. "Staying Alive Until 1973," *New Republic*, 162 (May 16, 1970), pp. cover, 7-8.

42. Stone, I. F., "McNamara and the Militarists," *New York Review of Books*, 11(November 7, 1968), pp. 5-10.

43. Swomley, John M., Jr., *The Military Establishment* (Boston: Beacon Press, 1964).

44. *The Value Line Investment Survey*, October 17, 1969, p. 102.

45. Weidenbaum, Murray L., "Problems of Adjustment for Defense Industries," in *Disarmament and the Economy*, ed. Emile Benoit and Kenneth E. Boulding (New York: Harper & Row, 1963), pp. 66-86.

46. Welsh, David, "Building Lyndon Johnson," *Ramparts*, 6 (December 1967), pp. 53-64.
47. Winn, Bill, "Marching Through Georgia," *Atlanta*, 8 (March 1969), pp. 63-68, 82-84.
48. Wolf, Charles Jr., "Military-Industrial Complexities," *Bulletin of the Atomic Scientists*, XXVII (February 1971), pp. 19-22.

CHAPTER FIVE

The Military, Science, and the Universities

When the American Chemical Society offered its services to the military during World War I, it was turned down on the grounds that the War Department "already had a chemist"[9, p. 58]. But by the end of World War II, *Business Week* [23, p. 19] noted, "partly by design, partly by default, federal support of pure science had come almost completely under military control"; most scientists remained in civilian garb, but funds for their salaries and laboratory equipment came from the military. By the time of President Eisenhower's farewell address on the complex, "the prospect of domination of the nation's scholars by Federal employment, project allocations, and the power of money" had come to be a danger "gravely to be regarded."

"The free university," Eisenhower[6, p. 1] said, "historically the fountainhead of free ideas and scientific discovery, has experienced a revolution in the conduct of research. Partly because of the huge costs involved, a government contract becomes virtually a substitute for intellectual curiosity." Potentially more dangerous than the military-industrial complex, Admiral Rickover warned almost a decade later, "is the close inner circle composed of researchers within the Department of Defense and those working for . . . Defense under contract"[27, p. 17]. Where the universities had been expected by some to form "an effective counterweight to the . . . complex by strengthening their emphasis on the traditional values of our democracy," instead Senator Fulbright[7, p. 36181] charged, they have "joined the monolith, adding greatly to its power and influence."

The price the universities paid for massive federal financing after 1945, without which some could not survive, was, according to Fulbright[7, p. 36181], "the surrender of independence, the neglect of teaching . . . the distortion of scholarship, and the taking into the Government camp of scholars . . . who ought to be acting as responsible and independent critics of their Government's policies."

Military support for research raised basic questions: Had the university been corrupted? Had scientists and intellectuals who had built weapons or supplied information become accessories to the Pentagon? Had intellect, former University of California President Clark Kerr asked, become a component part of the complex? Or, as defense scientists claimed, were they justifiably supplying the nation with badly needed skills, to maintain its world position against a totalitarian threat? They said the nation would suffer a severe setback if campus-affiliated defense research was halted. From this perspective, were the students and professors who expressed revulsion against weapons research showing more concern for the pristine purity of their ivory towers than for service to the nation?

• • •

How did this military-academic relationship develop? It is a far sharper break with precedent than the postwar development of a military-industrial complex. Private industry had been supplying the military's needs since Eli Whitney's time. But, other than ROTC programs (authorized in 1862), there was little military penetration behind the ivy-covered walls until World War I, and more significantly, during the 1939-1945 "physicist's war," with its developments in naval guidance, radar, airpower, and the 150,000-man Manhattan Project. In the selective mobilization of science during World War II, not only were physicists and other weapons scientists co-opted, but psychologists and other social scientists who devised military selection and training programs, staffed the propaganda and intelligence divisions, studied soldiers' morale, investigated the culture of Pacific islands, and manned the Strategic Bombing Survey. Entire research laboratories were drafted into war work; at one time, for example, three-fourths of the University of Chicago's staff and facilities were so involved.

Spending for research in pure science in 1938 totaled less than $40 million, with $23 million of that being done by universities. The first agency established to funnel government money to university laboratories was Vannevar Bush's Office of Scientific Research and Development (OSRD), which was placing $90 million a year in research contracts by midwar. In the quarter century after the war, research support was to grow fantastically. By the mid-1950s 85 percent of a $2-billion government outlay was for national security, and $120 million was for basic research. By the 1960s the national security agencies supported more than half of the nation's research, with universities getting a modest share. DOD financed only one-fourth of university research, compared with one-half of industrial R & D and three-fourths of governmental laboratory research. However, it supported a much higher percentage (40%) of university *basic* research than of industrial or governmental basic research. Even the best-endowed schools usually contributed little more than 10 percent of their own research budgets. By 1969 the Pentagon R & D budget had grown to more than $8 billion, or 16 times the 1946 figure, and it supported $400 million in basic research, or 10 times the national outlay of 1938.

But in 1945 the financial picture for laboratories, and for scientists who had come to be accustomed to the research affluence and prestige of wartime programs, was not optimistic. Without the unprecedentedly generous government funding which made Big Science a reality during the war, where was the support for on-going and dreamed-of programs to come from?

The military understood that it needed scientists more than it had in the past. Where military and industrial technology had been parallel before the war, e.g., the bomber and the airplane, military TNT and commercial dynamite, the post-Hiroshima and post-V2 scientific horizon promised more exotic weapons, which the military could obtain only by funding specific research projects relevant to its needs. As arms races became qualitative as well as quantitative, new developments threatened to upset military relationships. In a setting of atomic stalemate, technological progress was to become a substitute for battlefield victory. Thus the military felt it had no choice but to heavily support research with weapons potential. As universities were released from their wartime contracts and OSRD was disbanded, the Office of Naval Research stepped in to arrange financing on a cost-plus-nothing basis. (For 5 years after the war, the ONR was the chief agency for funding university basic research, usually on projects suggested by university personnel.) With the proposal for a civilian National Science Foundation deadlocked in Congress, universities and scientists could continue research under peacetime navy and army auspices or do without. Because of feelings of public responsibility, the intellectual excitement of being on the frontier of technology or in government, and the need for funding, most scientists continued their ties to the military.

SCIENTISTS AS LOBBYISTS

Weapons scientists in government work at three levels: (1) as "pure technicians"; (2) as planners and developers of strategic programs, in which technical components are only one part; and (3) as policy advisers[18, pp. 75-86]. Prior to World War II, administrator Bush said the military had no clear idea of what science could provide, and that scientists were ignorant of what the military needed. After the war scientists became increasingly important in advising the military and civilian superiors on weapons technology and the strategies which embraced or, in some cases, were molded by such technology. Through standing committees, special advisory positions, contract research, and semiautonomous operations research institutes, scientists participated in defense decision-making.

Mixed into the scientist's role as researcher and adviser was the scientist as a lobbyist. To differentiate these roles is difficult, because motivations inevitably are mixed and technical problems do not have neat boundaries. Looking at the "thinkers" as an interest group, which of them have developed stakes in the continuance of a large defense establishment?

1. Scientists and technicians who work directly for the Defense Department, in the service arsenals and shipyards, and in the Pentagon

2. Nonprofit research institutes under contract from the Defense Department, and the physical and social scientists who work for them

3. Physical scientists, especially the experimentalists, employed by the defense industry and universities, or those serving as consultants. For example, only one-third of the scientists and engineers added to industrial R & D staffs between 1954-1961 were supported by industry's own funds. Many of the nation's physical scientists and engineers were paid, directly or indirectly, by DOD in the late 1960s, and 290,000 worked for defense industry alone (prior to the 1969-1971 job cuts).[1] A Brookings Institution survey at 12 major universities showed that a quarter of the scientists received part of their regular salaries from federal funds; at one school 151 professors received their full pay from the government. In 1969 the Pentagon had 5000 contracts with individual scientists for on-campus research, including 200 classified projects, and it claimed to have requests for ten times more contracts than it could fill. The growth of the academic discipline of physics, and its severe depression in the early 1970s, were related directly to changes in military and space spending.

4. Universities which have become partly dependent on defense contracts and defense-related fellowship and research support. Massachusetts Institute of Technology, for example, has been among the top 100 defense contractors for years, with 69 percent of its 1968 research budget coming from the Defense Department and another 26 percent coming from other federal agencies; 19 of the top 75 Pentagon contractors were represented on the M.I.T. Corporation. Other schools received more than three-fourths of their research funds from national security agencies.

5. Strategists and social scientists, a smaller group.[2]

[1] Calculations of the number of engineers and scientists with defense jobs vary, depending on the subgroups examined. In 1970 an estimated 59 percent of all aeronautical engineers, 38 percent of nonprofessor physicists, and 22 percent of electrical engineers were employed on defense projects[25, p. 48].

[2] Galbraith[8, p. 334] believed that although deterrence, war games, and economic warfare were "fashionable" subjects for university research at one time, "the larger educational and scientific estate has not been strongly receptive to the Cold War imagery. . . . The Cold War specialists within the scholarly community have become an increasingly alienated group" and increasingly dependent on the Pentagon for funds and

As with the military-industrial relationship, we ask: Who initiates the contacts between these two public institutions, government and academe? Discussing foreign area research, a Pentagon spokesman said, "Approximately half of the research proposals are submitted by scientists seeking support of their individual research interests. ... Other proposals are generated as a result of discussions between knowledgeable persons within and outside DOD. Others are submitted by universities ... as a result of insight gained in current work. A few are the result of local government requests through U.S. missions personnel."[3]

Proposals in most fields are initiated by the researchers themselves. Johns Hopkins said 95 percent of its defense contracts originated from university suggestions. Admiral Rickover maintained that there "have been few—if any—instances where the technical people in the DOD—the ones who devise and produce weapons ... or field commanders—have asked for a particular (social science) research study." More broadly, Rickover said, he never had been asked if there was particular research that he would like to have done by think tanks or other researchers; "I believe that not many of their research projects have originated in the Armed Forces"[27, p. 18].

Scientists are no less interested in their careers than are other men. Professors, ex-academic Fulbright[7, p. 36181] said, "like money and influence ... having traditionally been deprived of both." Nor are they immune from pork-barrelling. Researchers and administrators have followed profitable research into new corporations, with 360 spun off from M.I.T. and Stanford alone. Research specialists cross over from academe to business and government, and former DOD officials become administrators of contract-dependent universities, e.g., California, Cal Tech, Rochester, and M.I.T.

• • •

Rickover's remarks suggest that little love is lost between many military officers and scientists, even when they recognize a mutual dependence. The military has attempted to placate scientists by permitting them to work in civilian research settings, under civilian supervisors, in civilian clothes, with civilian benefits, but antimilitary hostility remains within the scientific community.

After the war the military, "realizing that original research cannot be regimented, ... consciously (tried) to maintain a civilian feel in their outfits"[23, p. 21]. Scientists felt their contribution to victory had been indis-

---

recognition. Certainly, national security policy and related studies have suffered from a poor campus image since the Vietnam War began. The war led to a resurgence of traditional antimilitary feelings on campuses.

[3] In the social sciences, until recently, projects were more likely to be assigned or narrow "purchased" research, i.e., that originating in agency needs, rather than "sponsored" research, i.e., that proposed by scientists.

pensable and they deserved their status as national heroes. They believed they were successful because military regimentation, growing out of the organizationally conservative and noninnovative military mind, was largely absent. Manhattan Project Director Leslie R. Groves did not leave them alone; he instituted efficiency schemes which were notoriously ignored.

The military did not always conceal its disdain for scientists. It opposed granting them extensive postwar powers of independent initiative because of fears that, due to naïveté and lack of military experience, scientists might support a dangerously monistic weapons strategy[17, pp. 139-140]. Resentment of the scientist's new influence and prestige surfaced, for example, in officers' critical testimony during the security hearings for scientist-adviser J. Robert Oppenheimer. To Gen. Thomas White scientists and mathematicians involved in defense affairs were the "pipe-smoking tree-full-of-owls type."

Though sometimes permitting suspicions of one another to lead to conflict, usually they recognize that their interests are overlapping and interlocking. Military leaders have found that the academic world is a useful managerial compromise between industry and government, and that without it, they would be unable to tap the best scientific expertise. Although larger weapons research budgets benefit both, there have been harsh military-scientist disputes involving (1) control of postwar atomic energy development; (2) international control of atomic energy development; (3) the crash program to develop the H-bomb; (4) other controversies in the 1950s relating to "massive retaliation"; (5) responsibility for laboratories and scientific research; (6) control of space exploration; (7) nuclear testing and fallout shelters; (8) the use of chemical warfare, especially in Vietnam; and (9) the ABM and MIRV.

Control of postwar atomic energy development. The military wanted the program under army control, while the scientists demanded civilian control. Opposition to an army-sponsored bill led by the Federation of Atomic Scientists (FAS) convinced the military to accept the Atomic Energy Act, which gave at least nominal control over the use of atomic energy to civilians. The General Advisory Committee of the Atomic Energy Commission became the primary institutional presence of scientists in Washington. However, the other AEC advisory board was military, and the AEC disappointed these scientists by paying little attention to research projects concerning peaceful uses for atomic energy.

International control of atomic energy development. Forums, letter-writing campaigns, and elite lobbying were used by the FAS and the Committee for Atomic Information in support of international control of atomic energy development, but ultimately without success.

The first two postwar conflicts were born in the great military-scientific cooperative venture of the war: the Manhattan Project to develop an atomic bomb. Thirty years of development of the airplane had produced a vehicle

which could travel only about 25 times as fast as horse cavalry, but plutonium had an explosive force half a million times as powerful as TNT. Albert
Einstein's famous letter to President Roosevelt secured government interest in
atomic development; the administration supported the bomb project through
discretionary funds, eventually as the Development of Substitute Materials
project under the jurisdiction of the Army Corps of Engineers. Academic and
industrial scientists and engineers operated the facilities, isolated and insulated from the army and the government. When it became clear that Germany
did not have the bomb, some atomic scientists, later organized as the
Committee on Social and Political Implications, opposed use of the bomb
against Japan; most scientists in 1944-1945 restricted themselves to narrow
technical questions. After Hiroshima and Nagasaki, however, there was a
palpable feeling of guilt among the hero-scientists. "In some sense," Oppenheimer said, "which no vulgarity, no humor, no overstatement can quite
extinguish, the physicists have known sin and this is a knowledge which they
cannot lose"[5, p. 105].

   The crash program to develop the hydrogen bomb. After the 1949
detonation of an atomic weapon by the U.S.S.R., scientists disputed with
scientists, with the military supporting one faction. The disunity of atomic
scientists became clear. The initiative came primarily from scientists such as
Ernest Lawrence and Edward Teller, who were quickly joined by members of
the Joint Congressional Committee on Atomic Energy. "Although generally
favoring the bomb, the military were not the first to push it"[13, p. 300].
Because pro-"Super" scientists urged military leaders to express their interest
in the weapon, the Joint Chiefs of Staff strongly urged the development of a
hydrogen bomb at a meeting with the Joint Committee. Before the scientists
stimulated military interest, there had been few expressions of interest by the
services in more powerful weapons; Oppenheimer noted that military pressure
had been in the opposite direction, toward more weapons, not larger ones.
Skeptical scientists on the AEC's General Advisory Committee eventually
were overruled by nonscientists, as military support (e.g., from the air force
and the Weapon System Evaluation Group) grew stronger. The hydrogen-
bomb controversy was a turning point in military-science relations: it became
clear that opponents of high priority for the Super opposed it not only for
technical reasons (Oppenheimer thought it would be so large that it would
have to be transported by ox cart), but also for strategic and moral reasons;
they favored a more "flexible" strategy and were not pleased by the prospects of arms races and more destructive "city-busting" weapons. Scientists
favoring the bomb felt science should be followed wherever it led; critics say
this view is held today by the Pentagon and its supporters in industry and
Congress, that technological advancement is an end in itself. In 1954 Oppenheimer was stripped of his security clearance; the loyalty investigations of
1950-1955, Bush believed, demoralized much of the scientific community,
especially those critical of military programs.

Other controversies of the 1950s relating to "massive retaliation." Scientists associated with studies of tactical nuclear weapons, continental air defense, and other programs which the air force feared would undermine the threat of nuclear destruction through offensive airpower were distrusted. The Oppenheimer wing of the defense scientists often sided with the army and navy, favoring a balanced military capability. To them the air force hope of maintaining "superiority" was futile, given rapid technological change.

It was not until Sputnik (1957), and the establishment of the President's Science Advisory Committee and a special science assistant, that these scientists regained an important voice in making weapons policies. The PSAC, for example, led scientific opposition to air force proposals for crash programs to develop a nuclear-powered bomber and the B-70, and to deploy the Nike-Zeus antiballistic missile. The PSAC helped to establish a civilian space agency rather than one under air force control. It worked to unify control over military R & D. It also worked toward changes in U.S. disarmament policy and put before President Eisenhower the scientific rationale for opposition to nuclear testing. As the OSRD and the AEC's General Advisory Committee had been earlier, PSAC became the leading spokesman for the scientific community, attempting to overcome the more "parochial" views of service-attached scientists[19, pp. 161-162].

Responsibility for laboratories and scientific research. The scientists won civilian control of AEC laboratories such as Los Alamos, but overall direction of the government's basic science program remained in military hands. The services became the primary funding sources for research in nuclear energy and physics, materials science, oceanography, electronic engineering, and other fields. DOD, NASA, and the AEC could more easily obtain appropriations for all purposes than could civilian organizations and, until the late 1960s, these agencies did not have to justify items before a skeptical Congress; Defense Secretary Neil H. McElroy said his department supported basic research because it should be done and no one else had the money.

Control of space exploration. Scientific groups such as the American Rocket Society, the American Association for the Advancement of Science, the National Society of Professional Engineers, an International Geophysical Year panel, and FAS joined other civilian groups and a few military men to oppose military dominance of the space program. A civilian agency, NASA, was set up, but the air force continued to influence space policy.

Nuclear testing and fallout-shelters. Scientific groups, such as the Scientists' Committee for Radiation Information, publicized the dangers of nuclear fallout during the late 1950s and early 1960s, and opposed a national shelter-construction campaign. The scientists, such as Teller, who had pushed for development of the hydrogen bomb supported continued testing. Nuclear testing became a major presidential campaign issue in 1956, as other arms-related questions were to become in subsequent elections; scientific panels were organized for all presidential candidates, although the majority of scientific leaders were "liberal" (thus Democratic).[4]

The use of chemical warfare, especially in Vietnam. Again, criticism has come from scientific groups such as FAS.

The antiballistic missile and multiple independently targeted reentry vehicles. The technological complexities of the ABM and MIRV placed scientists in the center of the controversy. Former presidential and Defense Department science advisers wrote books and articles, and testified before Congress that the new weapons were dangerously destabilizing or would not work. For the first time scientists sought to block an administration defense program without support from dissident elements within the services or administration; the absence of expert dissidence from within made essential the respectability bestowed upon the anti-ABM congressmen by the outside scientists. Two science-oriented lobbying groups, the Council for a Livable World and the FAS, were active in coordinating opposition to the ABM. (In several localities during this period, defense industry technicians were organized to press their managements to convert to nonmilitary work.)

Cornell Vice President Franklin A. Long was rejected by President Nixon for the position of head of the NSF because of Long's opposition to ABM deployment. After adverse scientific and press reaction, the administration changed its mind and asked Long to accept the position but he declined.

THE UNIVERSITIES

Have the universities been bought by the Pentagon? Universities long have received support through ROTC programs (which have not touched as many as 40 percent of male undergraduates since 1945), but only since World War II has government research and fellowship support loomed so large for so many institutions. ROTC and military-industrial complex campus recruiting were sources of controversy during the Vietnam War, but the most serious form of "campus complicity" with the military was defense research and training for defense research.

Most of the schools involved heavily in weapons projects would be in a "Who's Who" of higher education. M.I.T., California, Stanford, Johns Hopkins, Rochester, Cornell, Michigan, Illinois Institute of Technology, Penn State, and Columbia were the ten top research contractors in 1969, receiving more than a third of federal R & D funds. Even for schools not in the top ten, the government was the major source of research funds: 84 percent for the

---

[4] Some scientists claim to be peculiarly sensitive to the instabilities of the arms race, because of their familiarity with the possibilities of nuclear accidents; they urged adoption of methods to insure the invulnerability of deterrent forces, urged development of "fail-safe" methods, and in the early sixties lobbied for a partial nuclear test-ban treaty. Most military leaders were reluctant to support the test ban, and some opposed it vigorously.

University of Pennsylvania in the mid-1960s, and nearly 30 percent of its operating budget. Ninety other universities had military research contracts in 1969. More than one-tenth of the top 500 defense research contractors have been universities and their affiliated centers. Universities often serve as administrators of Defense Department research facilities: the Jet Propulsion Laboratory at Cal Tech is operated under an army and NASA contract; the AEC's Radiation and Los Alamos Scientific Laboratories where nuclear bombs were developed are administered by the University of California; the Human Resources Research Office is run by George Washington; and the Argonne National and Brookhaven National laboratories as well as Rochester's affiliated Center for Naval Analyses are government-owned. Universities and nonprofit institutes work on major strategic systems, conventional weapons, and paper studies, e.g., on counterinsurgency. Without government money, a report of the Carnegie Foundation for the Advancement of Teaching noted, "the whole character of many universities' research programs (and in consequence their instructional programs) would change. Faculties . . . would shrink. Many research efforts would have to be abandoned completely (or) . . . curtailed"[21, p. 63]. "Government contracts represent a big part of our research efforts," the director of a Johns Hopkins research institute said. "It's a way of life"[11, p. 190].

Two sites of controversy in the late 1960s were the leading campus contractor, M.I.T., and Stanford. M.I.T.'s Instrumentation Lab, two blocks from the main campus, was established in the 1930s, as an adjunct of the school's aeronautics and astronautics department, to work on gyroscope navigational systems. One of the first interdisciplinary laboratories, it served as the research setting for generations of M.I.T. students. The guidance systems for aircraft, submarines, Apollo space vehicles, and missiles, including Polaris and the Poseidon MIRVs, were developed there. Its operating income rose from $16 million to $54 million between 1961 and 1969, when it became the target of student protests; it employed almost 2000 people, more than half of them degree-holding professionals. M.I.T.'s Lincoln Lab, a few miles away, was set up in 1951, at Defense Department urging, to develop the continental air defense system; it specialized in communication and radar. It employed 1800 and had about $65 million in military contracts (including work on the ABM). Half of both laboratories' contracts were classified.

In 1969 some of the students and faculty members protested: (1) classified research being done on campus (as being inconsistent with the openness of "free inquiry"), involving students who needed security clearance and intelligence agents making loyalty checks; (2) university ties to labs doing classified work, even if done off-campus; (3) chemical and biological warfare research; and (4) research tied to the Vietnam War, intensely unpopular on eastern campuses. M.I.T. responded by setting up a panel, which recommended that: (1) research energies be directed into more civilian projects, to provide a better military-civilian balance; (2) educational ties between the labs and the main campus be expanded; (3) classification and security barriers at the labs be reduced; (4) all research proposals at the two labs be reviewed.

The Lincoln Lab's director said he had sought nondefense work but funds were not available. Where the Pentagon, NASA, and the AEC were geared up to spend large amounts on research, he said, "agencies focusing on social problems have not matched this capability"[3, p. 69]. Later that year the Instrumentation Lab announced it would refuse weapons-system work (while accepting other defense work) and would seek contracts dealing with environmental and social problems. However, many of the laboratory's staff had specialized skills with little application to urban problems, and only 3 percent of the laboratory's research income came from social and medical research. Sporadic student protests continued. Six months later M.I.T. announced it would sell the Instrumentation Lab to a private corporation. "It is now clear," the university announced, "that it is not practical to anticipate that the laboratories could be diversified either wholly or in large part toward non-defense work. ... Funds are unavailable now to support large non-defense work in fields appropriate to the competence of the laboratories." The Lincoln Lab, doing more basic research, was retained by M.I.T., in line with its investigatory panel's recommendations[22, p. 24].

"The country's scientific and technological base rests in large part with the universities," the panel report had said, "and this base should be available to support advances in defense-related fields." While it did not suggest elimination of all defense work, it noted that heavy emphasis on defense research "detracts from similar efforts aimed at other urgent needs of society," and works against unclassified research. M.I.T. was urged to continue work on design of weapons, but to refrain from direct involvement in their production and deployment. For example, Lincoln's work on an advanced radar system able to see through heavy foliage was approved, but it was questioned whether M.I.T. engineers should go to southeast Asian battle zones to help in field tests.

Stanford is a major contractor in its own right, and until 1969, through its subsidiary Stanford Research Institute (employing more than 2000). The institute was created in 1946 to "improve the standard of living and the peace and prosperity of mankind," and was dependent for nearly half its research funds on DOD. SRI operated classified counterinsurgency projects in southeast Asia and Latin America in the late 1960s, developed new weapons, and played a major role in chemical and biological warfare research. Its Operational Technology Division included a navy-sponsored center for antisubmarine warfare and antiaircraft warfare, and it conducted experiments for the army's Combat Development Experiment Center. Scene of a 9-day sit-in in 1969 was the electronics and systems techniques laboratory of Stanford's engineering school. Soon afterward the university announced it was phasing out the lab's $2.2 million in classified contracts (principally in electronic warfare research) because of the controversy.

What can be given can be taken away, M.I.T. and Stanford were reminded in 1969. An AEC commissioner threatened to seek withdrawal of unclassified AEC research if the two schools decided against doing classified military research. The economic power of the AEC and NASA, if added to that of DOD, would be formidable indeed.

By 1970 the Defense Department, which a few years earlier (with Project Themis) had announced its plans to establish 200 new defense-related research centers at universities with little previous connection to the Pentagon, was seriously considering whether military research could continue to be conducted on campuses at all. At the University of Wisconsin an army mathematics research center was bombed, killing one researcher and injuring four others. Brief "research stoppages" were held at several schools. "If these federal research facilities on campus are causing administrators trouble," Defense Secretary Laird said, perhaps contract research centers should sever ties with universities[16, p. 2-A]. Harvard, Columbia, and Johns Hopkins (with special expertise in the self-deteriorating proximity fuse) began phasing out classified on-campus research in the late 1960s. Cornell wanted to sell its off-campus aeronautical laboratory to a private corporation, but was blocked for several years by legal embroilments. The University of Chicago had been divesting itself of military ties prior to the Vietnam War, leading its associate director of applied science laboratories and 25 scientists to quit in 1963. "The Department of Defense needs all the assistance of the finest scientific staffs it can assemble," the resigning official said. But he said the university administration would not invite faculty participation in defense research. "I think their last involvement in the development of atomic energy and the bomb [the first controlled nuclear chain reaction was sustained under the university football stands in 1942] left a deep scar on the moral fiber of this place from which it has not really recovered" [4, p. 28].

David Riesman and Christopher Jencks[14, p. 223] believed that the expertise of universities had been co-opted by the Pentagon indirectly, through the employment of university graduates in contract research. "By allowing these (graduates) to maintain non-military professional identities (e.g., as economists or engineers), the defense contracting system has co-opted many who would not have been willing to remain in uniform or under military discipline for more than a few years. In a sense, the contract system has been . . . a highly successful . . . alternative to ROTC." Almost half of the M.I.T. graduate students who accept industry jobs, for example, go to work for the 100 leading defense contractors. Physicist Teller, on the other hand[10, p. 2-A], warned that radical campus political movements were seriously jeopardizing the future of defense-related research. Many young scientists, he told the President's Commission on Campus Unrest, were being indoctrinated not to participate in defense research. Events of 1969-1970 had "practically cut the connection between the universities and defense-related industries," he warned. In Teller's view it was the socialization impact of antiresearch demonstrations that was important, rather than the cessation of the relatively small amounts of defense research actually conducted on campus. "The universities have a monopoly on the education of the young people."[5] If they will not take defense jobs, he said, defense work will come to a halt.

There was no sign in the early seventies that classified military research was going to be halted, but only redirected from university-affiliated labs on or near campuses to independent labs in anonymous buildings. The same personnel likely would continue their research under revised sponsorship and the same funding, and with less chance of their labs being taken over or their office files rifled. Most protests appeared to involve the alleged contamination of the university's academic purity, rather than serious efforts to block military research.

Research center directors claimed that the nation would lose a source of critical review if universities were prevented from doing military research. W. E. H. Panofsky, director of the AEC-funded Stanford Linear Accelerator Center (which was having funding difficulties related to center officials' anti-ABM position), called for university scientists to play an independent role in public scrutiny of defense policy. "It can't come from people who work directly for the Defense Department because they're obliged to live by official policy. It can't very well come from the contractors whose living depends on the Defense Department. So the universities are the only places with the technological expertise left. The real problem is how do you keep the universities from becoming captive in the process of furnishing this advice?"[26, p. 34]. Former Cornell President James Perkins believed the danger of captivity was real: "Acceptance of Government work and corporate donation," he said, "has been known to result in a slowing down of the university's critical faculties"[26, pp. 34-35].

GAS AND GERMS

In 1965 projects Summit and Spicerack were being handled by the University of Pennsylvania's Institute for Cooperative Research. Despite the pleasantness of the project titles, ICR was the only university laboratory involved in a form of classified research which was to become extremely controversial: engineering and systems analysis for defoliation and herbicides used to destroy food crops. It even evaluated potential defoliation targets in Vietnam, and measured the effectiveness of chemical and biological warfare (CBW). A student employee of the university bookstore noticed that ICR was receiving a suspicious array of books dealing with plant and infectious diseases and

---

[5] Defense corporations in the late 1960s, primarily through their acquisitions of existing companies, assumed an important position in the software (textbooks) and hardware ("learning machines") aspects of the education business.

with Asian studies; the controversy that followed, involving the most important academic research arm of the Army Chemical Corps, touched off a
national debate on the university's role in CBW.

More than 50 universities were involved in CBW research when the
campus unpopularity of the Vietnam War, where the use of napalm had been
widely reported, first focused attention on America's hidden arsenal. Ironically, napalm was invented at Harvard, rather than by its manufacturer Dow,
the target of anti-napalm protest. About $100 million was being spent on
CBW research contracts, and by 1968 it was estimated that the United States
spent four times as much on CBW (overall) as it did on cancer research, one
of the most generously-funded medical programs.

The rationale for university participation in CBW research was more
guarded than the rationale presented for more socially-acceptable military
research, but both boiled down to national service. The Pentagon said
universities should participate in CBW research because it "is necessary to
assure the security of our country against surprise attack or to minimize
surprise attack. In that regard, every university and every citizen has an
obligation to contribute"[11, p. 188]. More pragmatically, the Defense
Department said, universities benefit by having expensive government-
purchased computers, laboratory equipment, and training opportunities for
graduate students.

University justifications did not dwell on the need for defense research
to protect national security. When CBW first became a controversial issue,
most schools denied doing any such work; they said, "(1) The research was
basic work and had no connection with CBW. (2) The research was unclassified work that was available to all. (3) The research was strictly defensive in
nature"[11, p. 192]. The faculty debates at various schools on CBW, as those
on ROTC, tended to focus on procedural questions. In the case of ROTC,
faculty critics asked if military instructors should be granted academic status
and if the university had control over the content of the ROTC curriculum,
while the moral question of whether universities had any business being
involved in direct war support was left to student demonstrators. In the case
of controversial research, defenders of such programs spoke in the name of
academic freedom. "There is a broader university principle involved here,"
University of Pennsylvania President Gaylord P. Harnwell said, "the freedom
of the faculty to do research into any area they want to. . . . I can't tell
people what they ought to research. I don't presume to tell anyone that
certain kinds of research are inappropriate"[11, p. 196]. The moral
neutrality of this position was reflected in another comment by Harnwell:
"How or when or where new knowledge will find applications and whether it
be deemed for good or ill extends far beyond either the judgement or control
of universities or the men who compose them." Not the content of research
but its publishability, a neutral, "unemotional," and "nonpolitical" issue,

became the subject of a resolution by the university's faculty. Research contracts could be accepted, if they were unclassified.[6] For the military, Pentagon research chief John F. Foster, Jr., said, "Most of the value of university research is in the unclassified area"[11, p. 197].

THE THINK TANKS

Outside the universities there are a breed of noncorporate, nonteaching institutes which have stretched and bent, but not broken, their umbilical cords to the Pentagon: the think tanks. In various degrees of disengagement from government employment they all operate within the sponsoring agency's framework of interests and all are supported by DOD contracts. They have been attacked both by professional military men and from the Left.

The intellectual home of much of the systems analysis, cost-effectiveness studies, and strategic thinking that disturbs critics of various temperaments stands across the street from the Pacific Ocean: the RAND Corporation in Santa Monica. It is a continent away from the Pentagon and its working style is far removed from the Pentagon, too. Peopled in the 1960s by distinguished academics from the mathematical and physical sciences, engineering, economics, and the social sciences, RAND (professional staff: 500) is organized by skills rather than by categories of military operations. It was founded as the prototype nonprofit institute by the air force in 1948, but it prides itself on its intellectual freedom and autonomy, i.e., both external autonomy from air force pressure and internal autonomy for its researchers. It is the most successful of the 200 nonprofit research organizations, 1400 corporations, and 300 university centers which think about military problems and accept contracts to produce pieces of paper. Its funding doubled between 1960-1966. RAND technicians and strategists brief Washington officials, sit on dozens of government committees, lecture at war colleges and service academies, and in their first 15 years produced about 7000 research reports, memoranda, and technical papers. They helped to develop technical (e.g., "fail-safe") and managerial (e.g., program package budgeting) innovations. They "move freely through the corridors of the Pentagon and State Department, rather as the Jesuits moved through the courts of Vienna and Madrid, three centuries ago"[18, p. 252]. But critics have taken the Jesuit analogy and given it a different twist: RAND's studies should be accepted with the same caution with which one would greet a

---

[6] One University of Pennsylvania researcher chose not to publish his CBW results, and more often, research findings were "unclassified, but not available"[11, pp. 193, 196]. The FAS in 1967 called for universities to refuse secret research, but the Committee for Academic Integrity said the purpose of all war research was the same, whether secret or not, and all should be refused.

study of the Reformation by Jesuits based on secret documents in the Vatican; the bias is inherent in the commitment.

In-house research centers (civilian or military) are widely believed to be unable to produce long-term strategic thinking or innovative strategy-related technical work. At the same time, universities usually have been unable to organize professional skills into problem-solving units because of their departmental lines and nonresearch responsibilities. Thus the RAND-type organization is born. Most research funds to nonprofit corporations, more than $300 million a year, went to 16 institutes, which received 85 to 99 percent of their support from defense contracts. Personnel also provided a link to the Pentagon: seven of these institute presidents and five vice-presidents in 1969 once held high posts in DOD, including the president of the Institute for Defense Analyses (IDA), Maxwell D. Taylor, former chairman of the Joint Chiefs of Staff. Of the 18 professional staff members of the Logistics Management Institute, for example, six came directly from defense contractors, six were formerly employed by other defense-oriented research centers or acted as consultants, and one was a retired military officer.

The Office of the Secretary of Defense's IDA has been a unique combination of external and internal analytical units. Begun with the sponsorship of 12 universities, it was housed next to the Pentagon and participated in staff R & D work. It has been responsible for the Weapon System Evaluation Group (originally a military-dominated group reporting to the Joint Chiefs, later captured by the civilian DOD research office), and the secretary's Advanced Research Projects Agency which succeeded a military-dominated R & D board. IDA, structured around specific contracts, deals with basic technical and strategic questions. Even before university sponsorship was ended, its atmosphere was less academic than that of RAND, and it was less independent (e.g., in terms of accepting service assumptions). However, even its limited autonomy was believed to improve research results.[7]

Spun off from RAND was Herman Kahn's "soft data"-oriented, high-level-thinking-place, the Hudson Institute, which attempted to avoid close affiliation with any of its client agencies. "RAND is the loyal opposition," Kahn said, "and Hudson is not necessarily even loyal," with a minority of its staff being opposed to government or client agency policies[20, p. 349]. The

---

[7] Other types of research centers are government facilities managed by corporations, and think-tank divisions of corporations.

Research corporations tied to the military also include: the army's Research Analysis Corporation, successor to the Operations Research Office, liquidated in 1961 after 13 years of operations; and the Center for Naval Analyses managed by the Franklin Institute and growing out of a 1942 navy group. RAC and CNA were under tighter service control than RAND. The army and Johns Hopkins had fought over control of ORO research for years, with the university demanding autonomy. The army sought to maintain strict control in detail over the research process, and the tension finally became intolerable for both parties.

role of former RAND staff member Daniel Ellsberg in leaking the classified Pentagon Papers on the Vietnam War in 1971 led to some questions in the Pentagon about the loyalty of RAND opposition to national policies. RAND had helped in preparation of the Pentagon study. Secretary of Defense Laird, within a week of Ellsberg's arrest, ordered all classified information withdrawn from the custody of RAND on the grounds that it had allowed the leak. Special access to cryptographic material and intelligence information also was canceled.

At least 20 academic research centers have been active in strategic thinking, e.g., at Harvard, M.I.T., Princeton, Johns Hopkins, Columbia, Chicago, and Michigan. Academic centers contain a significant percentage of the total strategic community, a few hundred professionals.[8]

How much influence do the think tanks have? Are they really independent, and to the extent that they are, does this hurt or help them? Their nonprofit status theoretically makes their advice more objective since it is "unwarped by the hope of a sale"[2, p. 239]. "But in practice, they sometimes tell the military customer what he wants to hear to support his own preconceived conviction." They still have jobs and programs to protect.[9]

Despite continued reliance on the air force for the bulk of its funds through a blanket contract, RAND has exercised its own initiative in choosing study projects, and has been under no compulsion to pursue any project against its will. Some air force officers have resented RAND independence, and blamed RAND for undermining the air force's "massive retaliation" strategy of the 1950s with its limited war, airpower vulnerability, and civil defense studies. RAND was charged with supporting the graduated deterrence positions of the army and navy. But, because the air force wanted good advice, no sustained barriers were put in RAND's way, and it continued to

---

[8] Exceptions to the critical attitude of the Vietnam period were three centers characterized by critics as "hardline anti-Communist," "ideological" rather than "pragmatic," corporation-dominated, and "more prepared to accept military solutions." These included Stanford's Hoover Institution on War, Revolution, and Peace; Georgetown's Center for Strategic and International Studies; and the University of Pennsylvania's Foreign Policy Research Institute, the latter having been the principal adviser to the National War College. These centers, early in the Nixon administration, had personnel connections such as Adm. (Ret.) Arleigh Burke, the Georgetown Center's chairman, and Robert Strausz-Hupe, the director of the Foreign Policy Research Institute, both members of Nixon campaign task forces on security affairs; senior NSC staff member Richard V. Allen, on leave from the Hoover Institution; and other Hoover-Penn strategists brought into the DOD International Security Affairs office.

[9] Nieburg[19, pp. 245-256] believed that nonprofit institutes ("leashed intellectuals") present problems of absence of public control, evasion of the civil service system, conflict-of-interest, and possible pork-barreling. In their "cushioned, cost-plus nursery," he said, "profits" are used for perquisites and patronage, and in some cases to enable cooperative subcontractors to make a profit. Nieburg believed that, despite their advantages of short-term flexibility, all serve as agency advocates; they demonstrate objectivity in helping to divide up the defense contract market, he said, but not objectivity in protecting interests other than those of big corporations.

receive support for the same reason it had been established: The military felt that scientists would be unwilling to leave an academic and civilian atmosphere for the low salaries and the civil-service procedures of government employment.

RAND's relatively uncensored history was not for lack of air force efforts. Malcolm W. Hoag, of RAND's economics department, noted that the corporation's independent research "often puts us in violent conflict with the current prejudices of the client in question, whether it be the Air Force or the Office of the Assistant Secretary of Defense for International Security Affairs" [15, p. 234]. An example was the B-70 program: "There were a lot of generals in the Air Force who had dreams every night about flying at mach 3 in a B-70. And when suddenly the RAND Corp. began to shatter those dreams (with critical studies), they were very unhappy indeed. (My friends in RAND assumed that) there is cause and effect here, that the RAND Corp. scuttling of the B-70 program led to the difficulties that RAND experienced in having its contract renewed"[Shapero in 15, p. 407]. RAND's response was to start diversifying into other public policy work in order to avoid becoming the air force's prisoner.

Where the effectiveness of the navy center was due [18, p. 241] to its integral role within the Pentagon and its low-profile, navy-only working arrangements, RAND hoped to have as much influence with more objectivity. RAND attempted to conceal its impact on policy by convincing the client that ideas were products of his own thinking, since a negative result of RAND's great prestige could be that the air force would feel that it was losing control. Claims made for decisive RAND influence on policy probably have been exaggerated [8, p. 264] ; its independence sometimes deprives it of an effective voice. It also has been affected by antiwar sentiments among academics; RAND's president said in 1969 that the center was having difficulty recruiting staff for war-related work.

No yardstick exists to measure the extent to which think tanks affect military decisions,[10] especially those with long lead-time. The centers are most useful in supplying data for program disputes within the executive branch or with Congress, when rationalizing and defending decisions already made [18, p. 245] .

[10] An example of successful think-tank involvement in policy-making is the RAND air bases study of the early 1950s. The original air force request was for a study of the most efficient selection, construction, and use of overseas air bases for 1956-1961. An interdisciplinary team at RAND reformulated a routine logistical study into a broader strategic study, emphasizing the problems of vulnerability of deterrent forces and system-wide costs. On their own authority the researchers added new variables. Their conclusion was that under the existing basing system, i.e., reliance on advanced overseas operating bases, almost all of the strategic air force could be destroyed on the ground by a surprise attack. The air force adopted RAND's major recommendations 1 year after their formal presentation, not without substantial lobbying by the researchers themselves.

SOCIAL SCIENCE

Science and academe are not tied to the military only by way of weapons research. The Pentagon has sought strategic, social scientific, and foreign area research although the dollar amounts involved remain small (less than $50 million in outside contracts in 1970). In-house foreign area training, such as the army's Military Assistance Officers Program, also involved relatively small budgets. Many military leaders would not have been disappointed to have all civilian "whiz kid" contributions eliminated, from budgeting cost effectiveness, to strategies, to personnel motivation studies. "I have never heard of military people being themselves interested" in social science projects, Admiral Rickover said, and there has been chronic conflict between commanders and social science research staffs assigned to their units. The McNamara administration *was* interested; at a DOD-sponsored meeting of leading social scientists in 1967 it was agreed that the foreign area "missions of the DOD cannot be successfully performed in the absence of information on (a) socio-cultural patterns . . . including beliefs, values, motivations . . . (b) the social organization of troops . . . (c) the effect of change and innovation . . . (d) study and evaluation of action programs initiated by U.S. or foreign agencies in underdeveloped countries."

Looking at this report, I.L. Horowitz[12, pp. 90-91, 97-98] found three assumptions: (1) the Pentagon was engaged in "peacefare" (ideological conflict, pacification of total populations) as well as traditional warfare; (2) manpower, as well as weapons, is essential to a strong defense; and (3) "their professional autonomy will not be seriously jeopardized by the very fact of their dependence upon the DOD." The report, he said, "ignores questions having to do with social science autonomy as if these were products of misperceptions to be resolved by good will and better public relations between the DOD and the Academy." The social scientists seemed willing to accept most client premises. The U.S. foreign role was accepted, Horowitz said, and problems were "converted into a mechanical informational gap. . . . All efforts . . . are bent to maximizing social science participation[11] rather than to minimizing international conflict."

Military-related foreign area research in 1970 became a target of student protests at university centers, and in 1968-1970 of Senate investigations and restrictions. Pentagon-funded social science and basic scientific research that did not have a "direct and apparent relation to a specific military function" were banned. When compelled to cut back on controversial foreign

[11] One social science field receiving defense funds for many years is that of social psychology, as it relates to personnel and morale. Seventy percent of DOD social science research funds went into "human performance," "manpower selection and training," and "human factors engineering" studies. However, the services have resisted centralization of personnel selection and training, the heart of professionalism[17, p. 152] and research findings have had little impact on service programs. An exception may have been McNamara's program to draft 100,000 undraftables a year.

projects, DOD offered to transfer $400,000 of its $7.8 billion research budget to the state department, which had a research budget of only $125,000.

Researching methods of "controlling social change" became controversial in the late sixties, as some academics came to feel that such research put the Pentagon in better position to stifle "wars of liberation" in developing nations. Not only the function of such work, characterized by critics as scientific imperialism at best, but the source of funding became controversial. The army, for example, supported a nearly $2 million annual research program in counterinsurgency, military civic action and advisory functions, and psychological warfare at American University, and supported analyses of "third world" elites elsewhere. One of the most controversial was Project Camelot, in which the army sponsored a massive social science investigation to identify groups most likely to become involved in revolutionary activity, without revealing the sponsorship to host country authorities and participants. The project was canceled when its sponsorship was revealed in Chile, resulting in a sensitive foreign policy incident. The question American social scientists asked themselves, in the aftermath, was whether undertaking military-sponsored research amounted to support of the premises of official policy and, in this instance, whether the data would have aided counterinsurgents.[12]

CONCLUSION

Critics maintain that government dominance of research has created morale problems. A severe geographic concentration of research contracts despite Project Themis and other distribute-the-wealth directives, and the concentration of federal funding in the physical and life sciences and engineering, was said to undermine the already weak small schools and relatively underfinanced humanities and social sciences. There was an internal and external brain drain: Within universities, defense funds were believed to lure researchers away from underfinanced projects toward projects of interest to the Pentagon, leading to a decline in self-generated commitments to scholarly pursuits; and away from universities toward research corporations. Undergraduate teaching was thought to suffer relative to outside research and consulting or "community service" functions; some critics blamed student disquiet in the 1960s on the growing gap between students and their absentee professors.

Only a wealthy organization could be blamed for as much as DOD was charged with. To recapitulate: in 1950 federal R & D spending was $1.1 billion, and by 1961 it had increased almost ninefold; 1963's $12 billion was almost twice the total middepression federal budget, and more than two-

[12] Less ambiguous was a 1955-1960 Michigan State University project in South Vietnam, in which the 54 participating professors knew they were acting as a cover for the CIA.

thirds of that figure was for defense-related work. By the seventies, however, the other side of the disruption-of-universities charge was being voiced: Universities had become so dependent on the Pentagon that cutbacks hurt severely. Indirect costs of supporting government research continued to spiral, and the administrative headaches of operating controversial defense projects grew worse.

The dangers, then, are: "possible distortion of scholarly development, the imposition of external demands on research and education, the downgrading of teaching in favor of research, and the dependence of educational institutions on outside financing"[18, p. 10]. The root of these dangers can be located in the pre-seventies period of research funding abundance. The Defense Department was hardly the only culprit, but it does seem fair to lay some of the blame for these distortions, as well as for the distortions in business relationships, at the door of the Pentagon, if for no other reason than the extent of its financial penetration.

Scientists and academics have been eager accomplices in their own seduction into a military-university complex. They are not the innocents: the Pentagon has experienced little difficulty in finding recipients for its grants and consultantships.

Have science and academe, in fact, been militarized? They have gone some distance toward nationalization since 1941, but the pleas for seduction have not been acted upon fully. Universities are more independent than defense corporations.

The scientist still has a less certain place in the military establishment than the corporation executive. A member of the National Academy of Sciences' Defense Science Board is not comparable to a member of the Defense Industry Advisory Council, in terms of influence and involvement in a broad span of defense issues. The scientist is no longer in short supply, and his colleagues are by no means sure to agree with him on any given question. Although science remains vital to the military, greater care can be taken in choosing particular scientists. Civilian and military leaders can pick which expert scientific opinion they will put forward as authoritative. "The chosen scientists (often) provide a rationale and a justification for policies arrived at by other means"[19, p. 125]. Scientists are honored witnesses on matters of basic policy, as well as those which involve equations, but are less authoritative than they were earlier.

Scientists and the military men and civilians for whom they work often engage in polite deceit with one another: Scientists, like soldiers, claim they are best suited to make decisions on weapons selection, even as nonscientists cynically present rival experts. Politics, as Einstein said, is more difficult than physics, and scientists now have a quarter century of experience in the politics of science.

REFERENCES

1. "Arms Race: Scientists Question Threat from Soviet Military R & D," *Science*, 173 (August 20, 1971), pp. 707-709.
2. Borklund, C. W., *The Department of Defense* (New York: Praeger, 1968).
3. "Can Defense Work Keep a Home on Campus?" *Business Week*, no. 2075 (June 7, 1969), pp. 68-71.
4. "Defense Scientist Quits Chicago U.," *The Atlanta Journal*, June 6, 1963, p. 28.
5. Dupré, J. Stefan, and Sanford A. Lakoff, *Science and the Nation* (Englewood Cliffs, N.J.: Prentice-Hall, 1962).
6. Eisenhower, Dwight D., "Farewell Address," January 17, 1961 (SANE reproduction, 1969).
7. Fulbright, William, "The War and Its Effects—II," *The Congressional Record*, 113, part 27, pp. 36181-36184.
8. Galbraith, John Kenneth, *The New Industrial State* (Boston: Houghton Mifflin, 1967).
9. Greenberg, Daniel S., *The Politics of Pure Science* (New York: New American Library, 1969).
10. Halloran, Richard, "Teller Hits Campus Radicals," *The Atlanta Constitution*, July 25, 1970, p. 2-A.
11. Hersh, Seymour M., *Chemical and Biological Warfare* (Garden City, N.Y.: Doubleday Anchor, 1969).
12. Horowitz, I. L., "Social Science Yogis and Military Commissars," in *Peace and the War Industry*, ed. Kenneth E. Boulding (Chicago: Aldine, 1970), pp. 83-103.
13. Huntington, Samuel P., *The Common Defense* (New York: Columbia University Press, 1961).
14. Jencks, Christopher, and David Riesman, *The Academic Revolution* (Garden City, N.Y.: Doubleday, 1968).
15. Joint Economic Committee of the U.S. Congress, Hearings before the Subcommittee on Economy in Government,"The Military Budget and National Economic Priorities," (Washington: Government Printing Office, 1969).
16. Lengel, John, "Research at Colleges in Doubt," *The Atlanta Constitution*, September 3, 1970, p. 2-A.
17 Lyons, Gene M., *The Uneasy Partnership* (New York: Sage Foundation, 1969).
18. Lyons, Gene M., and Louis Morton, *Schools for Strategy* (New York: Praeger, 1965).
19. Nieburg, H. L., *In the Name of Science* (Chicago: Quadrangle, 1966).
20. Posvar, Wesley W., "Dispersion of the Strategy-Making Establishment,"

in *American Defense Policy*, 2nd. ed., eds. Mark E. Smith, III, and Claude J. Johns, Jr. (Baltimore: Johns Hopkins Press, 1968), pp. 340-361.

21. Raymond, Jack, "The Military-Industrial Complex," *Harvard Business Review*, 46 (May-June 1968), pp. 53-64.

22. Reinhold, Robert, "M.I.T. Will End Relation with a Research Lab," *The New York Times*, May 21, 1970, p. 24.

23. "Science Dons a Uniform," *Business Week*, no. 889, (September 14, 1946), pp. 19-23.

24. Smith, Bruce L. R., *The RAND Corporation* (Cambridge: Harvard University Press, 1966).

25. Udis, Bernard, ed., *Adjustments of the U.S. Economy to Reductions in Military Spending* (Washington: U.S. Arms Control and Disarmament Agency, 1970).

26. "The University Arsenal," *Look*, 33 (August 26, 1969), pp. 34-35.

27. U.S. Senate Foreign Relations Committee, Hearings on "Defense Department Sponsored Foreign Affairs Research," Part 2, (Washington: Government Printing Office, 1968).

CHAPTER SIX

The Military, the Media, Politics, and Public Opinion

Nineteen sixty-nine: a war that meandered on, bloodily but without decision, punctuated only by periodic expressions of official optimism; a hard-sell campaign to convince suburban Americans that they wanted an antiballistic missile for a next-door neighbor; a submarine that sank in the harbor; murder charges against American soldiers; a spy ship captured by a "fourth-rate military power"; lethal leak-prone nerve gas hauled by railroad back and forth across the country, through inhospitable cities and villages.

For years there had been warnings about the drift toward a militarized society, in which the people would not only acquiese in military dominance of national institutions and decision-making, but would demand it. American public opinion since 1945 had tended to embrace the military interpretation of international reality, and to support high levels of military spending. In 1969 and the early seventies, however, there was a sharp reversal of opinion— against the Defense Department, if not necessarily against the uniformed military. Was this a temporary reaction to close-to-home political and technological mishaps of the type cited above, to Vietnam, and to sloppy cost-controls in a recessionary period? Or was it the beginning of a return to the view that the military was incompetent *and* dangerous?

After a decade of war abroad and controversy at home, was the military seen as threatening or protecting? Hero or villain? Model for all of society or a semi-totalitarian institution? Did Americans believe their military had led the country into the endless war? Had it wasted billions of taxpayers' dollars in needless and ineffective weapons systems, which cost more than predicted and performed worse than anticipated? Or was the military, as the most visible group involved in international security affairs, being blamed for mistakes made by civilian leaders and institutions? Was the military being made the scapegoat for Vietnam failures and for anxieties caused by international and domestic tensions?

Traditionally, most writers assert, Americans have regarded the armed forces as an alien element in society. "Prior to World War II," Gen. David Shoup[45, p. 51] wrote, "American attitudes were typically isolationist, pacifist, and generally anti-military." According to Gen. Dale Smith[46, p. viii], "The American military has been maligned, stigmatized, and made out to be intrinsically dangerous to democratic government and American traditions." All that changed with Pearl Harbor and D-Day, Iwo Jima and Hiroshima. By 1949 journalist Baldwin [4, pp. 99, 119] believed "the military opinion now is given such weight by the people" that it is "time to call a halt."

As well as the possibilities of military-industrial elite conspiracy, President Eisenhower expressed concern about "an almost insidious penetration of our minds that the only thing this country is engaged in is weaponry and missiles" [15, p. 51]. Central both to Eisenhower's complex and to Lasswell's earlier "garrison state construct" was the idea that prolonged international crisis, the cold war in this instance, would lead to individual and mass insecurity. Perhaps insecurity could best be resolved by entrusting more responsibility to that security-insurance profession, the military.

Influence wielded by the military in the business community and governmental bureaucracy depends upon either acquiescence or support from Congress and the people. By the 1970s public acquiescence was no longer assured, but many believed that the military continued to mold public opinion. General Shoup (p. 51) felt it had successfully created a "militaristic and aggressive nation . . . with millions of proud, patriotic, and frequently bellicose and militaristic citizens." Usually the military was characterized as most powerful by its enemies and weakest by its friends.

In this chapter dimensions of public attitudes toward the military will be examined. Are people willing to allow the military to extend its control over individuals' lives? What are public attitudes toward extension of military control over allocation of national resources? How are these attitudes imbued, and what attempts has the military made to influence them?

THE PUBLIC AND FOREIGN AFFAIRS

Since the garrison state theory says attitudes toward the military are related to attitudes toward the international environment, wars, and crises, we will look briefly at those attitudes.[1]

[1] What is the size of the public which is attentive to such esoteric subjects as foreign affairs and the military? Levels of foreign policy salience and crisis awareness have been increasing [18, p. 359]. The "military policy public" in Wisconsin included 19

If continuing international conflict is expected, do people consequently feel a need for military protection? Is public deference toward the military related to perceptions of danger from abroad? Survey data is available for three indicators of perceived danger: (1) war expectations, without mention of specific enemies; (2) attitudes toward the officially designated enemy, the U.S.S.R.; and (3) attitudes toward the most threatening weapon, the nuclear weapon. However, substantial data over time is available only for the first.

Public expectations of imminent war are highly sensitive to changed behavior by Russian leaders, or more likely, to the recognition and verbalization of threat levels by American leaders. These expectations are likely to reflect the visibility and influence of the threat-identifying president. Contrary to the Lasswell construct, there has not been a secular trend toward more widespread expectations of war during the cold war. If anything, there has been a downward trend since 1948, with occasional sharp upward fluctuations, e.g., 1960-1961 with the U-2, Berlin, Cuba, and Laos. Expectations of a big power war were relatively stable after 1962. It is likely that years of continuing crisis—far from creating crisis nerves, or an "Armageddon complex," with people anxious for a showdown to end uncertainty—have made Americans believe they can live with international tensions. After all, they have survived past crises. Correlations between changing war expectations and changing attitudes toward defense spending over the years gives weak support at best to the notion that people are more willing to support high defense spending in crisis periods.

Available data on attitudes toward preventive war, use of the atomic bomb, "tough" or "soft" orientations toward negotiations, and "hawkish-dovish" attitudes toward limited wars do not support the garrison state

---

percent of all adults[14, pp. 203-204]. Twelve percent could minimally define "deterrence," and 10 percent knew something about the Polaris submarine; given the complexity and pre-Vietnam obscurity of defense issues, these are not small percentages. However, in some situations there may be recognition of an event or weapon, such as the atomic bomb—of which 98 percent of Leonard Cottrell's and Sylvia Eberhart's respondents had heard in 1946—without high levels of salience. Such matters may lack personal meaning: Cottrell and Eberhart [16, pp. 17-27, 100-112] found that people were not deeply concerned about the atomic bomb. Those interviewed expressed pessimism regarding the prospects for averting another world war and acknowledged the destructive capabilities of atomic weapons. Two-thirds said there was a real danger that atomic bombs would be used against America, and half of those saw at least a fair chance that members of their own families would be killed in such an attack. Yet only one-fourth expressed personal concern about the atomic bomb, one-half said they were not worried at all, and very few spontaneously mentioned the bomb in response to general world affairs questions. Their anxiety, of course, could have been repressed. Reasons given for not worrying about the bomb were that (1) there was no use worrying about something one could do nothing about, and (2) these were problems for government leaders and experts. Distinctions are made between threats to the political system and to oneself. The data to be reported here, then, includes opinions about issues which may not be highly salient; however, this problem characterizes most survey research on political matters.

hypothesis that continuing crisis leads to widespread trigger-happiness among the public. No trends can be found for this data: Support for first-use of nuclear weapons remained high and steady; belief that the United States was too soft in foreign affairs remained high and steady; support for preventive war rose slightly in the early 1950s but remained low. Attitudes tended to be "hard-line," but they had been that way since the immediate postwar period and did not increase with crises.

In the early sixties nuclear testing and construction of fallout shelters were offered to the public as possible responses to heightened international tensions. Despite military support for testing and shelters, and opposition to a nuclear test ban, the public remained skeptical of shelters,[2] and was divided on the advisability of continued testing.

A corollary to the garrison state linkage of crisis with support for the military and an Armageddon orientation is the widespread view that Americans respond to international events with unstable "moods." It is believed that they cannot tolerate extended uncertainty; supposedly they will react with irrational aggression or, if that is impossible, insistence upon withdrawal from foreign involvements. Gabriel Almond[1, p. 86] has written: "The superficiality and instability of public attitudes toward foreign affairs creates the danger of under- and over-reaction to changes in the world political situation. This unstable atmosphere surrounding our foreign policy makes anything better than a series of improvisations difficult to achieve." Edward A Kolodziej[32, p. 442] added, "It is precisely *because* the moods of the public often undergo rapid and radical permutations that significant limits are placed on the discretion of governmental officials in military and foreign policy. Long-range planning and swift adjustment to the vicissitudes of novel international conditions are seriously impeded." C. W. Borklund[8, p. 233] believed that public opinion provides a "strong check" on Pentagon power, causing officials to "devote a great deal of attention to it." Without "schooling in the basic elements of contemporary strategic problems," Kolodziej believed public support for government policies will be tenuous, and the nation's "bargaining power with its enemies will be correspondingly decreased. Political compromises may have to be reached that serve only to reinforce the public's skepticism and disdain of foreign policy and military involvement abroad." In the absence of instruction as to the need for rapid policy adjustments, ". . . large segments of the public are likely to become exasperated by the government's policies as they are seemingly drawn in first one direction and then another. Vacillating public moods will tend to replace stable expectations about the nation's foreign policies. The government's

---

[2] Gene Levine and John Modell [35, p. 272] found that the Berlin crisis more than doubled the number of people who said they had given thought to building a shelter. But after the Cuban missile crisis a year later the number returned to its pre-Berlin-crisis level. The shelter issue, Levine and Modell said, had not been fit into familiar patterns by national leaders, and was not salient.

flexibility abroad will be undermined by unpredictable oscillations and divisions in public sentiment"[32, p. 489].

This view was shared by American policy-makers during the Vietnam War. Presidents Kennedy, Johnson, and Nixon and their advisers consistently reiterated their view that the enemy planned to win the war not on the battlefield, but back home by the divisions of an impatient American public. Study of support for the war (both in terms of belief that the United States did not err originally in sending troops, and in support for the incumbent president's handling of the situation) shows that support remained relatively stable from year to year, with opposition to the war only gradually increasing. Most of the sharp and short-term changes in support for the government's Vietnam policy were associated with presidential public relations, e.g., President Nixon's appeal to the "silent majority" for support in November 1969 was followed by a 9 percent increase in support. To the extent that opinion on this subject was unstable, then, it was partly because presidents chose to make it so, for short-term political advantage. Only when avowed presidential policy changed from Lyndon Johnson's "nail the coonskin to the wall" to de-escalation and a negotiated settlement in mid-1968, did the number believing that intervention had been a wise action decline below 40 percent. It probably was not until 1971, when the Laotian invasion failed to generate even temporarily increased public support, that the war could be said to have lost the backing of the public.

Public opinion, far from being too unpredictable to provide support for international commitments, has been characterized by a "*strong* and *stable* 'permissive mood'" toward international involvement; it has given a "blank check" to the nation's leaders[10, p. 546]. It is important to be very clear as to which elites the public permits to act: It is the president and whichever civilian or military leaders he trusts. When the military supports an intervention policy opposed by the president it is unlikely that the public will contradict the president's definition of the situation as being not vital to the national interest. Questions probing for support for the president's handling of the Vietnam War invariably drew higher support ratios than questions which did not mention the president. Public attitudes toward military involvement abroad, if Vietnam is any indication, tend to be permissive once national prestige is involved.

Support for the Korean and Vietnam wars followed similar patterns: "In both cases initial support was high but this declined, as casualties mounted, to a level where support remained fairly constant and noticeably impervious to events. Both wars inspired about the same amount of support and opposition—although the anti-Communist element of the support for the Korean War may be weaker in Vietnam. ... An element of (the supporting group for both wars) appears to be willing to approve almost anything the leadership does"[39, p. 15].

President Johnson said Vietnam cost him 20 points in the presidential popularity polls. The popularity of both Presidents Truman (Korea) and Johnson were at their lowest during their last year in office, and the wars certainly contributed to their decisions not to seek third terms. However, Mueller showed that their decline in popularity started before the wars began, due to the gradual erosion of their "coalition of minorities." His analysis leads to the surprising finding that "the Korean War had a large, significant, independent negative impact on President Truman's popularity of some 18 percentage points, but the Vietnam War had no independent impact on President Johnson's popularity at all"[40, p. 28]. The explanation for this is that Korea became "Truman's war" to an extent that Vietnam never became "Johnson's war."

On unification of the armed services and on the need for a military draft, to take two more examples, the public has been acquiescent *after* the president and government have acted. After the beginning of Selective Service in 1940 support for the draft increased from 39 percent in October 1939 to 67 percent in July 1940.

Public opinion[3] commonly provides only general guidance for foreign policy; the public sets parameters within which officials can make decisions without much fear of arousing public concern.

THE PUBLIC AND CONSCRIPTION, CONTROL, SPENDING

How do Americans regard proposals to extend military control over individuals' lives? The most important form is the control exercised over enlisted men in the armed forces. The most extensive societal regimentation so far proposed would be *universal* military training (UMT), in which all men, and perhaps women, would be inducted into the services for a given period. National survey data [12, pp. 132-136] will be used to examine these and other attitudes toward the military.

[3] There are group differences of opinion toward security affairs based on one's social class, and psychological or situational factors. Davis Bobrow and Neal Cutler [18, p. 51] found greater similarity in national security opinions among persons belonging to the same cohort (birth in the same time period, thus aging through similar environments), as contrasted with life-stage or situational explanations. Differences between the attitudes of higher-class (center) and relatively lower-class (periphery) groups usually are thought to lie in the way opinions are held, i.e., their structure and not their content. In the periphery attitudes usually are seen as less stable, less informed, more "moral," and more absolutist; the periphery also is believed to favor the status quo, i.e., ideas emanating from the center some time ago, such as "containment" in the late 1960s. Bobrow and Allen Wilcox [7, pp. 139-140] did not find large differences in content of defense opinions between those with higher and lower education. Preferences for particular foreign policy outcomes among the mass public have not been found to have clear implications for popular support for weapons systems. Differences among the usual demographic and political groupings are much less pronounced for national security issues than for domestic matters.

Large armed forces based on universal conscription usually have been viewed by the public as deterrents against possible aggression, rather than as a threat to world peace. In 1945, 59 percent of those questioned in a national poll believed that UMT would reduce the chances of future wars, and only 12 percent saw it as provocative. UMT also has not been seen as a threat to individual liberties. Since 1945 most people have believed that "a year or two in the armed forces is good training and good discipline for any young man." Peacetime compulsory service, the National Opinion Research Center found in 1947, tends to be thought of "in terms of its potentialities for training and educating youth rather than as a means of building a strong military force." Military claims that better health, education, morals, citizenship, and physical training resulted from military service were widely accepted. Even among those who did not expect the United States to fight in another war within 25 years, support for compulsory training was high.

The issue was most salient from 1945-1953 and during the Vietnam War. The peak of governmental support for UMT came in the immediate post-World War II period, when President Truman, the military, and most congressional and civic leaders energetically sought passage of a UMT law. Yet public support then was no higher, and no lower, than it has been since. UMT was defeated then, and has not been instituted since, because the general public's support was of low intensity. Religious and educational elites, together with some congressional and labor allies, felt strongly about universal conscription and were able to block it.[4] Even after the draft controversies of the Vietnam War, in January 1969, UMT still was supported by Gallup's public: 79 percent favored it, and 16 percent opposed it. Even universal training for women was supported by 44 percent of those interviewed.

The stability of support for UMT is highly unusual for such a long period. Support for UMT was fairly low in the late 1930s, but rose sharply in early 1940. During the next 30 years support for UMT *never* fell below 60 percent, and only once rose above 79 percent.

Support for UMT contrasts with a sharp decline in public support for the existing draft system during the Vietnam War. Approval of the draft dropped 21 percent in 6 months early in the war, when publicity about draft inequities was widespread, although there had been no change in government action or draft calls. Ironically, those likely to be most resentful of the draft were among those who supposedly profited by it, the "heavy investors" in civilian education or careers who perceived themselves as vulnerable[19, p. 163]. Between 1945-1970 Americans consistently supported UMT over the draft, and the draft over a volunteer army; the operative feeling here was that

---

[4] Arthur Ekirch [22, p. 279], on the other hand, believed conscription, "as a concrete proposal," was no more popular after World War II than it had been previously. "The favorable verdict periodically recorded by opinion polls was open to question (because it) presented the issue of U.M.T. as an abstract question cloaked with an aura of preparedness and patriotism."

equality and fairness were best insured by universal training. An important reason cited during the sixties for support of UMT was that "every man has a responsibility to his country and should serve." Training and education of youth probably became a less important reason than it was in 1947, but support for UMT apparently has not been affected significantly by fears that wartime service in the military "hardened" youth, producing men for whom cruelty and suffering were commonplace.[5]

• • •

How far should civilian control go? When should war-waging and war-preparation decisions be left to the uniformed professionals? At what point do military-made decisions threaten civilian supremacy and, ultimately, democracy? Scattered data exists[12, pp. 127-132] on the questions of who should make decisions, whether civilian or military leaders are more to be trusted or blamed, and what are the attitudes toward the military man in politics.

During World War II Gallup asked whether Roosevelt and Churchill or the "military and naval leaders of the United Nations" should have "the final decision on the military and naval plans of the war." Despite the popularity of the two civilian leaders, only 21 percent felt they should decide, and 64 percent thought military leaders should decide. On atomic energy control the public was divided evenly; approximately the same number in 1949 believed army officers should control atomic development as believed it should be under civilian control of the type subsequently established. In national polls in the late 1940s less than 20 percent believed that military men had "too much say, in deciding our policy with other countries," and 33 to 40 percent believed they did not have enough influence. By 1962, however, there was substantial public support for the efforts of Secretary McNamara to assert firm civilian control over policy speeches by military leaders. Fifty-nine percent of those interviewed felt speeches should be "reviewed to see that they agree with U.S. foreign policy"; the government, they believed, should "speak with one voice." Twenty-seven percent said military leaders should be permitted to say what they wish.

The public tends to side with military leaders in the assignment of war-related decision-making authority, but to place the blame for mistakes on civilian leaders. Forty-four percent blamed "political men in Washington" for "the failure of our forces to be on the alert" at Pearl Harbor, and 21 percent blamed military men. In 1951, when asked to choose between President Truman and former Com. Gen. Douglas MacArthur, the public supported the general's position (usually by 2 to 1), saying Truman was wrong to dismiss him. (Perhaps, however, support for MacArthur was as much a reflection of

[5] A soldier who showed civic clubs his My Lai massacre photographs (before Calley was charged) said: "They caused no commotion. Nobody believed it. They said Americans wouldn't do this" [29, p. 81].

impatience with the way the Korean War was being fought, as it was an expression of nonsupport for civilian control.)

"The single event which best differentiates the impact of the Korean and Vietnam wars on Presidential popularity was President Truman's dismissal of . . . MacArthur. That move was a major factor in the politicization of the war as Republicans . . . echoed (the General's) complaints that it was the President's meddling in policy that was keeping the war from being won"[40, p. 29]. Richard Neustadt[41, p. 97] said: "Truman seems to have run afoul of the twin notions that a war-time Chief Executive ought to be 'above politics' and that he ought to help the generals 'win.' "

President Johnson, with repeated statements of support from former President Eisenhower and Com. Gen. William Westmoreland, avoided some of Truman's unpopularity. At least in the pre-Tet-offensive period of the Vietnam War, the public tended not to blame the military for war disappointments. As victory eluded the United States during 1967, Secretary McNamara's Harris poll approval rating for handling the war dropped from 47 to 36 positive to 42 to 45 negative in November. Westmoreland's November rating, by contrast, was 68 percent approval and 16 percent disapproval. Approval ratings for Westmoreland were significantly higher than for McNamara regardless of the respondent's position on the war. McNamara received majority support only from those who endorsed the administration goal of fighting a limited war in search of a negotiated settlement, and he was opposed by a majority of pro- *and* anti-escalation respondents. Westmoreland received majority approval even from the most dovish respondents.

Questions about preferred military or political solutions to the war found divided opinions. In November 1967, for example, a Gallup "military escalation plan" was the fourth most popular option from among six options. Forty-two percent favored and 48 percent opposed letting "the heads of the army run the war as they see fit, giving them all the men they say they need. Increase the pressures on enemy troops and step up the bombing . . . Go all out and use atomic weapons and bombs if the army believes we should." Mention of military leadership in the question failed to attract majority support—despite the widespread feeling that the war should be prosecuted more vigorously.

Table 3 shows opinions about the role of the military "during times like these." The president was acknowledged by a majority to be the ultimate authority over the military, and respondents lukewarmly endorsed the principle of civilian control. On war policy the military was given more deference than civilians other than the president. However, the 34 percent favoring civilian direction of wars (question 4)—even without mention of the president—might indicate that there has been a slight shift away from support for military direction since World War II.

What do people think of the military man as participant in domestic politics? "Are there any special groups you feel had too much influence over

TABLE THREE

Civilian Control of the Military: November 1967 Harris Poll

	Agree (%)	Disagree (%)	Not sure (%)	Total (%)
1. "When civilians tell the military what to do, too often politics rather than military action results."	73	10	17	100
2. "In Vietnam, the military has been handicapped by civilians who won't let them go all out."	65	10	25	100
3. "The President is the Commander-in-Chief, and all important military orders should come from him."	58	29	13	100
4. "In wartime, civilian government leaders should let the military take over running the war."	52	34	14	100
5. "If left unchecked by civilian control, the military could take over the whole government from civilian hands."	46	30	24	100
6. "Military men know how to start wars and fight them, but civilians have to end wars."	33	44	23	100

Source: The Washington Post, December 9, 1967.

Congress in the past year or so?" In 1944 less than 1 percent of a national sample volunteered the military. Will UMT result "in a group being formed of military men who will try to have too much power?" In a national poll in late 1945, 22 percent said yes. Only 9 percent in a 1945 poll said they believed that "our army leaders will try to run this country after the war." In 1944, asked in a poll about the propriety of military men running for the presidency, 26 percent said they liked the idea generally, 42 percent said they disliked the idea, and 20 percent said, "It depends on the man." In another poll there was substantial difference between veterans' support for two military men, MacArthur and Eisenhower, as potential presidential candidates. Support for Eisenhower was highest among combat veterans who had served with him in the European theater; support for MacArthur was *lowest* among combat veterans who had served with him in Asia, and highest among veterans who never left the United States. Transference of obedience to a military leader to the electoral domain depends on the man and on the war. Both MacArthur and Eisenhower were named in Gallup's Ten Most Admired Men poll every year between 1946-1962; through 1971, and with the exception of MacArthur, no Korean or Vietnam leader had made the list. After World War II, regrettably, survey organizations stopped asking questions about the military in politics.

• • •

Budgets reveal what people care about most; appropriating money is a de facto method of setting priorities, without incorporating them in a formal statement of goals. Defense spending has accounted for a large proportion of controllable government spending since the Korean War. Does this reflect widespread public support for giving much of the nation's financial and manpower resources to the military? Or does it reflect public lack of knowledge of or acquiescence in elite decisions? Again, survey data[12, pp. 137-144] will be used.

In 1960 President Kennedy was elected after a campaign in which he asked people to sacrifice for higher military and space spending, to catch up with the Russians. By the end of the decade voters in New Jersey and Tennessee, Indiana and Virginia, Minnesota and Florida, were grouping military spending, space exploration, and foreign aid together as the *least popular* government programs [51]. Did this represent a "popular groundswell" or were elites responsible for the shift and how sharp were opinion changes?

Despite the isolationism of the 1930s, the presumed antimilitary attitudes of the population, and the Depression, there was consistently high support from 1935-1940 for larger armed services. Support for enlarging any of the services never slipped *below* 65 percent (or 53 percent, if the respondent was asked if he was willing to have his taxes raised to pay for a larger military), and rose to 90 percent favoring a larger air corps in 1938. Of those with opinions in a 1937 poll only 9.9 percent said they believed larger armed forces would lead to war, and only 11.8 percent saw military spending as a "waste of money." Thus, the isolationist and "business pacifist" points of view were endorsed by less than a quarter of the population, at a time when the administration purportedly felt constrained by public opinion, and when the already small military forces were being starved. If political leaders were deterred from mobilizing military strength, it was not by the public, but by the press and Congress which purported to speak for the public.

Fig. One shows the fluctuations in defense-spending opinions. There was support for an expanded defense effort through the 1930s and 1940s, with larger numbers believing that defense spending was "about right" in the 1950s and 1960s.

The public, again, was blamed by political leaders for forcing the nation to demobilize after World War II. But in 1946 a majority of respondents in a national poll said America should have *more* military strength, "to accomplish what (they wanted) for the United States in the next 20 years."

The Truman and Eisenhower administrations often claimed to be under public pressure to cut defense spending to save money. But when given the choice in a 1946 poll 71 percent chose keeping the same level of military

FIGURE ONE
Does the United States Spend Too Much on Defense?

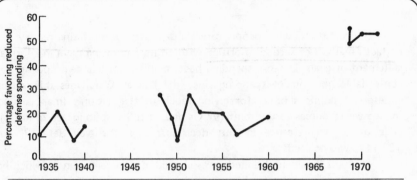

Source: American Institute of Public Opinion, and National Opinion Research Center opinion surveys.

Note: Figure line shows "too much," "favor less," or "decrease" responses to questions about whether the United States should increase, decrease, or maintain defense spending levels. Question wording varies over time.

Questions which ask about military strength, without reference to spending, are omitted, as are questions preceded by "filter" questions relating to information levels. Questions which include phrases such as "the taxes you pay" also are omitted here.

forces rather than balancing the budget, and 70 percent—a remarkable figure—chose maintaining existing forces rather than reducing taxes. After the beginning of the Korean War, support for military spending rose further: In December, 1950, 70 percent of those interviewed in a national poll favored doubling defense spending. The next year 84 percent favored continuing the defense program without reductions, even if the war was brought to an end. In 1953, as a Korean truce was negotiated, 74 percent of a national sample opposed reducing the military forces below 3.5 million men. In a poll after the Russian Sputnik was launched in 1957, 63 percent said they were willing to have their income taxes increased to build up U.S. military strength, again an unusually high percentage to acquiesce in higher taxes.

Once cuts are made in defense spending by *executive* leadership, the public tends to accept the reductions as compatible with the national interest [30, p. 240]. Seventeen percent in a July 1953 poll believed the nations's safety was being threatened by budget cuts, while 53 percent felt only waste was being cut. When budget cuts were being sought by congressmen in the early seventies, public confidence that only waste would be cut could not be assumed.

In 1961, after Kennedy's call for sacrifices, 28 percent said they were willing to sacrifice for improved armed forces—a smaller number than indicated a sacrificial willingness for the domestic welfare goals cited by Kennedy. But support for defense programs continued.[6]

What is most striking about this opinion stability is not that Americans strongly favored higher defense spending in the isolationist pre-1941 period (when U.S. forces were understaffed, underequipped, and generally unprepared for the coming war), but rather that support for larger defense outlays remained high into the 1960s. In 1964, after a substantial buildup of strategic and conventional forces, only 4 percent of respondents in a Gallup poll believed the level of military strength was too high, and 31 percent believed it was too low. Through the mid-sixties no more than 9 percent of a national sample ever *volunteered* defense spending as an area to be cut. If it were not for data from this period, it could be argued more easily that support for defense spending is simply a recognition of the objective dangers of international relations at different periods of history. But the continuance of support in the mid-sixties, followed in 1969 by strong opposition to defense spending, despite what many military men felt was a *deteriorating* strategic position relative to the U.S.S.R., undermines that argument. It suggests instead that attitudes of deference toward the military may be involved in responses to defense spending questions.

The Vietnam War led to strengthening of peace groups, and creation of such organizations as the Coalition on National Priorities and Military Policy (peace, church, and liberal groups), and antiwar, antidefense-spending academic, business, professional, women's, and labor groups. For the first time since the 1930s, such groups reached large numbers of people, and ceased to be viewed entirely as fringe radicals.

By 1968-1969 there was a sharp and unprecedented reversal of public opinion. In 1969 Gallup asked: "There is much discussion as to the amount of money the government in Washington should spend for national defense and military purposes. How do you feel about this?"[2]. Eight percent believed the United States was spending too little, 31 percent believed its spending was about right, and *52 percent* believed too much was being spent on the military. Gallup attributed the results to war frustration and the belief

[6] Huntington suggested that "the very continuity and breadth of (the popularity of) a large military establishment implies that it did not reflect a highly structured or discriminating set of attitudes." Support was consistent across most demographic, political, and attitudinal subgroupings. Huntington [30, p. 247] believed: "Strong military forces were a means which could be related to a variety of ends, the lowest common denominator among many conflicting foreign policies. . . . Increased American military strength may by itself be a source of satisfaction, pride, and excitement. Many citizens may . . . achieve psychological benefits from identification with the military might and achievement of their country." Consistency of opinion across standard groupings does not necessarily mean that Americans do not care about military policy, or that their opinions have no depth. That social and economic differentiations should be relevant to all security policy questions is an unproved assumption, and partisan distinctions probably are least important on security policies in which both parties usually have been implicated.

that the war was diverting funds from problems at home; procurement controversies also probably had an effect. Of the college educated, traditionally the group which supported internationalism and a strong defense posture, 60 percent believed military spending was too high. Opposition to defense spending continued high into 1971 [42, Table 1].

Even when overall strategies and methods were above reproach, opponents of military spending occasionally have been able to marshall opposition to specific weapons systems, usually on the basis of alleged duplication, excessive costs, or ineffectiveness. The antiballistic missile system (ABM), attacked on technical and strategic grounds and as an example of military expansiveness, was one of the few post-war weapons whose existence has penetrated public consciousness. Midway through 1969, however, 60 percent of respondents in a national poll had no opinion on the system; 25 percent approved of it. In several state surveys in 1969-1970 ABM was found to be less popular than overall defense spending, perhaps because for some people it had been made into a symbol of needless spending. These surveys showed some suspicion of "the Pentagon" and Pentagon "bureaucrats," and widespread acceptance of the view that there was considerable waste in defense spending. The existence of a military-industrial complex was acknowledged by about half the respondents in most states; they were divided as to whether such a complex was good or bad [51].

SOCIALIZATION

How have these attitudes, pro- and antimilitary, been nurtured over the years? What have been the relationships between the military and the important socialization media which influence the nature and permanence of attitudes?

Children are socialized through the family, peer groups, schools, and the mass media. The peace-minded pediatrician, Dr. Benjamin Spock, warned of militarizing effects from playing with war toys, which had been a staple consumer item for generations. Studies have attempted to measure the impact on children of television violence, but war toys have not been studied as closely. Sales of war toys, however, did begin declining suddenly in 1965, the year the Vietnam War escalated, and continued to decline to the point where a Toy Manufacturers of America spokesman told *Forbes* [52, p. 29] in 1971 that "you can hardly give them away right now." Toy soldiers, guns, tanks, battleships, and planes virtually disappeared from the marketplace. Presumably this reflected attitudes toward the war, although whether those of parents not wanting to teach their children to "play with death" or of children surfeited with war on television or some other explanation is unclear. Spock also criticized the glorification of the military, war, and violence in television, films, and comic books. He believed participation in activities such as air raid drills and fallout shelter construction in the fifties and sixties contributed to children's anxieties and aggressions. However, firm data on these hypotheses is lacking. Public schools seek to inculcate patriotism, but there is little study of recent military heroes.

Critics of the Junior ROTC program, as of UMT and "Americanism" seminars, suggested that teaching citizenship, grooming, and respect for authority be left to parents, churches, and schools. But the army justified high school ROTC on these socialization grounds: "It automatically guarantees the community a well groomed male student body . . . The program motivates the young man to be alert . . . to the world around him; it motivates him to (achieve); it encourages him to play a more active and meaningful citizenship role and to respect properly constituted authority. It develops patriotism and encourages a high sense of personal honor and deportment. Through this program the young man learns first to follow, then to lead, with increasing degrees of responsibility and authority"[Quoted in 27, p. 76]. After the First World War, when the American Legion sought to influence textbook content and to encourage placement of Junior ROTC units, some public school educators saw a more menacing prospect than that described by the army. Although senior ROTC increased its penetration of colleges from the 1920s until the 1960s—its existence being justified on different grounds —high school ROTC grew more slowly and erratically. At the end of fiscal 1969 there were over 700 Junior ROTC units (with plans to increase the total to 900 to 1200), with 133,000 students enrolled. Although strengthening of character and patriotism ("opportunity to learn about the . . . requirements for National Security and their personal obligations as American citizens to . . . contribute toward National Security") were the usual goals mentioned by military leaders, the high school program also was defended as a community relations tool. The commander of the navy program said it "exhibits the Navy to the public eye and introduces the Navy to the community through the youth of the nation"[7] [Quoted in 44, pp. 124, 126].

Adults are socialized not only by the family and peer groups, but by institutions and associations,[8] by the mass media, and through service in the military. General Shoup said of the mass media:

The American people have . . . become more and more accustomed to militarism, to uniforms, to the cult of the gun, and to the violence of combat. Whole generations have been brought up on war news and wartime propaganda; the few years of peace since 1939 have seen a steady stream of war novels, war

[7] Especially assigned officers also keep close touch with civilian youth organizations such as the Boy Scouts; the reason, an air force general said, is "to help assure our nation of capable leaders in the future" [44, p. 122].

[8] John Swomley [49, p. 210] believed that churches, which were influential opponents of UMT, "have been freer from military commitment and vested interests than any other major organized group in American life." But many religious leaders, such as Billy Graham and the late Francis Cardinal Spellman, have supported military activities.

movies, comic strips, and television programs with war and or military settings. For many Americans, military training, expeditionary service, and warfare are merely extensions of the entertainment of childhood. Even the weaponry and hardware they use at war are similar to the highly realistic toys of their youth[45, p. 53].

Some books and films, however, have gained popularity by ridiculing the military man, occasionally suggesting that he may go insane and start a nuclear war. "Dr. Strangelove; Or How I Stopped Worrying and Learned to Love the Bomb," a film in which the world was imperiled by a mad general, a wahooing-nuke-delivering pilot, and a Doomsday Machine, received critical acclaim. Similar films and books in the early 1960s included *Red Alert, Seven Days in May,* and *Fail-Safe,* as well as antiwar films such as "On the Beach" and "The Victors." Military men complained about being portrayed, in a colonel's words, as "clowns, clods, super-egotists, or villains," or in a sergeant's words, as "incompetent, negligent, vain, and self-serving, utterly stupid or cunning and sly, take your pick"[28, p. 27]. In 1969-1970, television's top-rated "Laugh-In" poked fun at "General Bullright," who proclaimed that "War Is Good Business—Invest Your Son," and "M*A*S*H" and "Catch-22" were "antimilitary" as well as "antiwar" films. (M*A*S*H", winner of the Cannes Festival Grand Prize and the National Society of Film Critics award for best picture of 1970, was banned by the army for screening to soldiers.) But that period produced another film hero: Gen. George Patton, a self-confessed military barbarian, in "Patton: A Salute to a Rebel" (titled "Patton: Lust for Glory" in Britain).[9]

In fact, the media norm continued to be one of presenting the military in a favorable light (often with use of Pentagon installations, ships, planes, and men),[10] despite the publicity given to the few antimilitary films and books. Most media portrayed the military either in heroic terms, e.g., the "12 O'Clock High" series, "The Longest Day" and "The Green Berets" films, and the "Steve Canyon" and "Buz Sawyer" comic strips, or in hale-fellow-well-met enlisted man's humor, e.g., *No Time for Sergeants,* and the "McHale's Navy," "Sergeant Bilko," and "Hogan's Heroes" television series. On the CBS-TV network, of 138 military characterizations during the first 3 months of 1970, 124 were judged to be favorable, eight comic, and six unfavorable. The unfavorable portrayals, the network maintained, did not reflect on the branch or service of the soldier-villain [28, p.29]. Louis Harris and Associates, after a 1965 opinion survey for the navy, concluded that the "Mister Roberts"-"McHale's Navy"-"Ensign O'Toole" type of entertainment had

[9] War critics pointed out that President Nixon had viewed "Patton" at least twice, shortly before his decision to send troops into Cambodia.

[10] The military refused to sell film or otherwise cooperate with disapproved films. But for John Wayne's "The Green Berets," two installations with men and weapons were provided for half the cost of one helicopter's service. Considerable naval facilities were provided for "Tora!Tora!Tora!" in 1969.

lowered the navy's image. "In the absence of popular fare to the contrary, the image of the Navy as a fun-loving, easygoing institution remains" [44, p. 127]. By contrast, Harris found the marines' prestige at a continued high level because of their image of toughness and discipline. (Several years later even the marines fell victim to media humor in the popular "Gomer Pyle" television series.)

A form of mass socialization which temporarily enjoys near-total control over individuals is military service itself.[11] By the late 1960s the nation had 23 million veterans comprising one-fifth of the adult population, and all had been under the socializing influence for months or years of officers, sergeants, and indirectly, the Pentagon leadership. The enormous armed forces television-radio network may be the leading source of information for servicemen stationed abroad, for example, and it is in wartime that the impact of military life is greatest. "In spite of themselves," former Marine Commandant Shoup [45, p. 52] wrote, many veterans returned from World War II "as indoctrinated, combat experienced military professionals . . . For better or worse, (they) would never be the same again." He continued, " . . . The creeds and attitudes of the armed forces are powerful medicine, and can become habit-forming. . . . For many veterans the military's efforts to train and indoctrinate them may well be the most impressive and influential experience they have ever had—especially so for the young and less educated . . . As they get older, many veterans seem to romanticize and exaggerate their own military experience and loyalties . . . (and become) pugnacious and chauvinistic." Military service, Senator Fulbright[26, p. 8] believed, "fosters . . . conformism, elitism, authoritarianism, and a certain romanticism about war."

Psychiatrist Bourne said, "The military establishment sufficiently indoctrinates the young men it inducts that when they are seeded back into civilian life, they carry with them values and attitudes which not only guarantee the perpetuation of the military system but enhance its slow and steadily increasing control over the entire society"[Quoted in 36, p. 4]. Veterans, Bourne said, retain identification with the military which leads them to feel that "any limitation of military power is an incursion of (their) own influence." They maintain an allegiance to the military, to what they have been through.[12] Shoup (p. 56) saw a "nation of veterans . . . adorned

[11] An even larger number of men, 45 million in 1968, were influenced indirectly by the military through their Selective Service registration. Draft officials operated under long-time Director (General) Lewis Hershey's "channeling" strategy, using deferments to encourage young men to stay in school or to train for occupations "useful to the national interest." Although local draft personnel were usually civilians, state and national Selective Service headquarters were manned almost entirely by military officers under DOD manpower guidelines.

[12] The Vietnam War, according to psychiatrist Lifton [36, pp. 1-4], led to particularly acute psychological problems for citizen-soldiers, rooted in "the theme of betrayal (by the generals and government leaders) and self-betrayal." The absence of

with service caps, ribbons, and lapel emblems ... —patriotic, belligerent, romantic, and well-intentioned—finding a certain sublimation and excitement in their country's latest military venture."

No firm relationship has been found between past military service and characteristics such as authoritarianism, however. Charles Moskos, in studying combat enlisted men in Vietnam, did not find attitudes which would appear to support militaristic values in later life, although Shoup's post hoc romanticization may occur nevertheless. Moskos found, not surprisingly, that soldiers tended to justify sacrifices already made in Vietnam, and that they were strongly critical of antiwar demonstrators.

He must at some level accept, if not the specific purposes of the war, then at least the broader rectitude of the social system of which he is a member. Although American combat soldiers do not espouse overtly ideological sentiments and are extremely reluctant to voice patriotic rhetoric, this should not obscure the existence of more latent beliefs in the legitimacy, and even superiority, of the American way of life. (However, combat soldiers consistently display) a profound skepticism of political and ideological appeals. ... They dismiss patriotic slogans or exhortations to defend democracy with 'What a crock'. ... When the soldier responds to the question of why he is in Vietnam, his answers are couched in a quite individualistic frame of reference. [38, pp. 147-149] .

EDUCATING THE PUBLIC

The military has been accused of attempting to mold civilian opinions through (1) community education programs (or Radical Right "brain-washing" forums) and (2) an elaborate public relations program. The question here has been: Should the military be permitted to carry its views directly to the people, without clearance from political superiors? Strategic views at variance from administration policy might be involved, or budgetary requests exceeding what the administration believes desirable. More recently, there has been controversy about military attempts to "sell" administration policies to the country and Congress.

Large public relations programs grew out of World War II, and for most of the post-unification (1947) period, there have been five military information programs: one each for the four services, and one for the Defense

welcoming parades, both collective and individual, for Vietnam veterans also was noteworthy. Lifton, while conceding that all veterans do not return as monsters or killers, said they have experienced "psychologically desensitizing" experiences and have been indoctrinated with a "dehumanizing military ethos." Personal identity is rejected, the organization is accepted as omnipotent and omniscient, the individual is convinced that he has no value except in his potential to become a soldier. "Dehumanizing" and "desensitizing" characteristics are difficult to locate empirically, of course. In any case, Lifton is talking about the rare case of completely successful indoctrination.

Department itself.[13] Civilian attempts to merge service operations in 1947 and to control military leaders' public speeches in the early 1960s led to military charges of "gagging." Officers, in "educating" the public to the dangers of external *and internal* communism and the concomitant dangers of unduly low defense spending, took part in "alert" seminars, "strategy for survival" conferences, and "freedom forums." In 1961 a concerned Senator Fulbright asked Secretary McNamara to stop military personnel from participating in "activities which undermine (the President's) policies. . . . There has been a strong tradition in this country that it is not the function of the military to educate the public on political issues. . . . Military officers are not elected by the people" [17, p. 267]. Reservists and guardsmen, military-support associations, veterans groups, business, and local schools had cooperated in these "Americanism" seminars, which often involved the advocacy of policies not in accord with those of the administration.

The seminars had grown out of a 1958 National Security Council directive urging the Defense Department to take positive measures to educate soldiers and the general public to the dangers of communism. (Indoctrination of troops was a subject of controversy after the unheroic performance of some American prisoners-of-war in Korea.) Although the directive was not rescinded, DOD in the 1960s did restrain officers' freedom to advocate rightist political theories and actions in official appearances by requiring prior clearance of speeches. Officers were discouraged from appearing at all in programs sponsored by political extremists. McNamara let it be known that top officers should support official policy in public, and that foreign policy was not the military's responsibility. Defense policy statements should be made by responsible officials, not by anonymous reports, McNamara ruled, as he sought to impose tighter control over the services' public relations activities.

The most dramatic "muzzling" incidents coincided with the rise of the John Birch Society and other rightist groups after John F. Kennedy's election. Maj. Gen. Edwin Walker, a decorated veteran of World War II and Little Rock, was the key figure. As commander of the 24th Infantry Division in Germany, he had initiated a "pro-Blue" campaign for his troops which included voting guidance for congressional elections and labeling of eminent Americans as communists. In 1961 Walker was judged by the army to have broken the law by trying to influence the outcome of an election through political indoctrination of his troops. Conservatives such as Sen. (and Gen.) Strom Thurmond saw the restraints on troop indoctrination as "a dastardly attempt to intimidate the commanders of the United States Armed Forces."

[13] Attitudes toward publicity vary by the service. Air force generals were prolific authors in the fifties and sixties. Admirals rarely write books; however, in 1959 the chief of naval operations had to direct them to avoid "showing the gold," i.e., holding their arms so their gold sleeve stripes were in prominent view when being photographed.

Thurmond led an abortive congressional investigation designed to show that the troops did not have a fully articulated and ideologically-based hatred of communism. Critics of the McNamara policies, President Kennedy said, "object quite rightly to politics intruding on the military—but they are anxious for the military to engage in politics"[17, pp. 266, 302]. Walker did not become a martyr, and military "education" of troops and the public was temporarily restrained. But a decade later Fulbright [27, p. 41] was uttering similar warnings in reference to the National Security Seminars sponsored by the Industrial College of the Armed Forces. They present "a simplistic, often outdated, and factually incorrect view of complex world problems," he said, and worse, they seek to "educate civilians on foreign policy issues (and) to teach them to be better citizens," neither of which is a proper function of the Defense Department. By 1970 300 2-week National Security Seminars had been attended by 180,000 civilians from business, professional, educational, and civic organizations, and reserve officers.

Walker was reprimanded, and generals' speeches were censored, *not* because they were attempting to influence their troops and the public, but because they were expressing attitudes and ideologies *contrary* to those of the incumbent administration. By the early seventies, however, the situation was reversed: Senator Fulbright was no longer disturbed that the military was not supporting the president's policies, but that the military *was* using its public relations capabilities to support administration policy. These efforts included "Silent Majority" pamphlets distributed to troops in Vietnam (to show pro-administration opinions from back home), "V-series" feature films (many in 1969-1970 dealing with the President's Vietnamization program, a pro-ABM program, and public speeches by military leaders attacking those who "seek peace at any price." Understandably, the Nixon administration was less concerned about military efforts to influence troops and the public than the Kennedy administration had been.

• • •

To reach the public, the Pentagon often must go through the national and local news media. Despite the liberals' concern about it being intimidated or seduced by the complex, and despite understaffing of Pentagon news bureaus, the national media sometimes exposes flaws in strategies, weapons systems, and military organization. Even before Vietnam, the military was not sacrosanct.

Critics have charged the national and local media with failing to uncover military scandals and being afraid to pursue those they uncover. Cost analyst Fitzgerald [25, pp. 2-4] said that "the media have been slightly less spectacular (in examining the military-industrial complex) than in reporting on the human interest stories." In 1969-1970 television networks killed revelatory documentaries on a weapons system scandal and a Marine Corps court-martial, Fitzgerald charged. Despite what he called "intense pressure to drop the story," however, CBS-TV carried an expose of cost overruns on a torpedo system. Seymour Hersh[29, p. 82], the writer credited with breaking the My Lai massacre story (through an obscure news service), said the handling of initial information on Calley's case brought "no credit either to the military—or to the press." First Pentagon news releases did not report that Lieutenant Calley was accused of murdering 109 Vietnamese civilians, only that he was charged with murder. Pentagon press officers "were prepared for a flood of questions that weekend from all news media, but it didn't come." It was not until a network interview with a soldier who had been at My Lai, 3 months after the first news release, that the press finally recognized the magnitude of the story.

On more prominent aspects of the war, similarly, the media tended to accept the government's version of events at face value. American reporters in Saigon were conspicuous critics of the pre-1963 government there, but after the war escalated, reporters were less troublesome. The "body counts" were treated as news, for example, and the 1966-1967 pacification program was usually described as a success. Media acceptance of what came off the military mimeograph machines in Saigon and Washington was gravely impaired by enemy successes in the Tet offensive of 1968. And in June 1971 *The New York Times* broke a story which was to portray the Kennedy and Johnson administration decision-makers in a distinctly unfavorable light. The purloined Pentagon Papers (see Chapter 9) were an account of American involvement in Vietnam, commissioned by Secretary McNamara in 1968 and classified as top secret since then. Apparently for the first time in American history, the federal government sought a court injunction to prevent a newspaper from publishing information in its possession. The *Times* soon was followed by other newspapers, three of which were temporarily enjoined from publishing stories based on the documents. The newspapers argued that the papers were historical and would merely "embarrass" the government, which the *Times* had tried to avoid doing in earlier international involvements, e.g., the U-2 flights and the Bay of Pigs invasion. The United States Supreme Court, in a 6 to 3 decision permitting publication of the documents, found that the government had not proved that national security would be damaged by publication.

Because the media generally and the television networks especially had been submissive in reporting about military affairs, government reaction to a 1971 CBS-TV prime-time documentary, "The Selling of the Pentagon," was unusually strong. Little of the content, relating to military public relations programs, was new;[14] what was new was the source. The program won

---

[14] Although a November 1970 administration memo directed the military to curtail its public relations activities, CBS charged that no significant cutbacks had been made. The network program also charged that officers violated Pentagon regulations prohibiting them from speaking to civilian groups on American politics or the foreign policy implications of Vietnam involvement.

several broadcasting awards, but Vice President Spiro Agnew called it "a clever propaganda attempt to discredit the defense establishment." He charged:

The many references to "the colonels," as though they were part of some totalitarian junta, the assembly of their statements totally out of context . . . were propaganda devices worse than those that CBS accused the Pentagon of employing. It is true that the network has the right to utilize . . . the subtle technique that implies that Army demonstration activities encourage violence in children . . . although most Americans will find these techniques less than admirable. But it does not have the right to cut and paste the widely separated statements of military spokesmen to create a false impression[9, p. 4-A] .

House Armed Services Committee Chairman F. Edward Hébert called it "the greatest disservice to the military" he had seen on television. A House subcommittee sought contempt of Congress action against the president of CBS, after he refused to provide nonbroadcast material used in production of the documentary, but the House voted against a contempt citation.

Media-theoretician Marshall McLuhan hypothesized that "our first TV war (Vietnam) has ended the boundaries between civilian and military life" [3, p. 13]. It seems more likely that, whatever else it did with daily carnage in living color, television coverage heightened awareness of the differences between civilians and the military. In interviews with 150 young army officers in 1971, television news was singled out as having treated the military most unfairly. The military may have come to perceive the mass media generally as its major institutional enemy. Journalist Lapham found that the officers with whom he talked directed their anxiety about "domestic confusion" and their hostility toward civilian society at "the media" and "the kids." The officers were said to feel that "The small-town weeklies still print the truth, but a great deal of dangerous trash gets published in the national newspapers or announced on network television. Even Walter Cronkite . . . has fallen from grace. . . . At the Pentagon it is fashionably humorous to refer to the *Washington Post* as *Pravda* . . .The press represents the cynicism of the big cities. . . . They are seen as emissaries from Sodom" [34, p. 84] .

The local media is less likely to be critical. The military has devoted much of its resources to community relations. Local advisory committees, made up of community leaders whom the military hopes to co-opt, are created in most base areas, and all installations have their own information office. The local leaders are used as base spokesmen and as informants on local reactions to military policies. Touring exhibits attract large audiences: Twenty-two army exhibits, for example, were said to have been viewed by more than 20 million people in 1970, and more than 12 million people a year see navy and air force aerobatic units.

Speakers are provided for all types of clubs; military TV-radio programs are carried by several thousand stations weekly; the Hometown News Center keeps communities informed of native sons; special ceremonies, parades, fly-bys, and firepower demonstrations can be arranged. The Army Air Defense Command's "Operation Understanding" flew influential local leaders (commissioned as "Ambassadors of Air Defense Artillery") to bases; the Navy Guest Cruise Program provided cruises to civilians; the Air Force Distinguished Visitor Program offered free trips for local opinion-makers; and the Joint Civilian Orientation Conference provided 8-day cross-country tours of military installations for civilians nominated by the president, the Pentagon, and congressmen.

The Pentagon says it does not conduct "selling campaigns," that it puts out large quantities of information only to maintain its credibility with the press, Congress, and the public. The bad news goes out with the good, Pentagon officials claim, including information known only to the military.

The military says tour programs cost taxpayers little and perform necessary public educational functions. "Operation Understanding" was begun in 1956 when the army found it necessary to convince urban residents that the air defense missiles being installed around cities were safe.[15] Other military programs are justified as "internal information tools." The army television series "The Big Picture," shown as a public service by 350 stations, was justified as a supplement to internal showings: to army wives, children, and retired soldiers living off base.

The anti-Pentagon position again involves (1) the size of public relations activity; and (2) its unneutral pro-military content.

A 1969 General Accounting Office study concluded that the Pentagon went far beyond responding to unsolicited requests for information which the Pentagon maintains is its primary informational task. In 1969 Congress barred the use of defense funds for "propaganda," a prohibition without practical effect, and Senator Fulbright unsuccessfully sought to cut public relations spending to $10 million a year. The public relations programs employed up to 6000 people, and trained 2000 specialists a year. Between 1959-1970, while the overall defense budget almost doubled, the department's reported public relations budget increased fifteenfold. With hidden costs (e.g., operations and salaries) included, Rep. Jonathan B. Bingham charged, public relations spending probably exceeded $70 million in 1970 [24, p. 1]. This probably was a conservative estimate. This figure also does not include the value of free publicity, estimated at tens of millions of dollars annually.

The most massive public relations effort remains the unsuccessful 1948 campaign for adoption of UMT. Support was enlisted from 370 national organizations, including the American Legion and Chamber of Commerce, and from 351 mayors. Almost 600 articles and editorials were promoted by

---

[15] "The public did not always relish the idea of troops and lethal missiles in their back yards," the Air Defense Command's public relations office noted. "Operation Understanding" won awards from two national public relations societies.

UMT supporters. A House subcommittee found the army guilty of using federal funds to influence Congress by producing pro-UMT films and sponsoring a touring civilian speaker who urged his audiences to write their congressmen in behalf of UMT.

C. Wright Mills [37, p. 221], in the mid-1950s, believed that "in all of pluralistic America . . . there is no possible combination of interests that has anywhere near the time, the money, the manpower, to present a point of view . . . that can effectively compete with the views presented by the warlords." Senator Fulbright felt the same way in the early seventies. He believed that the Defense Department was engaged in an effort to sell the administration's Vietnam policy to the public. He believed this was only one step away from using the public relations resources of the military establishment to rid Congress of those who questioned executive branch policies.

More recent examples were the campaigns in support of the Vietnam policies, the ABM, and the more limited efforts directed at Congress and the press in support of the F-111 and C-5A planes.

On the F-111 Secretary McNamara held a series of secret "Project Icarus" sessions (an ironic name to be chosen by the air force for a program involving a plane that crashed to earth with stunning frequency). He met with General Dynamics officials and Pentagon publicists to plan ways to obscure the plane's cost overruns and technical failures. (Later the notes of the meetings became public.) Efforts to influence "neutral reporters" appeared to have been successful: During December 1967, shortly before Congress canceled the navy version of the F-111, 65 percent of press articles were judged by the Icarus group to be "commendatory" and only 10 percent were "derogatory." Remarked General Dynamics president Roger Lewis: "The newspapermen want to be on the winning side." Pessimistic information known to the Pentagon was smothered in congressional testimony and press releases; in the secret meetings, there were frequent complaints about the "single-minded concern about specifications" in Congress and the press when the F-111 failed to meet speed, ferry range, and other specifications [33, p. 12]. In several appearances before congressional committees McNamara and the air force secretary denied knowledge of the cost and technical problems being discussed in the meetings.

On the war the military provided hundreds of television and motion picture tapes and films from their five Vietnam camera crews, to present the "positive side" of American involvement. Military speakers also were active. During the first 6 months of 1968 the army alone provided 1200 speakers on Vietnam, although regulations cautioned the speakers to avoid talking about the war's "foreign policy implications."[16] General Westmoreland spoke at 59 gatherings during his first 10 months as army chief of staff in 1968-1969.

[16] Some military speakers directly criticized war critics. Gen. Lewis Walt said, "Those who dissent . . . must bear a part of the responsibility for the losses of those gallant Americans" in Vietnam. Maj. James Rowe, an ex-POW, was active in talking to

Officers enjoyed two advantages as speakers on defense matters: the prestige of experts, and the ability to travel around the country.

Public revelation of a memorandum from ABM manager Lt. Gen. A. D. Starbird forced alteration of plans to sell the ABM system. The Starbird memo detailed ways by which magazine articles from cooperative civilian scientists could be solicited, supported covertly, and their publication obtained in scientific journals; classified briefings could be arranged for congressmen, journalists, and labor leaders (at least two unions carried pro-ABM articles in their magazines); and exhibits and orientation programs could be aimed at dubious ABM-site communities. The usual films, tours, speakers, and press releases also would be used. Criticisms of ABM, in the absence of a Starbird campaign, were answered by a national public relations effort sponsored by industrial contractors (with which Starbird had planned to cooperate).

INTEREST GROUP POLITICS

The basic weakness of the military as an interest group is its lack of roots in the nation. It is influential behind closed doors in Washington, and its civilian supporters may be influential in states with major defense installations. But the military itself is at a disadvantage in partisan politics, and sometimes in those aspects of national politics in which Congress and the pluralistic, middle-level, decentralized influence networks upon which Congress is based, have a deciding voice.

On national security policy the military is influential because many decisions never leave the Pentagon and White House, and never enter the public domain. It is also influential in support of its guild interests, e.g., perquisites, although these are more likely to come to congressional and public attention.

As an interest group the military is in a better position when the "scope of conflict" [43] is narrow, rather than broad. Navy officers, for example, are believed to prefer direct political contacts with Congress rather than indirect lobbying, i.e., going to the people to build pro-navy sentiments and to persuade *them* to influence their representatives. Direct contacts can be carried out so that "officers feel they are merely executing their responsibilities toward (their civilian superiors) without actually indulging in 'politics'."

To officers "the task of consciously cultivating public opinion was so unfamiliar . . . so uncongenial . . . because of its transparently political purpose," that public relations remained an "undignified" and controversial task within the navy[20, pp. 252, 265] . Political activity tends to increase

---

congressmen and publicly questioning the patriotism of Sen. George McGovern and other war opponents[27, pp. 132-139] .

during service crises (e.g., the postwar unification and bomber-carrier skir-mishes between the navy and air force) and when spurred by leaders, e.g., Navy Secretary James Forrestal ("Consider yourself a purveyor of informa-tion about the Navy. ... You have [an] obligation ... to [keep] the American people informed"), or Adm. Robert B. Carney ("A good program is worthless unless it's sold") [20, pp. 270, 276].

Political activity in the usual sense violates norms and laws. Political clubs and public discussion of politics are forbidden by the military code. Officers say there is little of the unofficial political activity which character-izes civilian governmental employees, e.g., in lobbying for higher wages; they say the military professional is circumspect and unlikely to assert himself politically. Although *partisan* politics is avoided, what the military would call proper discussion of its assigned tasks and national security problems involves politics in the more complete meaning of the term and it is here that the services are active.

Reservists, unrestrained by the laws which regulate professionals and unconcerned about role limitations, traditionally have been active in politics; their activity accounts for the continued existence of separate reserves and National Guards. Retired professionals have not yet become a politically dangerous "displaced class" (as they have been in some other countries) [5, p. 333]. They still are not particularly numerous except in states such as Virginia, California, Texas, and Florida, and lack strong local identities. But the most outspoken generals and admirals are men who have retired and been unleashed. There is a potential for political activity in this group, since many do suffer the economic, social, and psychological pressures of a downwardly mobile occupational group, after an enforced early retirement. If the post-Vietnam size of the military is reduced in accordance with "technological war" planning, there could be a sharp increase in the number of retired officers in the 1970s.

Veterans groups, i.e., organizations of nonprofessionals, and the simultaneously civilian-military National Guard are active in local politics. They support military and draft decisions but, mainly, they support them-selves. The guard used traditional states' rights and antimilitarist values, local service, and strong public relations programs to build a reputation for political influence. Like the Army Corps of Engineers, the guard has been a congressional sacred cow for local interest, not military reasons [21, p. 228]. Each of the services has had a professional association to present its viewpoint to the public: the Army and Air Force Associations (with 100,000 members each) and the Navy League. Since they are private organizations, unhindered by the requirements of civilian control, they can speak for the services when military leaders feel inhibited. They have well-developed public relations programs and congressional contacts.

Retired officers have been directly involved in partisan politics, but most continue to follow the apolitical standards endorsed by General

Eisenhower in 1948: "The necessary and wise subordination of the military to civil power will be best sustained . . . when lifelong professional soldiers, in the absence of some obvious and overriding reasons, abstain from seeking high political office" [47, p. 40]. Some officers who had supported Robert Taft (Eisenhower's convention opponent in 1952) joined a right-wing group, Pro-America, and others took part in right-wing activities in the 1960s. Military men have been involved in presidential campaigns in 1960 ("missile gap"), 1964 (test-ban dangers), and 1968 ("security gap"), by leaking information to candidates or warning of declining military strength.[17] Retired air force Gen. Curtis LeMay was George Wallace's American Independent Party vice-presidential running mate in 1968. A military hero, LeMay always had been controversial because of his efforts to make nuclear war thinkable; probably, he was added to the ticket more to pacify leading conservative supporters of Wallace than to gain mass support, and some believe he cost Wallace votes. Retired General Gavin was mentioned briefly in 1967 as a possible peace candidate. Neither professional association activities nor direct participation in politics, however, has served "to integrate the military into a unified political force" [31, p. 391].

CONCLUSION

Like any interest group the military tries to influence public opinion to support its programs. Together with its civilian allies, it creates images and sells policies. The Pentagon is able to sponsor more elaborate publicity than other governmental agencies; the effort represented by the films produced, flights arranged, letters answered, honor guards provided, press conferences held, and newspaper articles placed undoubtedly is matched only by soap or soft drink companies' advertising support for a new product. But the mere existence of such efforts does not mean that opinion necessarily is swayed by them on specific issues. More likely, the media and community relations programs of the services have a long-term, socializing influence on public opinion. Inadequate survey data prevents precise cause-and-effect conclusions, but we do know the general nature of opinions toward the military:

1. Garrison-state hypotheses are as yet only weakly supported by survey data, if at all, and the nature of linkages is uncertain. The public seems able to tolerate prolonged ambiguity in international relations without

---

[17] Sen. George McGovern proposed, during his 1972 presidential campaign, to reduce defense spending by $30 billion by fiscal 1975. Defense Secretary Laird called this a "white flag surrender budget." Defense spending was a major issue during the Democratic primaries that year, and in the general election campaign between McGovern and President Nixon. McGovern promised to "bring the military monster under control," and public opinion polls in summer 1972 showed that tax reform and cutting defense spending were his most popular issues.

reacting in a trigger-happy manner. But it is not clear what this means for public support for military positions on foreign policy.

2. The military is seen neither as threatening nor as totalitarian, but neither apparently has it been seen as a security-providing institution which can do no wrong. *People are not afraid of the military.* They are willing to give the military temporary control over their sons' lives (UMT and the draft) and to permit the military to direct limited wars in the way they see fit, with little civilian interference.

3. The only civilian whose judgment on security affairs is more respected than that of the military is the president.

4. People are much less willing than they once were to give the Defense Department carte blanche in the use of financial resources to ensure national defense. But it should be remembered that the secretary of defense and most top officials are civilians. Waste in the Pentagon is a widespread concern, but this may be attributed to civilian bureaucrats.

5. It is not clear to what extent the military has been blamed for Vietnam disappointments.

6. Public attitudes toward international events and toward the manner of American participation in limited wars have been *compatible with* military perspectives. Of course, this does not mean that such attitudes were *caused by* military-inspired brainwashing through the mass media and socializing institutions, although to some extent that is possible. For whatever reason, Americans have shown more patience and passive acceptance of elite-generated security policies than usually attributed to them.

REFERENCES

1. Almond, Gabriel, *The American People and Foreign Policy* (New York: Praeger, 1960).
2. American Institute of Public Opinion, survey number 784, Princeton, N.J., 1969.
3. "Announcing the Marshall McLuhan Dew-Line Newsletter," advertisement, *The Atlantic,* 223 (February 1969), p. 13.
4. Baldwin, Hanson W., "When the Big Guns Speak," in *Public Opinion and Foreign Policy,* ed. Lester Markel (New York: Harper & Row, 1949), pp. 97-120.
5. Biderman, Albert D., "Sequels to a Military Career: The Retired Military Professional," in *The New Military,* ed. Morris Janowitz (New York: Russell Sage Foundation, 1964), pp. 287-336.
6. Bobrow, Davis B. and Neal D. Cutler, "Time-Oriented Explanations of National Security Beliefs: Cohort, Life-Stage, and Situation," *Peace Research Society (International) Papers,* 8 (1967), pp. 31-57.
7. Bobrow, Davis B. and Allen R. Wilcox, "Dimensions of Defense Opinion:

The American Public," *Peace Research Society (International) Papers,* 6 (1966), pp. 101-142.

8. Borklund, C. W., *The Department of Defense* (New York: Praeger, 1968).

9. "CBS Avoids Reply to Barbs, Agnew Says," *The Atlanta Journal-Constitution,* March 21, 1971, p. 4-A.

10. Caspary, William R., "The 'Mood Theory': A Study of Public Opinion and Foreign Policy," *American Political Science Review,* LVIV (June 1970), pp. 536-547.

11. Christiansen, Bjorn, *Attitudes Toward Foreign Affairs as a Function of Personality* (Oslo: Oslo University Press, 1959).

12. Clotfelter, James, "The American Military and the Garrison State," unpublished Ph.D. dissertation, University of North Carolina at Chapel Hill, 1969.

13. Clotfelter, James, and B. Guy Peters, unpublished research, Emory University.

14. Cohen, Bernard, "The Military Policy Public," *Public Opinion Quarterly,* XXX (Summer 1966), pp. 200-211.

15. Congressional Quarterly Service, *Legislators and the Lobbyists,* 2nd ed. (Washington: CQ Service, 1968).

16. Cottrell, Leonard, and Sylvia Eberhart, *American Opinion on World Affairs in the Atomic Age* (Princeton, N.J.: Princeton University Press, 1948).

17. Cook, Fred J., *The Warfare State* (New York: Macmillan, 1962).

18. Cutler, Neal E., *The Alternative Effects of Generations and Aging Upon Political Behavior* (Oak Ridge: Oak Ridge National Laboratory, 1968).

19. Davis, James W., Jr., and Kenneth M. Dolbeare, *Little Groups of Neighbors: The Selective Service System* (Chicago: Markham, 1968).

20. Davis, Vincent, *The Admirals Lobby* (Chapel Hill: University of North Carolina Press, 1967).

21. Derthick, Martha, "Militia Lobby in the Missile Age: the Politics of the National Guard," in *Changing Patterns of Military Politics,* ed. Samuel P. Huntington (New York: Free Press, 1962), pp. 190-234.

22. Ekirch, Arthur, Jr., *The Civilian and the Military* (New York: Oxford University Press, 1956).

23. Farber, Michael, "The Armageddon Complex: Dynamics of Opinion," *Public Opinion Quarterly,* XV (Summer 1951), pp. 217-224.

24. Farney, Dennis, "Pentagon's Promotion of Its Own Activities Upsets Many Critics," *The Wall Street Journal,* November 13, 1970, pp. 1, 21.

25. Fitzgerald, A. Ernest, "The Pentagon and the News Media," address to the Businessmen's Educational Fund, New York, April 14, 1970.

26. Fulbright, J. William, "Militarism and American Democracy," Owens-Corning lecture at Denison University, Granville, Ohio, April 18, 1969.

27. Fulbright, J. William, *The Pentagon Propaganda Machine* (New York: Random House, 1971).
28. Hamrick, Tom, "Coping with the Boob Image," *Army,* 20 (July 1970), pp. 26-30.
29. Hersh, Seymour M., "My Lai 4," *Harper's,* 240 (May 1970), pp. 53-84.
30. Huntington, Samuel, *The Common Defense* (New York: Columbia University Press, 1961).
31. Janowitz, Morris, *The Professional Soldier* (New York: Free Press, 1960).
32. Kolodziej, Edward A., *The Uncommon Defense and Congress, 1945-1963* (Columbus: Ohio State University Press, 1966).
33. Landauer, Jerry, "The F-111: A Saga of Pentagon Puffery," *The Wall Street Journal,* May 25, 1970, p. 12.
34. Lapham, Lewis H., "Military Theology," *Harper's,* 243 (July 1971), pp. 73-85.
35. Levine, Gene N., and John Modell, "American Public Opinion and the Fallout-Shelter Issue," *Public Opinion Quarterly,* XXIX (Summer 1965), pp. 270-279.
36. Lifton, Robert Jay, "Vietnam and the Militarized Society: The Human Cost," SANE pamphlet, 1969.
37. Mills, C. Wright, *The Power Elite* (New York: Oxford University Press, 1956).
38. Moskos, Charles C., Jr., *The American Enlisted Man* (New York: Russell Sage Foundation, 1970).
39. Mueller, John E., "Patterns of Popular Support for the Wars in Korea and Vietnam," unpublished paper, University of Rochester, 1968.
40. Mueller, John E., "Presidential Popularity From Truman to Johnson," *American Political Science Review,* LXIV (March 1970), pp. 18-34.
41. Neustadt, Richard E., *Presidential Power* (New York: Wiley, 1960).
42. Russett, Bruce, "The Revolt of the Masses: Public Opinion of Military Expenditures," paper presented to the Inter-University Seminar on Armed Forces and Society, Chicago, 1971.
43. Schattschneider, E. E., *The Semisovereign People* (New York: Holt, Rinehart and Winston, 1960).
44. Shearer, Derek, "The Pentagon Propaganda Machine," in *The Pentagon Watchers,* eds. Leonard S. Rodberg and Derek Shearer, (Garden City, N.Y.: Doubleday, 1970), pp. 99-142.
45. Shoup, David M., "The New American Militarism," *Atlantic,* 223 (April 1969), pp. 51-56.
46. Smith, Dale, *The Eagle's Talons* (Washington: Spartan Books, 1966).
47. Smith, Louis, *American Democracy and Military Power* (Chicago: University of Chicago Press, 1951).
48. Spock, Benjamin, "Dr. Spock Speaks on War and Peace," SANE pamphlet, undated.

49. Swomley, John M., Jr., *The Military Establishment* (Boston: Beacon Press, 1964).
50. Verba, Sidney, et al., "Public Opinion and the War in Vietnam," *American Political Science Review,* 61 (June 1967), pp. 317-333.
51. William R. Hamilton and Staff, unpublished polls, Washington, D.C., 1968-1970.
52. "Who Needs Gallup or Harris?", *Forbes,* 108 (December 15, 1971), p. 29.
53. Yarmolinsky, Adam, *The Military Establishment* (New York: Harper & Row, 1971).

CHAPTER SEVEN

The Military and Congress

"Congressmen are generally in favor of science and defense in the same way they are united in their opposition to cancer and the common cold" [25, p. 11]. Critical legislative scrutiny of the defense budget was abandoned during World War II, and it was not reinstated until the early seventies. During the war "the armed forces got what they wanted to such an extent that they had about $50 billion in unused appropriations at the end. ... Congress was disposed to 'trust in God and General Marshall'" [5, p. 55]. The sense of international urgency following the war, combined with the increasing technical sophistication of defense choices, made it more difficult for strict congressional controls to be reimposed. Sometimes by lobbying for defense projects, more often by acquiescing in administration requests, Congress nevertheless has played an essential part in the growth of the military establishment.

In the debates of the early seventies, critics within Congress accused it of being a pushover for the Pentagon, of being dominated by the military-industrial complex. Sen. Gaylord Nelson said $70 billion defense budgets would pass with less than an hour's floor discussion, "on the theory that the military knew best and that we really were dealing with purely technical military matters and not with political matters" [26, p. 12]. As ex-Congressman Stewart Udall said, "We simply did it because men who knew and who had the information had made these decisions." Often legislators said they felt the defense budget was so large and sacrosanct that it could neither be investigated adequately nor challenged. "Senators and Congressmen have other things to do," Fulbright said, "and they don't wish to tilt at windmills." Sen. Barry Goldwater agreed that "we almost took as gospel . . .anything that came from the Pentagon, without really looking into it in depth" [21, pp. 259, 130, 471]. Even a powerful member such as the late Mendel Rivers, chairman of the House Armed Services Committee, felt that the Defense Department sometimes did not treat Congress as a full partner in making national security policy. "There are times," he said, "when the

148

Department of Defense forgets that Congress exists for reasons other than to provide a blank check"[2, p. 256].

Politically, it was not easy for congressmen to resist those who claimed the virtues of toughness and patriotism. "If you vote against anything the military wants," Rep. Otis G. Pike said, "you are being 'soft on Communism'" [37, p. A-2]. The defense budget had been wrapped in the American flag.

The "power of the purse," investigatory powers, and the responsibility to set military organization all give Congress potential influence over the armed forces. Between 1945-1960 congressional committees often were occupied with settling interservice disputes, acting almost in a judicial role. During this period Congress never vetoed directly a major administration-proposed strategic program, force-level recommendation, or weapons system, except when confronted with competitive service programs[19, p. 133]. Kolodziej[22, pp. 419-420] pointed to a decline in congressional initiatives in defense policy in the early 1960s, due to favorable international conditions, forceful Defense Department and presidential leadership, reduction in the service rivalries which permitted and encouraged congressional intervention, and a generally rising defense budget which gave the military and its congressional allies less ground for criticism. But even under more propitious circumstances in the late sixties, comprehensive congressional involvement was difficult to achieve. Congressmen themselves pointed to the near-monopoly of intelligence data and technical expertise held by the Pentagon.

Congressional controversies usually have involved some combination of interservice rivalries (e.g., Thor-Jupiter), rivalries within the defense contracting community (e.g., the F-111), and rumors of scandal or mismanagement. All provide precious information and options for congressmen. Congress has been interested in military organization, manpower policies, and construction, but until recently little sustained interest (relative to their importance) was shown in strategic and general policy matters. Until the Vietnam War provoked opposition to defense requests, congressmen depended on their committees, the Bureau of the Budget (later the Office of Management and Budget), and the president to evaluate the massive defense programs. And strategy was something that came out of the Pentagon.

WHO ACTS FOR CONGRESS?

"Congress" does not act, of course. Congressmen act or certain congressmen in key positions act. In defense, as in all areas of legislation, standing committees and their chairmen are the most important actors; their recommendations usually win approval after perfunctory examination by the full houses.

Specialization is a virtue nurtured by committees and subcommittees, and specialization and attention to detail are highly regarded in Congress. In military affairs, because of the layman's hesitation to involve himself in the technically esoteric and politically sensitive area of national security, committees have enjoyed not only dominant but sometimes exclusive control over legislation and appropriations. Data gathered by committee hearings usually provide the only basis for developing and choosing between alternative programs.

Of predominant influence are the Senate and House Armed Services committees and defense appropriations subcommittees. Since neither house has centralized its national security policy organization since 1946, other committees and subcommittees sometimes have become involved in defense controversies: government operations, foreign relations, government information, veterans affairs, merchant marine, space and aeronautics, foreign aid, military justice, military construction, and defense production. The Joint Atomic Energy Committee played a leading role in atomic energy affairs in the 1940s-1950s. The committee supported development of the hydrogen bomb; later it was blamed (or credited) by some for blocking agreement in Geneva disarmament negotiations by refusing to amend regulations to permit U.S. compromises on the protection of nuclear secrets.[1]

Usually, however, the armed services and appropriations committees have controlled what the houses are given to vote upon, and what kinds of options are available to the rest of the members. William Proxmire, chairman of the JEC subcommittee on Economy in Government, said, "Only when we get into some inquiry into the military does anybody . . . challenge (our) jurisdiction." (The subcommittee had done six staff studies, held 12 sets of hearings, and issued nine reports on waste and inefficiency in military procurement between 1951-1969.)

Members of the armed services and appropriations committees have acknowledged the difficulty of trying to oversee the Pentagon. The House Armed Services Committee in the fifties studied waste, the location, construction, and transfer of installations, and personnel problems because of a "fear of lack of competence" in more technical and less strategically peripheral matters [11, p. 100]. Rep. Richard Bolling in 1969 characterized both armed services committees as real estate committees. Until 1960 the appropriations subcommittees were left relatively free from specific authorizations by the substantive armed services committees; the House subcommittee tended to review administration and avoidable waste, while the Senate appropriations body focused on military policy. The Senate and House Armed Services

_____

[1] The committee was an in-house lobby on behalf of nuclear weapons, using visits to executive officials, solicitation of interest group support, release of information to the press, and speeches to influence executive decisions. It "was well enough informed about developments in the nuclear field to bring pressure upon the executive before decisions were made" [19, p. 136].

committees attempted an occasional broad review of military policy through hearings.

Section 412 (b) (1959), which strengthened the armed services committees' relative standing by making authorization a strict prerequisite for defense appropriations, was seen by Kolodziej [22, p. 423] as weakening congressional cohesion by emphasizing committee divisions against a centralized DOD. The overall capacity of Congress to control the Pentagon budget was not bolstered by the committee changes, even though in the sixties the armed services committees more actively examined detailed defense plans and procurement authorizations. Appropriations subcommittees continued to play a significant role in examining military policies; overlapping appropriations-armed services membership in the Senate discouraged rivalries there.

Investigations by the armed services committees commonly have been intended to develop a case for increased spending, e.g., the 1956 Symington airpower hearings and the 1957-1958 Johnson missile hearings. After hearings in 1968 a report of the Senate Armed Services preparedness subcommittee called for prompt decisions to deploy additional strategic weapon systems and to improve existing systems. Other hearings have sought to present a military viewpoint which had lost in intraexecutive disputes, e.g., the 1951 MacArthur hearings, the 1962 "muzzling" investigations, and the 1963 hearings to present the military's negative attitudes toward the test-ban treaty. Rep. Don Edwards, critical of the armed services committees' tendency to structure one-sided hearings, said in 1969 that he studied 3000 pages of testimony of 300 witnesses; 298 of the witnesses worked for the Pentagon, and the other two came from the National Rifle Association. "There is not even an effort to have a devil's advocate," he said [26, p. 48].

Committees have other means to orient their work in preferred directions. When the president in 1966 set up an advisory commission on Selective Service which looked as if it favored a lottery to select military inductees, the House Armed Services Committee set up its own civilian advisory panel to support its antilottery position.[2] Investigatory and overseeing responsibilities potentially damaging to the military can be placed in the protective custody of the armed services committees by congressional leadership, to ensure that inquiry will not be carried too far. This was done in 1969 with a congressionally mandated study of defense profits and a required investigation of the need for another nuclear aircraft carrier: A joint study group from the committees recommended funding for carrier construction.

In recent years, under criticism from other congressmen, the armed services committees and their new subcommittees began to explore weapons systems and strategies in more complete and critical fashion. McNamara was

[2] That year Congress prohibited imposition of a lottery without its approval, guaranteed student deferments, protected local board autonomy, and otherwise limited presidential discretion.

credited by some legislators, although not committee chairmen, with educating them to the strategies and weapons selection methods of the Pentagon. His explicitly detailed annual "posture statement" set out the intellectual premises on which the military budget was based.

Who sits on these committees? These are prestigious assignments, generally going to able, senior, and conservative members. Most believe with the late Sen. Richard Russell, that "there would be little merit to a course that would win a war against poverty in our backyards if we jeopardized the security of our very home" [37, p. A-2]. The full House leadership and part of the Senate leadership in the early 1970s was firmly pro-Pentagon, i.e., the "whatever our boys need" school of belief. This leadership chooses committee members who can be expected to make the "correct" decisions; helping to insure this conservative coloration has been liberal legislators' tendency to seek appointment to committees dealing with domestic social problems.

Most committees place great importance on gaining widespread committee support for legislation before it is reported out, and so committee members tend to support that legislation on the floor. Not only will a member of a relevant committee have been involved in the consensus-building process; not only will his attachment to his committee's record of success be at stake in the full house's votes on legislation reported out; in addition, he probably would not have been placed on an important committee in the first place if he had not been thought to be both sympathetic to the interest (e.g., defense) involved and responsive to leadership wishes.

Conservative southern Democrats and midwestern Republicans dominate the military committees. Dealing with the small-town Southerners disproportionately represented in military leadership was a southern quadrumvirate; Russell of Georgia, Stennis of Mississippi, Rivers of South Carolina, and Mahon of Texas headed the four committees in 1970. When Rivers and Russell died, their places were filled by two Louisianans. Rep. William Moorhead charged that these chairmen "have dealt so long with the military and with the defense contractors that they begin to think they are without fault"[28, p. 106]. Typically, their districts are bulging with bases and defense plants, with Rivers's Charleston district the classic example: Fifty-five percent of the area's payroll was accounted for by defense business, and Rivers claimed to be responsible for most of the military installations in his district. There were 12 bases, stations, centers, and shipyards, and five smaller installations, and during Rivers's 6 years as chairman five defense plants were located in Charleston. The six ranking Democrats on his committee had 43 military bases and plants in their districts. In the Senate, on the other hand, the association between the level of economic dependence on military payroll of a senator's constituency and 1969 membership or immediate past membership on Senate defense committees (armed services, appropriations subcommittees on defense and military construction) was barely significant statistically. (Using the military contracts form of dependency, the association was even weaker.) Factors in addition to constituency dependency must be considered relevant in assigning senators to defense committees. This also may indicate that members are generous in approving military spending for states not represented on the committees, perhaps through "log-rolling" arrangements.

The importance of defense installations and contracts to localities has been discussed in Chapter Four. "Under the Johnson Administration defense spending became an agent of redistribution of income in favor of some of the poorer areas of the country, especially the South, and most particularly Texas" [31, p. 69]. Georgia, which became a major beneficiary, at one time had the chairmen of both armed services committees (Russell and Carl Vinson). Local officials from Marietta, Lockheed-Georgia's home, credited Russell with helping to get the C-5A contract for Lockheed. At the plane's 1968 roll-out ceremonies, President Johnson said, "I would have you good folks of Georgia to know that there are a lot of Marietta, Georgias scattered throughout our fifty states. All of them would like to have the pride that comes from this production. But not all of them have the Georgia delegation" [8, p. 53].

On the afternoon of November 18, 1964, after announcing plans to close 80 installations within the United States, Secretary McNamara received telephone calls from 169 affected congressmen. He was accused by some of a "breach of faith" because he did not give them an opportunity to "comment" beforehand on his proposed shutdowns. Intervention by key legislators has been instrumental in keeping several shipyards and bases in operation despite their decreasing duties.

Senators such as Henry Jackson of Washington, the home of Boeing, and Russell publicly associated themselves with the interests of their states' contractors and military installations, and often cooperated with lobbyists and service leaders to secure contracts or missions. The payoff could be substantial: as few as 29 major ABM contractors in 1969 operated 300 plants in 172 congressional districts in 42 states, and it was estimated that 15,000 firms eventually would profit from full deployment. On the other hand, Senator Fulbright has remarked, "Having so little participation with the military in my State, it has never been a matter of primary significance as a Representative from Arkansas. The principal installation in my State was the germ warfare plant, which has never attracted my sympathy very much." When a witness before Wisconsin Senator Proxmire's subcommittee (also including members from Michigan and Pennsylvania) suggested that reduced defense spending would hurt Pacific Coast states, Proxmire asked: "It might help Wisconsin, Michigan, and Pennsylvania, and not some of the other states?" [21, pp. 121, 152]. Five of the six senators who altered their positions on the ABM during 1969-1970 were moving toward positions more consonant with their states' dependency levels.

Studies by Russett and the author have pointed to constituency dependence on military installation spending as a more important factor in senatorial voting on defense measures than the more publicized dependence on industry contracts. For example, the highest correlation between Senate votes on a 1969-1970 scale of support for the ABM and a constituency dependency measure was with the military payroll indicator. But states' dependence on military contracts were not significantly associated with their senators' votes on ABM, and similar results were found with general defense policy voting scales. Russett noted: "Perhaps military bases, because they are stable and enduring, exert a political influence on Capitol Hill that here-today, gone-tomorrow contracts cannot. . . . Direct hire by the Defense Department may more strongly mold the attitudes of workers. . . . (Perhaps) defense weapons and equipment contractors, unlike local suppliers of military bases, try to exert political influence on key Senators from other states as well as their own" [31, p. 85] . Bases have been subject to close congressional control, not only when they are established or closed, but when major changes in manpower or assigned tasks are made. Military uniforms and vehicles are highly visible. Many procurement contracts, on the other hand, may not be visible as *military* programs, because they are awarded to chemical and automotive plants usually perceived as commercial. This may reduce the constituency impact of contracts and reduce their impact on congressional behavior.

Where dependency explanations break down most noticeably are with congressmen from low-dependency states who support defense legislation anyway. For example, 25 of 36 senators from states with more than one-and-a-half times their "share" (based on their percentage of national income) of military payroll supported ABM on all 1969 votes; however, 12 of 42 senators from states with less than their share also supported ABM on all votes. It is for the latter group in particular that other explanations, such as party, region, executive influence (through electoral strength, or promises or threats relating to patronage, contracts, and bases), institutional factors (e.g., relating to house leadership, seniority, committee membership), other constituency and personal characteristics, ideology, and attitudes toward domestic priorities must be seen as playing decisive roles. Some congressmen are members of law firms which work for defense companies, and others are associated through service on boards or staffs of banks and business firms; 60 of the 274 representatives who reported their stock holdings in 1969 held stock in defense firms. However, it seems doubtful that personal financial interests play an important role. Log-rolling, or vote trading, may help to explain the behavior of legislators from low-dependency states. Also, congressmen may vote differently on different kinds of defense issues: (1) hardware procurement; (2) decision-making procedures, research methods, and civilian control; (3) manpower and deployment; and (4) military construction.

Pork-barreling and log-rolling are not practices confined to defense programs, of course; they are found in all areas of American politics. And some representatives become supporters of the military not for reasons of pork but for patriotism: Continued close association with generals and admirals leads them to believe that the nation must strengthen its military posture and give its uniformed, beribboned experts a greater voice in policy-making. Long-time House Armed Services Committee Chairman Vinson considered "the military establishment and national security too important to be left to civilians such as the President and his advisers. (Policies) should be decided by civilians in Congress on the basis of the best advice of the professional military leaders, without the intervention of the Bureau of the Budget"[32, p. 255]. He looked to the Joint Chiefs, not to the president. Years later Vinson wrote a young colleague: "Some things proposed by the Executive Branch are virtually impossible to change. This is particularly so in the area of defense. I personally am reluctant, and indeed refuse, to substitute my judgment on a military matter for the judgment of those so much more qualified to make decisions of a military nature"[37, p. A-2]. Men like Vinson develop a proprietary interest in the services, having been responsible for so much of their appropriations over the years; Vinson was "Mr. Navy," "the admiral," and "father of the modern Navy" while he was chairman of the pre-unification naval affairs committee. Men in uniform, Rivers said, "don't have a lobby like some of the other people have. The only lobby they have is the Committee on Armed Services" [27, p. 22]. Not only are committees agencies for the exercise of congressional authority over the military, but they are channels for military influence on Congress.

For liberal congressmen "many good and liberal things—foreign aid, technical assistance, travel grants, fellowships, overseas libraries—could be floated on the Communist threat" [14, p. 54]. National defense has been used as a cover by congressmen interested in promoting other programs. Ex-Representative Udall said "we couldn't do . . . the things we wanted to do to improve the life of people in this country, to improve our educational system . . . unless we got the defense banner out" [21, p. 256]. The interstate highway program was passed as a "defense highway act." The first major aid to education bill was passed after Sputnik, with its name changed from the Elementary Education Act to the National Defense Education Act.

A congressman's experience in the military also has been cited as a factor working toward support for defense legislation. Louis Smith pointed out, however, that in the post-World War II Congress a majority of each house were veterans (most having held nonregular commissions below the rank of colonel.) "It does not appear to have given a military cast to the thinking of members of Congress or . . . to have made them subservient to their former commanders"[32, p. 231]. In 1969-1970 about two-thirds of the congressmen had served in the military. There was no significant association between congressmen having had active or combat service and voting for or against defense legislation. Congressional membership in the military reserve and

National Guard became a subject of legal controversy in 1970 when the Reservists Committee to Stop the War filed suit to order 122 congressmen expelled from the reserves, including 35 on ready or active standby status and 29 sitting on defense, foreign affairs, or appropriations committees. Including retired officers, 39 of the 100 senators held officer ranks. The group cited a Constitutional provision against persons "holding any office under the United States" being members of Congress. The group claimed it was "deprived of the unbiased judgment of the members of Congress on war and defense policy." The courts have not so far agreed.

● ● ●

Committees have sought to insure that their close ties to the professional military are not cut, by trying to insulate officers from civilian administration pressure when testifying before committees. The National Security Act of 1949 gave the service chiefs legal authority to take their independent views directly to Congress, although no effective device has been available to protect officers from the executive's retaliation.[3] Sometimes, officers have cooperated with friendly committees by permitting themselves to be led into lines of questioning whereby, "in good conscience," they are forced to tell congressmen that the military really needs more money and weapons than the administration recommended. Such contrary testimony occured, for example, during hearings on nuclear-powered carriers and the B-70 bomber. Some officers have openly opposed administration programs, and escaped punishment, while others have defended policies they disliked. Service manuals warn that frank testimony can result in transferral from one's post of duty, although the official reasons for transferral may be different; the House Armed Services Committee at least once protested that military witnesses had been intimidated by the administration.

More recently there have been equally unsuccessful congressional efforts to protect witnesses critical of the Pentagon's high spending. The Proxmire subcommittee investigated the air force's alleged reprisal in firing A. Ernest Fitzgerald, a celebrated deputy for management systems and self-described "parsimonious hawk." After his initial testimony had touched off the C-5A cost overrun controversy, the air force changed C-5A cost figures to be submitted by Fitzgerald to the subcommittee; denied him permission to present written statements or supplementary materials; and sought to restrict the topics on which he could testify. Prior to his testimony Fitzgerald had been informed that he was to be given civil service status; 2 weeks afterward he was told that the previous notice had been a "computer error", the first of

---

[3] Several years earlier Vinson had succeeded in writing in a statutory responsibility for the chief of naval operations to "keep his military machine in readiness . . . (even if this meant that he) might feel impelled to come to the Congress . . . against the wishes or the approval of his civilian boss" [16, p. 272].

its kind, according to defense officials. The retroactive revocation of his civil service status denied Fitzgerald an opportunity to challenge the decision. A memorandum prepared for the air force secretary detailed alternative methods for terminating Fitzgerald's services, including one conceded to be "rather underhanded." However, the air force denied that the memo had adverse implications for Fitzgerald, although its wording was conceded to be "unfortunate." Within a year he (1) had all major weapons system work removed from his responsibility ("I just wasn't invited to the meetings and reviews," Fitzgerald said, something Proxmire termed "isolation"); (2) was assigned to study mess hall costs and cost overruns in construction of a serviceman's 20-lane bowling alley in Thailand (Air Force Secretary Robert C. Seamans said, "Proper supervision of recreation facilities is not to be taken lightly"); and (3) was dismissed for "efficiency" reasons[21, pp. 790-792]. Fitzgerald charged the air force with putting investigators on his trail to try to discredit his character.

After some backing and filling about "reorganization" of his duties, the Pentagon admitted that Fitzgerald was fired. Unable to find evidence to support his charge, Seamans retracted an earlier statement that Fitzgerald had provided Congress with classified documents, which would have violated federal law. A bipartisan group of 60 congressmen protested Fitzgerald's firing, and Proxmire unsuccessfully sought to get the Justice Department to bring charges against air force officials for attempting to "influence, intimidate, or impede" Fitzgerald from testifying accurately before Congress. The American Civil Liberties Union charged that the dismissal of Fitzgerald violated the Constitution, civil service regulations, and federal laws regarding interference with congressional witnesses and government employees' right to testify. (A federal court agreed that Fitzgerald should have received a public hearing.) Congressional protest prevented the air force from replacing Fitzgerald with an auditor whose firm worked for C-5A manufacturer Lockheed, but Fitzgerald did not get his job back.

•   •   •

Chairman Rivers believed that the United States should build any weapon desired by the military that was technologically feasible. He once attacked McNamara, who declined to build several sophisticated systems, for "having the effrontery to try to hold back the state of the art" [1, p. 53]. But committees have not always felt such a close bond to the military. Senator Harry Truman's Special Committee to Investigate the National Defense Program, which earned a reputation for willingness to defer to the military on strategic matters during World War II,

shared the traditional American distrust of the military. ... The committee saw the military mind as rigid, shortsighted, and ignorant of the complexities of the economy. It saw itself as an instrument for helping to shake the military loose from 'hidebound' ways . . . and for . . . helping to keep the insatiable demands of the military within reasonable bounds. It resisted the demands, not out of a desire to protect the civilians or merely to save money, but because it regarded the services as slow, inefficient, and incredibly wasteful when they entered fields other than those concerned with military matters [29, p. 158] .

In the 1970s committee leaders who shared the Truman Committee's views of the military (e.g., those of Senate Foreign Relations and the Joint Economic Committee) occupied peripheral positions in the military appropriations framework.[4]

Favorable committee action is necessary and often sufficient for congressional passage of legislation because of the deference to committee expertise. If the four key military committees agree on a policy opposed to that of the administration, the administration may have to come to terms. But more commonly there is some disagreement, permitting the administration to choose the congressional demands to which it will respond. Disagreements could be found even among defense supporters during the Nixon administration. When Chairman Mahon charged that "the military has made so many mistakes, it has generated a lack of confidence" (citing the navy's recent record of sinking a $50 million submarine under construction in San Francisco Bay, the loss of two Polaris submarines, the Pueblo incident, two disastrous carrier fires, an American ship's collision with an Australian ship, and an attack on an American ship in the Mediterranean), Rivers immediately responded, "This is the way to tear down the military! That is one of the most popular things you could say. Keep on saying it, and the enemies of the military will love you for saying it!" [24, p. 833] .[5] In the Senate, Chairman Stennis ordered public hearings into the cost of the C-5A (built in Chairman Russell's Georgia), as Russell continued to oppose construction of a Fast Deployment Logistics Fleet (potential rival to the C-5A in moving equipment to troublespots), which would be built in good friend Stennis's Mississippi. But committee leaders usually agreed in the 1960s and early 1970s that the military needed as much or more than the administration was willing to request, and all favored a strong military-industrial establishment. Stennis and Mahon were critical of Lockheed's management during the C-5A financing

---

[4] In 1951 Louis Smith believed Congress held "for the military lobby all those habitual fears it has for administrative agencies which proclaim their own virtue at public expense," in addition to anxieties about improper military influence over democratic government[32, p. 235]. In the mid-fifties Lewis Dexter found widespread distrust of the military among members of presumably friendly defense committees (although most members felt that their colleagues were more pro-military than themselves) [11, pp. 105-107].

[5] Congressional decorum reasserted itself later, however: both chairmen altered their remarks for publication in The Congressional Record. In the new version Rivers was quoted as saying that Mahon's words had given "wings to the very things I was talking about."

debate in 1970, for example, but both agreed to help nurse the company through its difficulties.

REBELLION

In 1969 the reputation of the four military committees as conduits for translating Pentagon requests into legislation provoked a rare rebellion against established congressional procedures. Traditionally, armed services committee hearings produced recommendations which coincided with those of the Defense Department, sometimes going beyond on particular systems and making slight overall cuts, and which were seldom challenged by other congressmen. In 1969 the Senate Foreign Relations Committee, with some of its members expressing dissatisfaction with 1968 armed services hearings on the ABM (which had heard almost exclusively from supporters of deployment), opened hearings of its own to present critics of the ABM and MIRV. An ad hoc foreign relations subcommittee, headed by Stuart Symington (also a member of armed services), began investigating U.S. security commitments. The JEC Proxmire subcommittee, which had begun hearings on procurement policies in 1968, urged a $10 billion defense cut. The House Foreign Affairs Subcommittee on National Security Policy and Scientific Developments (which had not held hearings in 11 years) was reactivated by a previously friendly congressman to investigate MIRV, ABM, chemical and biological warfare research, and defense policy; it recommended a freeze on MIRV testing. A House Government Operations subcommittee investigated defense contracting procedures and budgetary surveillance of the Pentagon. Its hearings contributed to passage of a bill creating an outside study of the federal acquisition process.

Under pressure the Senate Armed Services Committee set up subcommittees to deal with various weapons systems and held more extensive and critical hearings. Investigations touched on Pentagon contracting procedures and research, the F-14 contract, the Manned Orbiting Laboratory (MOL), increasing costs of weapons, My Lai, and desertion rates. In 1970 the draft, a continuing concern, was the subject of Senate hearings. Even the friendly House Armed Services Committee held critical hearings on an army tank program during which it found that the army had put $2 billion into a tank that would not be a significant improvement even if it worked, had released misleading information, had ignored test failures, and had rushed into mass production to avoid budget cuts. It also studied the costly, trouble-plagued Cheyenne battle helicopter, My Lai, the submarine sinking, and the Pueblo incident. Ad hoc congressional groups were organized to study defense policy and national priorities. The Senate Government Operations Permanent Investigations Subcommittee held hearings on irregularities in the operations of army noncommissioned officers' clubs and on black-marketing and currency manipulation in Vietnam.

Most 1969 cutbacks, however, were ones volunteered by the administration. The Johnson budget was reduced by $3 billion by the Nixon administration, and the Cheyenne and MOL were scrapped for technical as well as for cost reasons; the final appropriations bill (minus some Vietnam funding) was cut to $69.6 billion. Although the non-Vietnam military budget actually may have risen, and the Nixon "savings" were partly illusory, the $5 billion cut by Congress for fiscal 1970 had been matched only by $5 to $6 billion cuts in fiscal 1954 and 1969. And never had such an economy drive been generated in Congress with so much public support and attention. In 1970 the procurement authorization bill was reduced by $600 million, and the House Appropriations Committee deleted $2 billion from the appropriations bill (from the AMSA or B-1 bomber, the nuclear carrier, and research programs). The Senate Appropriations Committee ignored administration requests to restore House-cut funds, and cut another $300 million, persuading the Senate antimilitary spending group to offer no further objections to the $66.4 billion fiscal 1971 appropriations bill. Most of the programs reduced were ones for which the Pentagon did not fight vigorously; for example, pending a National Security Council study of the possibility of reducing the aircraft carrier fleet from 15 to 12, Congress knocked out funds for starting a new carrier. While giving the Pentagon most of what it wanted in 1970, the House Appropriations Committee warned it to reform its procurement and management practices: "What this country needs is more defense for the dollar, not necessarily more dollars for defense" [15, p. 2-A].

Important developments in 1969 and 1970 were the increased willingness of the Senate Armed Services Committee and the appropriations subcommittees to cut defense spending, and their growing expertise in dealing with military programs. The broader economic problems of 1969-1971 encouraged a more economy-minded attitude. But the House Armed Services Committee preferred to add unrequested funds for navy shipbuilding. In 1969 Secretary Laird did not formally request appropriation of navy funds that were authorized by Chairman Rivers and the House, so the next year, to insure funds would be appropriated and spent, Rivers secured prior agreement from the administration. It would spend an unrequested $300 million dollars, in return for Rivers' support for an expanded ABM program. The House committee also sought to discredit other committees' critical testimony on several weapons.

Within his committee Rivers, not hesitant to use his power as chairman, rarely was opposed by more than three members. For example, on the 1970 adoption of an authorization bill only $34 million less than the administration sought, the vote was 33 to 3 for. Whatever anyone thought of him and his committee, Rivers said in 1969, one could not criticize success; he claimed never to have had 150 votes cast against him on the floor on a committee recommendation. "And Caesar in all his glory can't make that statement." (The next year he suffered his only defeat, in a 130 to 100 vote, since assuming the "toga" as chairman, on a minor procedural question.) In the larger House, committee reports are challenged less often than in the Senate, and the committee's power is enhanced accordingly.

Russell defended the record of the Senate Appropriations and Armed Services committees (both of which he had chaired) in examining the military budget. He claimed to have held complete hearings and to have cut almost $9 billion from Pentagon requests between 1964-1970. Nobody has been "just slap-happy dashing it through," he said. Pentagon officials claimed only 17 percent of civilian program outlays in 1970 were controllable by Congress, whereas almost all DOD programs were subject to annual revisions. During one year (1967), for example, a committee was investigating defense operations on more than 70 occasions, with questions ranging over more than 200 subjects. Secretary McNamara himself averaged more than 100 hours of testimony a year during his 7-year term, requiring at least four hours in preparation for each hour of testimony. In the first six months of 1967 leading DOD executives spent more than 6000 hours in actual testimony [2, p. 249].

Rarely has more than 5 percent been cut from recommended budget levels, however, and Russell conceded that Congress had problems in overseeing the budget. He said McNamara's success in consolidating power in his office had lessened the interservice competition which congressmen depend upon for information as to budgetary struggles and feasible policy alternatives. He also allowed that "there is something about preparing for destruction that causes men to be more careless in spending money." In 1969 Russell told the Senate that his committees had "allotted vast sums to the Navy (for ships) before we knew we had a missile that would work on them" on the basis of "unqualified" testimony from "everyone in the Department of Defense and in the Navy. ... It probably cost the taxpayers $1 billion, because they have had to rebuild those missiles three times" [34, p. 10]. Russell conceded that his efforts to serve as watchdog were limited by inadequate staff. The armed services committees have the responsibility for annual authorizations almost as large as those coming from all other committees combined. The Senate defense appropriations subcommittee had only two or three staff members to deal with the entire defense establishment. Congress, Udall said, was "pathetically understaffed" and became a rubber stamp because it was not equipped to challenge the Pentagon [21, pp. 264, 268].

POWERS

What can be done by committees and by Congress? Congress has the power of the purse, although most congressmen see it as insufficient without other powers. The annual budget review elicits information. It has been used to express dissatisfaction with military assistance programs, and sometimes foreign policy directives are attached to authorization and appropriation bills. Generally, however, Congress has refused to deny funds to "our boys in the field" during wartime, and has been hesitant to do so in peacetime. Supporting the money power is the investigatory power. By this means testimony can be developed which will lead to publicity adverse to the administration or to particular military programs. Congress has the authority to declare war, but the fashion of declaring wars has declined since 1941. The Senate has the power to ratify treaties and otherwise take part in making foreign military commitments, although here executive agreements have placed more authority in the president's hands. Congressional groups also act to represent others in the executive branch, nongovernmental elites, and the general public; most often, they serve as appeals agents for the losers (especially disappointed military men) in intraadministration disputes.

Through informal negotiations with the White House and Pentagon, or even by indirect signals, key legislators make known what they will tolerate and what they cannot, what they will insist upon and what they will compromise on. The implied threat of public controversy or behind-the-scenes unpleasantness sometimes makes the administration modify its proposals, but most concessions on defense policy are minor. An exception has been ABM policy. President Johnson's 1967 decision to order deployment of the ABM could be credited in part to prolonged congressional pressure. Republican efforts in Congress led wags (looking at the 1968 election) to say the ABM was to be deployed more against American Republicans than against Chinese communists. The newly elected Republican president in 1969 then modified Johnson's proposed system to make it less objectionable to Democratic critics.

Congressional influence tends to be negative; it can block changes easier than it can secure positive innovations in weapons or strategy. Its negative impact was seen in its power to block the reserves-National Guard merger, for example. [Also 23, p. 470.] On money matters, of course, Congress has a potentially powerful veto.

Influence is impossible without information, and the most valuable information is knowledge of disagreements among others. The primary lever Congress has to influence military policy, therefore, is the surfacing of disagreements within the military and within the Defense Department. Congressmen need options laid out for them to choose from *early* in the process, so they actively encourage interservice disputes. They want independent services with overlapping functions; a clean bureaucratic flow-chart would severely limit congressional participation. Thus, committees have wanted to retard the growth of centralized power in the Pentagon. Since the unification issue was first raised in Congress in 1944, Congress has been asked to permit several reorganizations; each time, it was reluctant to see more centralization, but each time the change was accepted with modifications, and without challenge to the need for "rational" centralized control [16, p. 382]. Limits placed on centralization by Congress have proved ineffectual, allowing the secretary of defense to increase his control over the services and unified commands.

The assured independent existence of services with detailed, congressionally specified missions and with direct access to Congress is a reflection of congressional concern that it not be left without alternatives to simple ratification of administration proposals. In the late 1940s the interests of the navy, for example, coincided with those of congressmen who wanted to maximize their institutional influence by insuring that disputes were not papered over before they reached the Capitol. The B-70 and nuclear propulsion programs were other instances where disputes between the services and between the technologists permitted early congressional involvement.

Secrecy and incompletely reported technical and budgetary information complicate congressional ability to play a major role. Even some members with "top secret" security clearance, sitting on relevant committees, have not been permitted to see information on defense programs. "If we can't get the facts," Rep. Lester L. Wolff said, "we can't make the decisions." Congressmen with access to prestige-conferring secret information tend to be those favorable to the military case, and they are given a powerful advantage over their colleagues. (Chairman Rivers once told a critical representative: "If you knew what I know about the Soviet Union, you wouldn't be standing up here . . . "and then walked off the floor [26, pp. 29, 33]. In 1970 a $200 million "contingency fund" for troubled Lockheed Aircraft was quietly lodged in a $544 million general authorization request. In March 1968 (8 months before C-5A overruns were revealed) an air force assistant secretary told a House committee the plane was between target and ceiling costs. In 1969 the army admitted in a closed committee session that the cost of CBW research had been scattered clandestinely through the defense budget for years. Aid for Thailand and other sensitive foreign aid programs have been hidden under other programs.

Congressmen also are reluctant to demand full information, even when national security is not thought to be involved. In 1970, for example, the Senate handily defeated Proxmire's amendment requiring the Pentagon to tell Congress if it was following the "fly-before-you-buy" policy formally announced by Secretary Laird 3 weeks earlier. "Why shouldn't they tell us whether they're carrying out their own policy?" Proxmire asked [33, p. 1]. Congress is not provided with major defense-planning documents, such as the 5-year program and the Joint Strategic Objectives Plan. And there is the common tendency of administration spokesmen to underestimate anticipated weapons costs.

Related to adequate information is the importance of expert support for congressional attempts to impose alternative strategies or structures.

Outside experts or dissidents within DOD[6] usually have been necessary allies because of congressional hesitation to cross swords directly with military men. "I would not like to substitute my judgment for the judgment of General Powers or General Wheeler, or some of the other experts in our defense structure," Rep. Robert L. Leggett, who favored lower defense spending, remarked in 1969. If several weapons systems were proposed, he said, "I would rather not have us decide on a political basis which of them to deploy. I would rather that the decision be made by the professional soldiers" [26, p. 15].[7] Congress has tried on occasion to set up panels of scientific advisers, e.g., a ceremonial House Science and Aeronautics Committee panel in 1960, and proposals for independent review and audit boards in the early seventies.

Huntington is correct in thinking [19, p. 132] that it is political capabilities, not technical expertise, which Congress lacks. In this view committees simply cannot bring together all conflicting parties; they can become advocates or critics of a few particular programs at particular times, but they are unable to arrive at an overall program. Nevertheless, legislators *believe* that lack of technical expertise is a major problem for them.

Until the ABM-MIRV debates of 1969-1970 no congressional committee ever had assembled the technical expertise necessary to oppose administration defense policy, without the aid of elements within the Pentagon. In the ABM dispute, however, the Senate Foreign Relations Committee, the Joint Economic Committee, and various ad hoc groups served as the organizing foci for scientists, academics, some of the McNamara generation of DOD whiz kids, and former Democratic administration officials (ex-insiders) critical of the ABM. Some who had supported McNamara's holding action against the ABM from within now criticized from without. This was particularly important since the interservice disputes which characterized the forties and fifties had largely disappeared.

If Congress is told a missile system is necessary, but cannot be assured it will work, Senate Majority Leader Mike Mansfield said, Congress must be willing to "judge independently its necessity." Congress cannot be "taken in by what the Joint Chiefs of Staff or the Secretary of Defense say they must have," he said, because they never can be satisfied. Outside experts, who became the dissident congressmen's "own" experts, probably were most valuable not for their expertise but for their respectability, the cover they provided against being dismissed as know-nothings.

[6] Outside criticism of administration policies, it has been asserted, can be effective only if supplemented by inside opposition, and vice versa [19, p. 175]. This suggests the C. P. Snow model of "closed politics" [38].

[7] As an alternative to item reductions, which the Pentagon contended could only be made by defense specialists, an across-the-board 7 percent cut in Pentagon spending was proposed in 1970 and defeated by the Senate 42 to 31. The ceiling approach was defeated soundly by the Senate in 1971.

STRUCTURE AND STRATEGY

At one time Congress had wide powers to determine what the military *should be,* while the executive decided what the military *should do* [2, p. 247]. During the forties and fifties Congress continued its prewar pattern of investigating the "how," not the "why," of military policy. Congress remains active on matters involving men, materiel, and management, especially those relating to military structure, i.e., UMT, the draft, the volunteer army, organization of the services and general staffs, unification, the National Guard and reserves ("part-time soldiers but full-time voters"),and individual constituent complaints. On these matters administration requests are treated critically, with some being blocked or rejected, although even here congressional preeminence is doubtful because of DOD's greater specialization.

How the services are manned, what uniforms soldiers wear, how much money they are paid, and from whom they take orders are questions on which congressmen feel reasonably secure. Dollars are dollars and bosses are bosses. But hydra-headed MIRVs and "counter-force versus counter-value" strategies are beyond the normal world of congressmen, and it is here that matters usually have been left to the professionals, i.e., the administration and the military.

Until the Vietnam years congressmen involved in military affairs raised few questions of military policy in terms of their meaning for national or international political objectives. Where Congress has appeared to concern itself with overall policy, these usually have been cases where it "feels it is able to judge between clamoring claimants—usually different military services—and give one or another of them a larger slice of the available pie . . . (or) where Congressmen are concerned with some local situation, usually . . . employment"[11, p. 95]. Congressmen sometimes assume the arbiter role in disputes between technologists, but most have been unwilling to involve themselves in military strategy and technological questions. "Who are we to say 'no' to the military people?" one congressman asked Dexter [11, p. 101]. The military are the experts on organization, command, and war plans, and they have been regarded with a deference which congressmen rarely show to other experts. Congressmen favor varying overall levels of military strength, but more serious problems come when they must deal with qualitative, rather than purely quantitative, choices. Now they must choose between rival types of weapon systems capability, between weapons within a given category, or in the early 1970s, between going ahead on a new weapons approach (MIRV) or holding back.

The military's views have not always been accepted, but between 1941-1960 items labeled by the Joint Chiefs of Staff as "strategically necessary" (e.g., the wasteful Canol Project investigated by the Truman Committee during World War II) usually were taken out of the reach of Congress. The Truman Committee never considered questioning the motives of military leaders, because it would undermine public confidence. However, it saw as one of its major tasks the maintenance of the dominance of civilian agencies over the military in industrial mobilization; over a wide range of bureaucratic conflicts, it pressured the military to stay within the confines of its professional role. In the 1960s, as the Joint Chiefs encountered competing civilian strategists, congressmen often objected that civilian DOD officials gave too little weight to military opinion on strategy. But fear of undermining public confidence became less effective in deterring criticism of the services.

The congressional investigatory power has been used to probe strategy, but more effectively, it has been used to investigate matters relating to construction, manpower, or procurement methods. (Table Four shows the range of congressional defense controversies since World War II, and indicates the importance of committee investigations.) For example, most congressmen support spreading defense contracts around geographically and giving a significant share to small businesses. A recurrent theme of congressional investigation has been that too much of the defense dollar goes to a few large firms. During World War II the House and Senate set up a Select Committee on Small Business to study the impact of contract distribution on small businesses. The Truman Committee reflected his concern about undue concentration of defense contracts. "The little manufacturer, the little contractor, and the little machine shop," Truman said in February 1941, "have been left entirely out in the cold. The policy seems to be to make the big man bigger and to put the little man completely out of business. . . . Seventy to 90 percent of the contracts let have been concentrated in an area smaller than England." In the late 1960s Senator Proxmire, with his small business committee and the JEC subcommittee, used investigation to press home the same concerns about small businesses. No committee since has been as influential in procurement affairs as was the Truman Committee, because the latter operated in a political vacuum caused by President Roosevelt's preoccupation with foreign affairs and strategy [29, pp. 12-13, 28].

CIVILIAN CONTROL—BY WHOM?

One of the oldest tenets of American civil-military relations is that the professional soldier must be under civilian control. Civilian control has been used to justify changes in force levels, choices between weapons, service and departmental reorganization, and changes in relations between cabinet officers and the president and his military advisers. The Constitution presumably enshrines civilian control and strict separation of civilian and military spheres by its provisions that (1) the president shall be commander-in-chief of the armed forces; (2) Congress shall "provide for the common Defense," "declare War," "raise and support Armies," "Provide and maintain a Navy," "make Rules for the Government and Regulation of the land and Naval forces," and "provide for calling forth . . . organizing, arming, and

TABLE FOUR
Selected Congressional Defense Controversies, 1945-1970

Years	Issue	Issue content and participants
1945	United Nations ratification, Article 43	Article pledged U.N. members to deploy troops at request of Security Council. Effort to require prior Congressional approval.
1945-1946	Control of atomic energy development	Military or civilian composition of Atomic Energy Commission governing board. Scientists and military initially lobbied against each other.
1945-1946	Pearl Harbor	A special joint committee investigated the attack in an effort to fix blame.
1945-1948	Draft and UMT	Extension of draft through war; draft or volunteer army after war; army proposals for UMT. Opposition from peace, labor, and religious groups.
1949	Ratification of NATO	Congressmen questioned whether ratification would commit Congress to approve any military assistance programs later submitted, and extent to which obligation to rearm Europe was being accepted. Military and civilian administration officials supported ratification.
1949	B-36 and the "Revolt of the Admirals"	Interservice conflicts on allocation of service shares of relatively fixed budget, given differing concepts of the new nature of warfare. Air force-navy competition over control of airpower (the bomber versus the aircraft carrier); navy rallied congressional supporters to maintain its missions. Air force supporters sought 70 (versus 48) groups; compromise of 58 groups. "Unification and Strategy" hearings, resulting from interservice rivalries unresolved by National Security Act of 1947. Principal reliance on airpower versus balanced forces.
1950-1952	Preparedness investigation	Senate Armed Services subcommittee hearings on waste, theft, and cost overruns in military construction; witnesses from corporations and services.
1951	"The Great Debate"	Republican senators' efforts to limit presidential deployment of troops in Europe under NATO without prior congressional approval was unsuccessful.
1951	MacArthur recall	Senate Foreign Relations and Armed Services committee hearings on the president's recall of MacArthur, following the general's triumphal return to the United States and address to a joint session of Congress. Joint Chiefs supported Truman position.
1951-1952	UMT	Armed Services committees revived UMT proposals, supported by the administration, the National Security Training Commission, the Joint Chiefs, and reserve and veterans organ-

167

TABLE FOUR, continued

Years	Issue	Issue content and participants
		izations. Opposed by church, farmers, peace, and labor organizations. House vote to recommit UMT bill effectively ended efforts.
1951-1958	Conventional war capabilities	Congressional opposition to administration cuts in army and Marine Corps manpower. Formal and informal floors set for manpower levels.
1952	Cataloging Act	House and Senate Armed Services Committees and subcommittee of Senate Government Operations investigated varying costs for "identical" products for the different services; effort to standardize procurement practices.
1953	Ammunition shortage	Senate Armed Services preparedness subcommittee investigation of alleged inadequacies in army procurement policies thought to lead to critical shortages of ammunition in Korea.
1954	Army-McCarthy hearings	Senate Government Operations permanent investigations subcommittee dealt with two questions: (1) had Senator Joseph McCarthy used improper means to secure preferential treatment for a former subcommittee consultant, Pvt. G. David Schine; and (2) did the army try to pressure McCarthy into calling off his investigation of alleged communists in the army?
1955-1956	Airpower	Senate Armed Services Committee examination of relative airpower of U.S. and U.S.S.R., especially regarding B-52s. "Sufficient" versus "superior" airpower. Defense Department leadership disputed air force charges of insufficient airpower. Appropriations subcommittees supported airpower emphasis.
1955-1958	Reserves and the guard	House Armed Services Committee studied laws designed to strengthen reserves. Opposition to administration efforts to reduce guard strength.
1956	Talos missile	Eisenhower vetoed military construction bill because of restrictions on Talos missile sites placed by armed services committees.
1957	Status of Forces Treaty	Soldier to be tried by Japanese for shooting a Japanese woman on a firing range. Efforts within House Foreign Affairs and Armed Services committees to change the Status of Forces Treaty with Japan to have Americans tried by Americans; opposed by president. In 1953 Bricker Reservation to NATO treaty would have revised section making military personnel stationed abroad subject to jurisdiction of indigenous courts.
1957-1958	Missiles	Johnson investigations: beginning of the "Missile-gap" charge; response to Sputnik.

Years	Issue	Issue content and participants
1957-1958	Military pay	Senate Armed Services hearings and Cordiner committee discussion of scaling salaries on basis of skills, not seniority.
1958	Unification	Armed services committee hearings; congressmen uneasy about administration proposals that appropriations to services be made through the secretary of defense, and that members of the Joint Chiefs be restricted from appealing directly to Congress.
1958-1963	Nike-Zeus, Nike-X	Senate Armed Services Committee study of which antimissile systems were obsolete.
1959-1960	Personnel cross-over	Special investigations subcommittee of House Armed Services hearings on alleged influence of retired civilian and military officials working for defense contractors. Contractors and service associations opposed regulation changes.
1959-1960	Bomarc	Appropriations subcommittees studied allegedly obsolete ground-to-air missiles.
1961	Construction and housing	Hearings and floor and conference fights over: (1) construction bill provision to transfer the army's Food and Container Institute away from Chicago (opposed by Illinois legislators); and (2) a scandal-ridden housing project.
1961-1963	B-70 (RS-70)	McNamara refused to spend funds appropriated on grounds that bombers were useless in missile age. House and Senate Appropriations and Armed Services committees involved, especially Chairman Vinson.
1962	"Muzzling" the military	Senate Armed Services preparedness subcommittee hearings to examine the extent of civilian censorship of military speeches.
1962-1970	TFX (F-111)	Senate Government Operations permanent investigations subcommittee held hearings and released staff studies at various times during this period; DOD officials, air force and navy officers, and corporations were involved. Alleged conflict-of-interest and political pressures in selection of General Dynamics over Boeing, preferred by the services. Later revelations of technical deficiencies in the aircraft.
1963	Joint Chiefs terms	House Armed Services subcommittee study of possible retaliation by Kennedy administration against two of the Joint Chiefs who had testified against its budget requests on specific items.
1963-1964	X-22 (V/STOL)	Senate preparedness subcommittee examination of contract award for navy aircraft to Bell Aerosystems instead of navy-favored Douglas Aircraft.

Years	Issue	Issue content and participants
1964-1965	Missiles versus manned bombers	House and Senate Appropriations and Armed Services committees examined McNamara-air force dispute on relative obsolescence of missiles and bombers. Funds were authorized for both.
1965-1966	Military base shutdowns	President Johnson vetoed a congressionally-approved provision requiring the secretary of defense to submit closure plans to Congress prior to taking action (and giving Congress veto power.) The hostile House and Senate Armed Services committee hearings and legislation marked a turning point in McNamara's dealings with Congress.
1965-1967	Reserve-guard merger	McNamara's plan to reduce the size of the reserves and National Guard, and to combine them for increased military effectiveness was blocked by House and Senate Armed Services subcommittees. Congressmen were angered at not having advance warning that the plan (opposed by the Reserve Officers Association and the guard) would be implemented.
1965-1968	Nuclear navy	Conference committees on authorizations and appropriations in 1965 evidenced displeasure over DOD concentration on missiles and planes, in comparison with nuclear surface ships and other navy programs. House and Senate Armed Services and Appropriations committees and Joint Committee on Atomic Energy hearings in 1968 concern McNamara's decision to end construction of nuclear attack submarines after fiscal 1970 and Secretary Clifford's "go-slow" policy.
1966	Manned bombers	McNamara planned to retire all B-58s and over half of the B-52s and to replace some with F-111s. Air force and House Armed Services subcommittee were critical. Funds for an advanced manned bomber were authorized.
1966-1967	Vietnam debate begins	Senate Foreign Relations Committee became the center of opposition to Vietnam policy.
1966-1970	ABM deployment	Congress authorized funds for ABM in 1967, and charged administration with delay. Administration stressed cost, unreliability due to lack of testing, and possible danger to arms-control agreements. House and Senate Armed Services and Appropriations and Joint Atomic Energy subcommittees were involved in initial stages (on Nike-X, later Sentinel), and other committees became involved (with Safeguard) in 1969-1970.

Years	Issue	Issue content and participants
1966-1970	Military manpower	Hearings on draft deferments, the lottery system, and the volunteer army. Congress restricted presidential discretion in altering Selective Service System, later defeated legislation to abolish the draft.
1967-1970	Indochina	Continued congressional concern about Vietnam, Laos, and Cambodia policies, especially in Senate Foreign Relations subcommittees. Debate on Foreign Military Sales Bill, 1970, to which the Cooper-Church "no troops in Cambodia" amendment was attached.
1968-1969	Cheyenne helicopter	Conflict-of-interest charges by representatives (involving a former Lockheed vice president serving as army assistant secretary for research and development, who returned to his Lockheed job the year after the contract was awarded to Lockheed), and later investigations of technical problems by the House Armed Services Committee.
1968-1969	C-5A	Revelation of cost overruns on plane before the Joint Subcommittee on Economy in Government; air force cost analyst who made the relevation was fired.
1968-1970	Security commitments	Senate Foreign Relations subcommittee examined U.S. commitments to Laos and other countries in a series of hearings.
1969-1970	Overruns in military procurement	Committee hearings on overruns in SRAM, Minuteman III, Sheridan tank, F-111, and other programs.
1969-1970	MIRV and ABM (Phase II)	Senate and House Appropriations, Armed Services, and Foreign Relations (Affairs) committee hearings, the latter to present anti-administration viewpoints.
1969-1970	Chemical and biological warfare, and nerve gas disposal	CBW accidents led to House hearings on extent of U.S. CBW production. Controversial army plan to transport "obsolete" nerve gas canisters through populated areas and dump them in the Atlantic was investigated by oceanography subcommittees of Senate Commerce and House Merchant Marine and Fisheries. Conservationists opposed army plan.
1970	Army data banks and surveillance	Senate Judiciary Subcommittee on Constitutional Rights and a House subcommittee investigated army surveillance of and information-gathering about civilians.
1970	Military embarrassments	Hearings on the Pueblo incident, the Green Berets murder case, and My Lai.

disciplining, the Militia;" and (3) no one "holding any office under the United States" (e.g., a military officer) shall sit in Congress.

But, as Huntington pointed out, the "maximizing of civilian power always means the maximizing of the power of some particular civilian group or groups,"[20, p. 80] at the expense not of the military, but of *other* civilian groups. The president and Congress each identify civilian control with its own control. Congressional warnings of development of a "Prussian General Staff" in the JCS structure, for example, reflected fears not of military power over civilians but of growing executive power.

The congressional role in military affairs has been variously defined as to control, not command; to appraise management, not to manage; to veto objectionable changes; to set the existence, size, and composition of forces but to leave their command and administration to the executive.[8] The post-war expansion of the defense establishment made the soldier's position more difficult in regard to the "separation of powers" (actually the *sharing* of powers between separated institutions) by shifting the focus of congressional-military relations from military supply units to the professional service heads. The military man owes partial and overlapping loyalty to two civilian institutions. As in most institutional conflicts, reference to the Constitution does not solve the problem. Final authority is left to be worked out not in courses in constitutional law but in political conflicts in Washington.

Attempts to assert congressional control are supported by the power of the purse. The usual congressional role (i.e., perspectives adopted over time by institutional actors) is that of budget-cutter. For example, the House Appropriations Committee's paramount task was perceived to be that of guarding the federal treasury against all assaults [12]. Or, rather, *almost* all assaults. As on civilian programs, defense economy was something to be practiced in someone else's constituency. Moreover, on defense, committees and Congress have tended to assume a reversed role, that of advocate. Instead of "Do you really have to have it?," Rivers's committee asked military witnesses: "Are you sure you have enough?" In committee Rivers said: "Let's get to missiles. Are there any questions on airplanes? We need them so bad I can't conceive how there can be. Let's get to the missile program." Or on the House floor: "I will not discuss the AMSA. I will not discuss Russia's plane. I tell you on my own responsibility the Russians do have a bomber and we need an AMSA whether Russia has one or not" [37, p. A-2, and 1, p. 127].

The General Accounting Office was created by Congress in 1921 because of "profiteering" and loose procurement practices in World War I. Its powers were expanded over the years, as Congress relied upon it for surveil-

---

[8] Congress has sought to avoid writing too much detail into defense laws, allowing the Pentagon flexibility, especially in the more nebulous areas of strategy and weapons system management. One cannot legislate efficiency into DOD management, Senator Russell once remarked.

lance of executive spending. It became an important weapon in the hands of legislators who believed that administrators were inherently wasteful. Secretary McNamara began to use GAO audits as a DOD management tool to work for greater efficiency in defense contracting.

In 1965 a subcommittee of the House Government Operations Committee investigated the GAO, in response to contractor complaints. Nieburg charged [25, p. 374] that the committee cooperated with contractors and the air force to weaken the GAO: The comptroller general resigned, and the GAO was instructed to restrict itself to "general administrative problems" rather than public identification of contractor overcharges and underperformance. In 1968-1970 Senator Proxmire frequently chided the GAO for its reluctance to endorse measures designed to permit closer supervision of the Pentagon budget (e.g., uniform accounting standards), and for its claims to have insufficient manpower or statutory authority to conduct studies he desired. Sixteen percent of the GAO professional auditing staff worked on defense procurement and contracting, and about 40 percent worked in the overall defense area. Comptroller General Elmer Staats said the amount of work done for the armed services and defense appropriations committees increased sharply in the late 1960s. But the GAO could not duplicate the Pentagon's own audit system, Staats emphasized, so Congress would have to be content with getting most of its information about DOD from DOD.

In the early 1970s there remained some question as to whether most congressmen wanted the GAO to serve as an independent watchdog over the Pentagon. Certainly the Pentagon opposed any encroachment on its basic reporting functions (e.g., information on weapon system costs) which it believed were executive responsibilities.

The primary goal of Congress, most liberals and conservatives in that body have agreed, is national security, not efficiency in government. Until the Vietnam War expanded, however, Congress was not particularly successful in sabotaging McNamara's economy moves, except for his efforts to close military installations in 1964-1965.

The committees sometimes appropriate more for weapons systems, especially for the air force and navy, than the administration requested; in 1965 Rivers also gave the Pentagon a considerably larger pay raise bill than had been requested. Congress has on occasion attempted to force the administration to spend money for programs by appropriating unrequested funds. In the cases of research and development funds in 1946, the 70-group air force in 1949, increased Marine Corps funds in 1955, another B-52 wing and the B-70 in the 1950s, the money simply was impounded and not spent by the administration. Funds appropriated in the 1960s for the B-70 (or RS-70), AMSA, a nuclear frigate, and several versions of the ABM were not spent. Vinson considered "mandating" (ordering) President Kennedy to spend $10 billion for the RS-70, but the president averted the mandate by promising to reappraise the bomber.[9] A decision on ABM deployment was held up for more than 2 years, despite congressional approval of $500 million to begin deployment in 1966. "The most prominent Congressional role is that of prodder or goad of the Administration on behalf of specific programs or activities" [19, p. 135]. In House Appropriations Committee Chairman Mahon's view, Congress was most useful not in raising or lowering the defense budget, but in "redirecting, re-emphasizing, and accelerating key defense programs having a direct relation to our ability to survive," while cutting marginal projects [2, pp. 256-257].

The administration can stunt congressionally-favored programs by refusing to spend the money appropriated. But "where Congress objects to a DOD program, the Pentagon is often successful in going ahead, anyway, particularly if the program does not require any new budget funds," [2, p. 247] as happened on a part of the reserves-National Guard reorganization.

The congressional role as defender of military budget requests against Office of Management and Budget or civilian Pentagon reductions is facilitated by the military professional's attitude toward the legislative and executive branches. Close relations with Congress has been the navy's number-one political goal. Lobbying Congress does not "involve violation of the protocols of hierarchy and chain-of-command" involved in lobbying within the administration. The military "regarded the Congress as a mother-figure—warm, affectionate, and permissive—while the father-figure, the President, was more formal, aloof, and commanding" [9, pp. 252, 265]. Where the executive usually has been concerned about "more bang for the buck," the basic congressional view has been that waste is preferable to risk, that supplying too much military hardware is better than running the risk of disaster with too little hardware. For this reason many congressmen were concerned about McNamara-style efficiency. "If I'm wrong we lose the money," Rep. Elford A. Cederberg told an ABM opponent in 1970, "but if you're wrong we could lose the country" [18, p. 12-B].

HOW MUCH CHANGE?

Before Vietnam Congress had a double standard. As Senator Nelson remarked, it was an established tradition that a defense bill would be rushed through Congress in a matter of hours, while a program to help advance

[9] Mandating that particular funds shall be spent, or that particular forces shall be maintained at specified strengths, as has been done for the National Guard and reserves, is the fourth strongest of six pro-military options cited by Huntington. The most permissive, from the executive's viewpoint, are resolutions without the force of law; authorizations of higher levels of weapons or forces than the administration requested; and increased military appropriations above administration requests. The least permissive options are formal legislative prescriptions of the minimum strengths for services, as was done for the Marine Corps in 1952, and prohibitions in appropriations acts against the use of funds to reduce programs or forces [19, p. 140].

the interests of the poor would be scrutinized, debated, and amended for weeks.

The bill to authorize appropriations for weapons procurement for fiscal 1970 was 888 words long: it authorized $22.5 million a word, almost $173 million a line, and $4 billion a page for a total of more than $20 billion. But in 1969 things had changed: The bill did not pass until 11 weeks after it had become the business of the Senate, and efforts to cut spending lasted 8 months. "The days of the Defense Department asking and receiving are over," Senator Mansfield said [37, p. A-2]. For the first time in years defense policy was discussed by legislators who did not sit on any of the military committees and who were not recognized specialists on defense policy. Unable to secure reductions in authorizations from the armed services committees, liberals (especially in the Senate) went outside the committee structure to seek support for their proposals from the public and press and on the floor. There were significant violations of Senate folkways, e.g., passage of an amendment (providing for review of defense contracts) which had not been studied first in committee, introduced by three freshmen senators who belonged to the president's party.

Certainly it was the first time since the 1930s that leadership for opposition to military proposals had come from Congress, but was it the beginning of a revolt against the military committees, a broader revolt against the defense establishment, or a fruitless gesture? Things were changing, but not precipitously, and suggestions that a new critical attitude characterized Congress exaggerated the liberals' successes. Congress did repeal the 1964 Gulf of Tonkin Resolution which authorized unlimited U.S. military intervention in Southeast Asia (passed in what ex-Sen. Ernest Gruening called a "papa knows best" mood.) The Senate passed a National Commitments Resolution opposed by Nixon, 70 to 16, and in 1970 urged President Nixon to take the lead in proposing a broad arms limitation agreement, especially on the MIRV. The disarmament subcommittee of the Senate Foreign Relations Committee in 1969 promised open-door, televised hearings on the ABM and forced the Senate Armed Services Committee to open its usually closed doors and invite witnesses critical of ABM. Armed Services split 10 to 7 in favoring Nixon's ABM program and insisted, among other things, on more detailed reporting from the Pentagon on major weapons contracts. On the ABM, for the first time in years on major legislation, a minority report was filed.

The ABM and MIRV were the first weapons systems which were attacked because they were considered *dangerous, even if they worked.* Until then (with the possible exceptions of the hydrogen bomb and civil defense, among elites) there has been no such thing as "too much" national defense, just as in civilian pork barrel few believe there can be too many public works projects. The only questions had been whether the weapons were technologically feasible, whether the economy could stand the requested level of appropriations, or were the economic rewards being evenly distributed, or were there minimal levels of efficiency in procurement. Now, like labor or civil rights legislation, defense programs could be good or bad. The ABM and MIRV were opposed for all of the customary reasons but also because even if they worked and costs were modest, critics felt they would dangerously affect international relations. They would be strategically destabilizing, would escalate the arms race; in short, they would *weaken* national security. Critical senators asked of the ABM: (1) Do we want it? (even if costless); and if so, (2) is it too expensive?; and (3) will it work? Most answered no to all questions.

The ABM also was opposed and supported for reasons that had little to do with military strategies. A congressman's party is important in most areas of roll-call voting, and it was found to be the most important variable in a study of House roll calls on military appropriations between 1945-1962 [17, p. 760]. Julius Turner in 1951 classified the "armaments" issue as one of "moderate (party) cleavage, inconsistent;" Republicans, reflecting the suspicions of Senator Taft, supported defense when in power, opposed it when out of office [35, pp. 69-70]. By the 1960s party positions on defense policy had been turned around, with the Republicans supporting military spending under Democratic and Republican administrations, and the once pro-defense Democrats becoming more skeptical. Republicans charged that Democratic senators showed sudden concern about weapons systems in 1969, after years of acquiescence under Democratic presidents; six Democratic senators supported President Johnson's Sentinel on several votes in 1968, then opposed Nixon's Safeguard (described by the press and legislative leaders as the first key test of Nixon's legislative strength), and others moved from inconsistent positions to opposition. Only one Republican senator switched from opposition in 1968 to support in 1969. The relationship between party and Senate ABM voting in 1969-1970 was weak; however, the relationship between pro-ABM voting and membership in or voting association with the "conservative coalition" of Republicans plus Southern Democrats was much stronger. The South has been characterized as the most "jingoistic" region of the country [6, p. 364], and it is true that few Southern legislators opposed defense measures in the 1960s. Two who did, Sen. Ralph Yarborough of Texas and Sen. Albert Gore of Tennessee, were defeated for reelection in 1970.

Despite the sound and fury about new priorities, the Senate in 1969 defeated *all* challenges to major weapons systems: the manned bomber, the C-5A plane, nuclear carriers, the F-14 plane, and the ABM. The closest vote, 50-50 with Vice President Agnew breaking the tie, was on the ABM. The reformers won only on several procedural votes (e.g., giving the comptroller general subpoena power over defense contractors' records, and the quarterly auditing requirement) and several token budget amendments (e.g., restrictions on CBW research and on use of ground forces in Laos and Thailand, and reduced independent research funds.) All fund cuts were restored, at least partially, by the Senate-House conference, whose $20.7 billion procurement authorization bill left out no major weapon and seriously restricted none. (The administration had asked for $21.9 billion.) Also restored were additional funds for a helicopter gunship, an antitank missile, a supertank, and radar programs for bomber defense. The conference committee cut out the subpoena power and audit amendments, revised the Laos-Thailand amendment, and eased CBW restrictions. Critics may have won indirectly on the C-5A, because several months after the vote the air force announced it was reducing its C-5A order from 120 to 81. But two-and-a-half months of debate had won Senate critics a mere $70 million in budget cuts, over those made by the Stennis committee.

In 1970 congressional critics also lost all major weapons votes, but did succeed, for one of the few times in modern history, in imposing statutory limitations on the president's war-making powers. After months of debate Congress passed a modified Cooper-Church amendment, prohibiting the president from using any funds to introduce ground combat troops or military advisers into Cambodia. These attempts to redress the balance of power between the executive and Congress, relating to the commander-in-chief powers, were probably the most important events of the 91st Congress. In 1971, faced with new restrictive legislation, Secretary of State William Rogers presented a legal brief denying that Congress had the Constitutional power to pass legislation requiring its consent before American troops were committed abroad. He said Congress should assert itself only through the drastic method of cutting off funds; Senator Fulbright charged that this was as bad as a Johnson administration statement that the power of Congress to declare war was old-fashioned in the nuclear age. Legislation to force a 150,000-man troop cutback in Europe and various restrictions on Vietnam policy (e.g., no use of draftees in combat) were defeated in 1971. The Senate went on record for the first time in favor of a complete withdrawal from Indochina (within 9 months, subject to release of prisoners), but there was no cutoff of funds. Various end-the-war amendments were defeated in 1969-1971. Some senators, including Stennis, indicated they would be more receptive to legislation limiting the president's war-waging powers *after* the Vietnam War was over. The rebellion against military spending and presidential prerogatives did not extend to the House, where no more than 100 votes could be obtained in 1969-1970 for any significant measure to restrict defense spending. Some legislation (such as a 2.5 million-man ceiling on active military personnel) which conformed to administration plans, however, permitted the president less flexibility than in previous years.

The 1969 ABM vote proved to be the critics' high-water mark for at least two years.[10] And the ABM debate was justly characterized as a light slap on the wrist for the military, not the beginning of tight control.

---

[10] Rising unemployment between 1969-1971 showed the political importance of defense jobs. Some liberal congressmen indicated they would prefer their constituents to be working on defense projects of questionable value than to be unemployed.

LOBBYING

Congress is a target of all lobbying campaigns on national programs, and its members often are more vulnerable to political and economic pressures than are executive branch officials. Congressmen traditionally have been sensitive to expressions of local sentiment, while recognizing that some of it springs from nationally coordinated campaigns.

On the ABM the lobbying was significant, but not fevered; most contractors apparently avoided direct contact with congressmen, leaving that to the administration and several "citizens' committees" made up of business-men and former government officials. Against the ABM in 1969-1970 were religious, scientific, liberal, and antiwar groups, two large unions, and organized suburbanites (e.g., "SCRAM" or Sentinel Cities Reject Antiballistic Missiles) in seven cities genteelly angered by plans to locate ABM sites in their "backyards." For the general public the ABM probably became the most controversial weapons issue since civil defense. The earlier controversy resulted in the Kennedy administration abandoning a planned fallout-shelter program. Both, significantly, involved construction of facilities in heavily-populated areas.

More typical of defense policies, however, was the 1970 alignment of lobbyists on the issue of contracting procedures. While most of the new-priorities groups were busy with the headlined issues, industry groups (e.g., the Electronic Industries Association) lobbied for higher research spending and against authorizing the comptroller general and a blue-ribbon panel to establish uniform accounting standards. (Admiral Rickover claimed uniform standards could save $2 billion a year.) Restraints on defense research spending imposed in 1969 were loosened in 1970. The uniform accounting legislation, which had passed the Senate by 69 to 1, was scuttled under intense industry pressure in the House Banking Committee.

Contractor associations oppose cost-cutting measures within the administration, and contractors seek similar goals in Congress. The Aerospace Industries Association (with a $2 million annual income in 1970) had said earlier: "We don't even dream of buying any influence of any kind" [8, p. 57]. All groups indicate innocence of any pressure or relationship to procure-ment; the Aerospace Industries Association claimed in 1969 never to have endorsed a specific weapons system (including the ABM) and said they merely educated and informed congressmen and the public. "Usually," Con-gressional Quarterly Service noted, "defense industries lobby in Congress by indirect means. They seek to convince top ranking (military) officers of the need for a particular weapons system and leave it to (them) to sell the program to Congress" [7, p. 93]. After initial contacts between constituent businessmen and key congressmen, industry officials may request military personnel to make follow-up contacts with unconvinced legislators.

The Pentagon tries to insure continued congressional trust by helping congressmen with information and with the personnel and procurement matters often referred to them by constituents. Military legislative liaison officers "expedited" 140,000 constituent letters a year in the late 1960s. Regulations prohibiting "unauthorized" contacts between officers and congressmen did not affect the more than 300 liaison officers assigned to Capitol Hill by the Pentagon in the early 1970s to brief and socialize with congressmen and their staffs. The annual Pentagon lobbying budget was fourteen times the reported lobbying expenses of the biggest-spending private group required to report costs. McNamara sought to coordinate service liaison with Congress, but congressmen continued their traditional dealings with the services; DOD made only minor service budget cuts and personnel reassignments, for fear of alienating legislators.

Industry groups such as the American Ordnance Association and the National Security Industrial Association cooperate with the service-identified associations and related groups (e.g., the Marine Corps Reserve Officers Association and the Infantry Association), the American Legion and the Veterans of Foreign Wars, the National Guard Association, and most labor unions.[11] However, much of the lobbying that occurs is ritual letter-writing and petition-publishing with little impact. Narrow service associations are discounted in interservice disputes. The general patriotic and veterans clubs are too large and diverse to be able to bring their influence to bear too often.

Contractors routinely brief many congressmen on the local economic impact of pending defense legislation, sometimes at the congressman's initiative. And on issues with sizable financial impact on the specialized segments of defense industry, industry lobbying probably does affect congressional decisions. As in other legislative areas the lobbying alignment often comes down to groups with immediate and vital stakes (pro-spending) against groups with more diffuse interests (anti-spending), and the former usually prevail.

CONCLUSION

The congressional debates of 1969-1971 on Indochina and the "Maginot Line in the Sky" (critics' label for the ABM) raised two basic questions about defense policy: Who should decide, and what should be decided. The "who" referred not only to the committees or individuals within Congress which should have more or less influence, but to the institutional prerogatives of the legislative houses themselves versus those of the executive. Congressional control preferences were nothing new for congressmen, but what was new were the corollary demands from some that this control be exercised in a rigorously skeptical manner.

[11]Executive officials of most service and industry groups are retired military officers.

If the budget stringency of the early 1970s continues, there could develop more intense interservice rivalry than there was in the 1960s. With the services fighting for budget shares, and spokesmen for civilian priorities being increasingly outspoken, congressmen again may find themselves with sufficient information and choices to assume an independent judicial role, if they wish to do so.

REFERENCES

1. Barnet, Richard J., *The Economy of Death* (New York: Atheneum, 1969).
2. Borklund, C. W., *The Department of Defense* (New York: Praeger, 1968).
3. Caraley, Demetrios, *The Politics of Military Unification* (New York: Columbia University Press, 1966).
4. Clotfelter, James, "Senate Voting and Constituency Stake in Defense Spending," *Journal of Politics,* 32 (November 1970), pp. 979-983.
5. Coates, Charles H., and Pellegrin, Roland T., *Military Sociology* (University Park, Md.: Social Science Press, 1965).
6. Cobb, Stephen A., "Defense Spending and Foreign Policy in the House of Representatives," *Journal of Conflict Resolution,* 13 (1969), pp. 358-369.
7. Congressional Quarterly Service, *CQ Guide to American Government,* Spring 1970 ed. (Washington: CQ Service, 1970).
8. Congressional Quarterly Service, *Legislators and the Lobbyists,* 2nd ed., (Washington: CQ Service, 1968).
9. Davis, Vincent, *The Admirals Lobby* (Chapel Hill: University of North Carolina Press, 1967).
10. Dawson, Raymond H., "Congressional Innovation and Intervention in Defense Policy," *American Political Science Review,* 56 (March 1962), pp. 42-57.
11. Dexter, Lewis A., "Congressmen and the Making of Military Policy," in *Components of Defense Policy,* ed. Bobrow, Davis B., (Chicago: Rand McNally, 1965), pp. 94-110.
12. Fenno, Richard F., Jr., "The House Appropriations Committee as a Political System: The Problem of Integration," *American Political Science Review,* LVI (June 1962), pp. 310-324.
13. Froman, Lewis, *Congressmen and Their Constituencies* (Chicago: Rand McNally, 1963).
14. Galbraith, John Kenneth, *How to Control the Military* (New York: Signet Books, 1969).
15. Hall, John, "$2 Billion Cut From Defense," *The Atlanta Constitution,* October 7, 1970, p. 2-A.

16. Hammond, Paul Y., *Organizing for Defense* (Princeton: Princeton University Press, 1961).
17. Havens, Murray C., "Metropolitan Areas and Congress: Foreign Policy and National Security," *Journal of Politics,* 26 (November 1964), pp. 758-774.
18. "House Bars Bid to Halt ABM," *The Atlanta Constitution,* June 12, 1970, p. 12-B.
19. Huntington, Samuel P., *The Common Defense* (New York: Columbia University Press, 1961).
20. Huntington, Samuel P., *The Soldier and the State* (Cambridge, Mass.: Harvard University Press, 1957).
21. Joint Economic Committee of the U.S. Congress, Hearings before the Subcommittee on Economy in Government, "The Military Budget and National Economic Priorities," (Washington: Government Printing Office, 1969).
22. Kolodziej, Edward A., *The Uncommon Defense and Congress, 1945-1963,* (Columbus: Ohio State University Press, 1966).
23. Masland, John W., and Laurence I. Radway, *Soldiers and Scholars* (Princeton: Princeton University Press, 1957).
24. "Members Rewrite History," *Congressional Quarterly Weekly Report,* 27 (May 23, 1969), p. 833.
25. Nieburg, H. L., *In the Name of Science* (Chicago: Quadrangle, 1966).
26. "The Power of the Pentagon," *The Progressive,* 33 (June 1969), entire issue.
27. "The Power People," *Look,* 33 (August 26, 1969), pp. 20-27.
28. Proxmire, William, *Report from Wasteland* (New York: Praeger, 1970).
29. Riddle, Donald H., *The Truman Committee* (New Brunswick, N.J.: Rutgers University Press, 1964).
30. Ries, John C., *The Management of Defense* (Baltimore: Johns Hopkins Press, 1964).
31. Russett, Bruce M., *What Price Vigilance?* (New Haven: Yale University Press, 1970).
32. Smith, Louis, *American Democracy and Military Power* (Chicago: University of Chicago Press, 1951).
33. Smith, Robert M., "Senate Refuses to Require Laird to Report on Buying," *The New York Times,* August 18, 1970, pp. 1, 19.
34. Stone, I. F., "The War Machine Under Nixon," *The New York Review of Books,* XII (June 5, 1969), pp. 5-12.
35. Turner, Julius,*Party and Constituency* (Baltimore: Johns Hopkins Press, 1951).
36. U.S. Senate Armed Services Committee, Hearings before the Preparedness Investigating Subcommittee on "Status of U.S. Strategic Power," (Washington: Government Printing Office, 1968).

37. Unna, Warren, "Doubts Rise on Hill Over Arms Needs," *The Washington Post,* March 23, 1969, pp. A-1-A-2.
38. Westerfield, H. Bradford, "Congress and Closed Politics in National Security Affairs," *Orbis*, X (Fall 1969), pp. 737-753.

CHAPTER EIGHT

The Military and the Defense Department

Civilian control of the military, while a general concern of congressmen, can be a conscious day-to-day goal in the Defense Department. The prize is determination of defense policy: Who decides between rival military strategies, which entail substantially different internal allocation of resources; who decides on the advice to be given the president and Congress on prospective foreign policies and weapons policies; and who controls implementation of these policies by the nation's largest bureaucracy.[1]

DOD is involved in all stages of an idealized picture of defense policy-making and implementation: (1) the president and the National Security Council make policies (inextricably "foreign" and "defense"); (2) the Defense Department's civilian and military leaders formulate a military strategy to support those policies, and determine (within the president's budget) the levels of manpower and appropriations necessary for such a strategy; (3) Congress approves or disapproves appropriation requests; (4) business provides the weapons funded; and (5) DOD executes the policies.

Viewed from the pinnacle of the Pentagon, what does the defense establishment look like up to this point? It rests on several foundations: (1) the strength and abilities of the military profession itself; (2) support in corporate, labor, and academic America; (3) close cooperation with the committees and leadership of Congress; and (4) traditional public acquiescence. Is it true, as critics say, that the establishment operates without checks

---

[1] Neat distinctions between Defense Department dominance in making national policy and dominance by the uniformed military are difficult to make, because expanded influence within the executive branch for DOD also is likely to mean expanded military influence. Similarly, the military is an indirect beneficiary of most expansions of executive responsibility vis-à-vis that of Congress.

and balances? Societal attitudes set broad limits on military influence, but these attitudes are rarely salient enough to force government to curtail military programs. Despite severe criticism from a congressional minority, and recent spending restrictions imposed by congressional allies, the military is not in immediate danger of being brought to heel by Congress. In fact, Senate vote margins on 1971 challenges to military programs showed that critics had lost strength for the second consecutive year. ABM deployment, which passed the Senate by one vote in 1969, passed by 64 to 21 in 1971. Even if the military already is under moderately tight control, and has a diminished influence over national policies, control is a continuous process; once imposed, it must be maintained. The executive branch, sometimes accused of being the most acquiescent to military demands, must be the routine enforcer of checks and balances on the military. How strong are checks within DOD, and what are the military's strengths there?

It is in the Pentagon that the military's previously discussed methods of influence are brought to bear, e.g., its claim on expertise (Chapters 5 and 7), its ability to appeal to the public (Chapters 6 and 7), and its close ties to industry and labor (Chapter 4). Within the Pentagon its outside strengths are duplicated and supplemented. Military men are regarded as the experts on the use of military force in behalf of national interests. They have great organizational strength, which permits them to take on new tasks. They are thought to "know more," because of their access to strategic intelligence not available to most civilian policy-makers. Their allies outside of the executive branch, such as those in defense industry and the scientific community, have representation within the Pentagon as well. Finally, since the president is an elected official with a wide range of legislative responsibilities, the military's ability to appeal to the public and to important congressmen must be considered. Usually, however, decisions within DOD are made in a "closed politics" setting in which only the losers go to the public and Congress. The military's following outside the executive branch is more important for the caution it imbues in civilian leaders in the Pentagon than for the ability of congressional and public supporters of the military to alter DOD decisions, once made.[2]

THE SECRETARY AND THE JOINT CHIEFS

The relationship between the president, the military, and the civilian heads of the military departments has varied considerably since the navy and war departments' founding in 1789. At times the department head was responsible only for administration and fiscal controls, the military leadership for defense planning and operations, and both dealt with the president. At other

[2] Army critics of the New Look emphasis on airpower appealed outside the executive in the 1950s and military critics of weapons decisions and Vietnam policies did the same in the 1960s, but with little success.

times the department head has been included in the chain of command, between the president and the military chiefs. Military leaders have been involved in policy-making and administration, as well as in more strictly professional matters. Civilian control at times has been synonymous with presidential control, something lying entirely outside the departments.

The United States came out of World War II with a Joint Chiefs of Staff which had been intimately involved in strategic, diplomatic, economic, and administrative questions: Should allied forces deal with representatives of Vichy France; should Soviet or allied armies liberate Prague; should a limited supply of machine tools be used to produce heavy cruisers for the navy or planes for the British; or how could General Joseph Stilwell be restored to the good graces of Chiang Kai-shek [7, p. 10]. No bureaucracy surrenders conquered territory unless it becomes too costly to hold. With new world responsibilities and a dynamic weapons technology making military considerations a daily concern in Washington, the military was no more likely to give up all of their new roles than were civilian policy makers to demand that they do so.

The war had forced the services into closer cooperation than ever before, and formal unification was pushed by the army and some civilians in the late 1940s. The navy and marines along with their congressional supporters resisted, fearing a merged service would take away their missions and reduce their force levels. The National Military Establishment which emerged in 1947 retained separate services with their own civilian secretaries and departments. Placed on top was a new Department of Defense, whose secretary's job was to manage the establishment at a time of intense interservice rivalry. The first secretary of defense, James V. Forrestal, committed suicide. Subsequent secretaries under Truman and Eisenhower, until Thomas S. Gates, Jr. in 1958, usually perceived their role to be budget cutter for the president, occasionally spokesman for the military, but never chief strategist. Military chiefs submitted funding requests for their services which not only took little cognizance of the other services' requests, but usually far exceeded what the president believed desirable. It was the secretary's job to cut down these "wish lists," usually accomplished through imposition of a monetary ceiling (see Figs. Two and Three). Except during the Korean War the ceiling was more likely to be a cause of, than a result of, the selection of strategies and foreign policies. Since President Eisenhower believed economic strength (as represented in part by a balanced budget) was essential to national security, it was not unreasonable for money decisions to dictate force levels which in turn influenced strategies. Below the ceilings, uniformed chiefs were given wide latitude in deciding which programs should be expanded and which cut back.

Legislation and administrative practices between 1949-1960 increasingly centralized the Department of Defense. The civilian secretaries of the constituent army, navy, and air force departments were relieved of respon-

FIGURE TWO

Defense Spending, 1939-1970

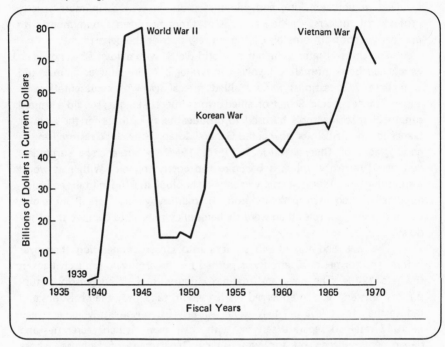

sibilities relating to making defense policy, despite the services' fondness for their own departments. The secretary of defense was given greater control over operational commands, his office was expanded to include interservice agencies such as Defense Research and Engineering, and he was given a larger staff. The secretary, as the president's representative, became the symbol of civil authority within DOD.

• • •

Military men work with civilians in most DOD offices; they are well represented in those dealing with policy-making and weapons development (e.g., DR & E), and are less well represented in budgeting and administrative offices (e.g., comptroller).

At the highest level the Joint Chiefs are the secretary of defense's "immediate military staff," according to the National Security Act, as well as being the "principal military adviser" to the president, the secretary of defense, and the National Security Council. The chiefs have a right of access to the president independent of the secretary, and consider themselves to be the military advisers to Congress as well. The chiefs have no formal authority of their own; they act in the name of the president and the secretary of

FIGURE THREE

Defense Spending as % of GNP

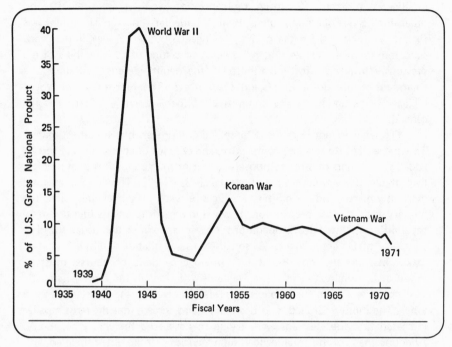

defense.[3] The chiefs represent the services' views, as well as being advisers and administrators. Under Gates, McNamara, and Laird, they met regularly with the secretary and the deputy secretary to exchange views in the Joint Chiefs' conference room.

The chiefs and services have their own strategic planning units, JCS Joint Staff has 400 officers, in an overall JCS organization of 2000 people.

Of the joint defense commands and agencies to which the chiefs are attached, the most important has been the Defense Intelligence Agency. Secretary McNamara, suspecting that the services provided partisan intelligence (e.g., what to the air force looked like missile silos in the U.S.S.R. looked like tanks to the army), centralized all service intelligence agencies into the DIA. Centralization did not slow the operation's growth, nor insure useful and accurate data. In 1971 about $3 billion was spent on military intelligence (excluding the funds for the Central Intelligence Agency) and about 150,000 military personnel were involved in intelligence.

After a year's study in the Office of Management and Budget, the

[3] Vietnam was the first war which the Joint Chiefs, as a body, was charged with running for the secretary of defense.

Nixon administration in 1971 announced that Richard Helms, director of the partly civilian-run CIA,[4] would henceforth coordinate and review all national intelligence programs. Extensive reorganization would place the DIA and other intelligence operations under Helms's budgetary control. The intent was to cut $1 billion from the overall intelligence budget. A new intelligence subcommittee was created under the NSC, consisting of the members of the previously informal "forty committee": the deputy defense secretary, the chairman of the Joint Chiefs,and four others. The reorganization would replace Helms on the "forty committee" with his deputy, a Marine Corps general.

To what extent does the defense decision process bias threat estimates? To what extent do secrecy, complexity, and absence of countervailing forces, added to conflicts of interest, appeals to patriotism, and institutional rigidity, help the military secure what it wants? [13, p. 20]. Threat estimates are inevitably biased, and the military intelligence system *is* self-serving: Since the military feels it must prepare for the worst in regards to enemy identities and capabilities, its intelligence operations look for the worst, and usually find it. Secretary of Defense Charles Wilson used to say that the military tried to make the Russians look 8-feet tall. Intelligence data, of course, must be interpreted; usually the military evaluates situations in the most pessimistic way possible, e.g., in the public interpretation given to the Russian SS-9s in 1969. The military argued, and Secretary Laird agreed, that the large missiles indicated that the Russians were trying to develop a first-strike capability. Announcement of this intelligence finding, critics pointed out, coincided with the congressional debate on ABM deployment. But former Assistant Secretary of Defense Paul Warnke aptly pointed out that it was the military's job to find threats. What else would they be expected to find?

Since the DIA through 1970 was partly controlled by and reported directly to the Joint Chiefs, this source of intelligence could be subject to organizational bias, emanating from the top or from the field. The chiefs maintain there are countervailing forces: the CIA and the rest of the intelligence community. The CIA did present a contrary picture of what could be expected from bombing North Vietnam, and was consistently more pessimistic about U.S. prospects in Vietnam than were the Joint Chiefs. But the fact that CIA evaluations were largely ignored (see Chapter 9), and that secrecy limited their impact, suggests that the military has dominated the intelligence area. And it is the effort to develop countervailing forces, such as the CIA, which has been at the core of much of the internal Pentagon conflict of recent years.

The military is expected to advise civilian leadership on the nature of probable military threats now and in the future (through 5-year plans and

---

[4] Although the CIA has no organizational tie to the chiefs, its first three directors were professional officers, many CIA agents previously served in the military, and the JCS traditionally has had access to its strategic intelligence data.

longer-range studies). In recommending strategies to cope with these dangers, military men inevitably will consider national policies as well as the instruments for implementation.

The military, for example, has been intimately involved in governmental discussions on disarmament and arms control since World War II. The military usually has opposed major arms limitations which lack strict surveillance, inspections, and controls—the type of controls the U.S.S.R. has not wanted to accept. The military favored attempting to retain U.S. monopoly of atomic weapons in the late 1940s, argued against policy suggestions made by disarmament adviser Harold Stassen and other civilians in the mid-1950s, and was very hesitantly persuaded to accept the nuclear test ban treaty of 1963. The latter was a rare example of military advice on strategic-political questions not being accepted. In 1970-1971 the military, supported by Secretary Laird, urged extreme caution in the Strategic Arms Limitation Talks with the U.S.S.R.

CIVILIAN CONTROL UNDER KENNEDY, JOHNSON, AND NIXON

Just as interservice rivalry has provided information for congressmen, it has been a method of civilian control within the Defense Department. Service rivalry was not instigated by civilian policy-makers; it grew out of the bureaucratic loyalties and ambitions characterizing all large organizations. But it nevertheless prevented formation of a united military front against civilians who wanted to cut budgets or change strategies. Minority opinions within the military leadership can be used by civilian leaders to justify and to support their own positions. Or disunity can be a rationale for ignoring military recommendations altogether: If the experts disagree, then is there an expert opinion?

Interservice rivalry is an inefficient means of civilian control; the price may be duplication of weapons, inadequate interservice planning, or pressure for higher budgets. Of course, service differences also provide civilian policy-makers with a wider range of options, and can point to pitfalls or opportunities which unified opinions might obscure. President Kennedy's secretary of defense was determined to impose stronger civilian control while restraining interservice rivalry; to do this McNamara brought in civilian budgetary, weapons, and strategic planning specialists as his own experts. He particularly sought to end the military's virtual monopoly on strategic planning. McNamara imposed his own bureaucracy on top of the existing Pentagon bureaucracy; he commanded a work force of 67,000 headquarters civilians, and higher-echelon civil service jobs in DOD increased from dozens to perhaps thousands. Many were in centralized supply, communications, and auditing agencies, but the most controversial were the "whiz kids" brought into the Office of International Security Affairs (ISA, called "McNamara's State Department"), the Office of the Comptroller, and the new Office of Systems Analysis.

The systems analysts were credited with rationalizing the Defense Department to the point where President Johnson ordered all other federal agencies to adopt similar techniques. But their "cost-effectiveness" method of analyzing weapons was only as good as its assumptions. Intangible and nonquantitative considerations were often ignored—especially such traditional military factors as "morale, esprit, confidence in one's equipment, the status of training, tactics, the deterrence to the enemy that the very existence of a weapon creates, or the value of a human life" [2, p. 45]. The effort was to maximize objectives for given resources, or minimize resources for given objectives, or simply to get dollars into the calculation at an early stage. Systems analysts helped to abort the nuclear-powered airplane while encouraging the TFX concept (to achieve "commonality" between air force and navy) and the C-5A [14, p. 60], a mixed record at best. The TFX (later the F-111) contracting decision was made finally on the basis not of sophisticated analysis, but on the secretary's own business experience. Professional soldiers were highly critical of systems analysis methods of studying and choosing weapons, and similarly resented the intrusion of "defense intellectuals" into strategic planning.

The Office of Systems Analysis, under McNamara, made the first and most important review of the goals and plans of the Joint Chiefs. Program objectives memoranda, instead of originating with the military, originated among McNamara's whiz kids, to be sent down to the Joint Chiefs for comment (in a specified form). JCS objections often were footnoted rather than included in the text of memoranda. The chiefs' Joint Strategic Objectives Plan (JSOP) received less attention. The pain of such treatment was eased by increased spending for strategic as well as conventional forces. Since all services prospered, unlike during the lean administrations that had gone before, the incentive and the rationale for military complaints were eroded. But in the face of competition from McNamara and his aides, the military closed ranks. In 1963-1965 the chiefs split an average of 45 times a year, or on 2.9 percent of the issues decided. By the end of the decade, with the exodus of Air Force Chief of Staff Curtis LeMay (1961-1965), the last advocate of a one-weapon solution, all JCS members supported a strategic mix. The Joint Chiefs then split on only four to six issues a year, or an average of 0.5 percent.

The Nixon administration had a different attitude toward the professional military. The Joint Chiefs were to be included earlier and more closely in decision-making, not controlled and "layered" through the use of civilian analysts. ISA was downgraded and the Office of Systems Analysis was restricted to review and comment. Lloyd Norman reported, "Secretary Laird's new budgeting policy for the first time in years gives full play to the Joint Chiefs' role as strategy planners. He has salvaged the JSOP from oblivion" [9, p. 25]. Although Laird came into office with prospects for stabilized defense budgets, he showed more respect for the military leaders' views, official prerogatives, and personal prestige,[5] and the chiefs were said to feel they had greater influence on policy. Laird supported JCS proposals such as B-1 (AMSA) bomber development, new fighter programs, and a reoriented ABM—where McNamara had repeatedly blocked AMSA and ABM. But Laird canceled the Manned Orbiting Laboratory and pushed for substantial troop withdrawals from Vietnam. In 1969 he acquiesced in budget cuts by the Defense Program Review Committee, which included officials from the White House, DOD, JCS, the Budget Bureau, and CIA, but he advocated higher spending for 1971-1973.

The Nixon administration vowed to root out the whiz-kid approach to weapons selection and to correct Pentagon overcentralization by transferring more decision-making on contracts and on postcontract management from high-level DOD civilians to the military. The three civilian service department secretaries also were to be given more responsibility, which Laird said would mean greater civilian control.

Whether, as Laird's defenders said, he retained the overall control which McNamara supposedly imposed, was unclear. But Laird's system was a partial return to the Truman-Eisenhower ceiling approach, in the sense that the military chiefs had a strong voice in suggesting where funds were to be spent within monetary limits. In the Eisenhower years, Gen. Maxwell Taylor complained, initial plans were prepared without regard to resource limitations. Budget ceilings imposed political compromises between competing service ambitions while strategic planning was left out in the cold. McNamara and Hitch felt that civilian control suffered too, because the president and secretary of defense were denied essential budgetary information. Therefore, McNamara combined military capabilities into "program packages" cutting across service lines; this let policy-makers know how much was being spent on all general purpose forces, for example, to make it easier to identify redundant programs or undersupported areas. The method was said to avoid "concealed, parochial, and de facto decisions in the lower echelons," and to force "the military to define and justify its objectives, to point out alternate ways of accomplishing them, to calculate the cost and . . . effectiveness" of alternatives [8, p. 358].

Has civilian control been increased or decreased by organizational and policy changes within DOD? From the time McNamara entered the department with a list of special projects to be undertaken (his "99 Trombones") the organization was alerted to his determination to gain control. Soon after

[5] The importance of flattery, for encouraging military support for administration policy, should be neither exaggerated nor ignored. When President Nixon paid his first call at the Pentagon after taking office in 1969 he said: "I always feel a bit embarrassed when an admiral comes up and says, 'Sir.' I think it should be the other way around. I am sure the Secretary (Laird) has the same problem . . . I do not presume to be a specialist in this field and I am going to rely, when it comes to purely military matters, on what military advisers tell me should be done" [4, pp. 33-34].

his 1968 departure his admirers and enemies (both were legion) were amazed that "Super-Mac" had had much less impact on the Pentagon than they had supposed.

Although McNamara was acutely conscious of his political vulnerability in fighting the Joint Chiefs and their congressional allies, and picked his fights carefully, his 7 years had seen many battles (see Table Five). His refusal to deploy the B-70 bomber almost brought on a constitutional crisis, after Congress provided the funds, and that was only the beginning of weapons conflicts. Congressional committee chairmen came to distrust him mightily, e.g., for TFX, budget sleights-of-hand, and ignoring military opinion. McNamara felt he had to persuade, not order; he argued with the Joint Chiefs for a full week before persuading them to support the nuclear test-ban treaty. Dependent on presidential support, McNamara held it on most issues; but congressional and Joint Chiefs pressure cost him the president's backing on two big decisions: the missile buildup (1961-1964) and "thin" ABM deployment (1967). For 6 years McNamara had resisted pressure to deploy various ABM systems, which he correctly maintained would be outmoded before they could be deployed. He canceled or delayed other systems, but they cost money nevertheless. He overruled the military and his own systems analysts on selection of General Dynamics to build the TFX, for what Senate investigators later charged were political (the Texas location of the General Dynamics plant) and conflict-of-interest (business ties between the company and DOD civilian policy-makers) reasons. But McNamara felt he could not take on the military at every turn; he stabilized the number of U.S. offensive missiles, and warned prominently of the dangers of an arms race (which he felt would bring not more but less security) but not until the United States had responded to a nonexistent "missile gap" by adding more than 500 missiles to the 450 already deployed. (The Joint Chiefs wanted 3000.) Arthur M. Schlesinger, Jr. said McNamara "did not believe that doubling or even tripling our (ICBM) striking power would enable us to destroy the hardened missile sites or missile-launching submarines of our adversary. But he was already engaged in a bitter fight with the Air Force over his effort to disengage from the B-70. ... After cutting down the original Air Force missile demands considerably, he perhaps felt that he could not do more without risking public conflict with the Joint Chiefs and the vociferous B-70 lobby in Congress" [11, p. 6]. When McNamara retired, weapons systems still cost more than expected, and military experts still were at the right hand. McNamara had claimed credit for massive savings by cutting the Joint Chiefs' proposed budgets, closing bases, and economizing on all purchases, but defense spending in 1968 was almost double that of 1961. What military men felt was an occupational force in the Pentagon had departed and the five-pronged building still stood. McNamara had not dramatically altered the nature of communications between the Joint Chiefs and Congress [6, p. 21],

TABLE FIVE
Selected Events, Policy Disputes, and Strategic Changes, 1946-1970

Year	Events	Policy disputes involving Pentagon	U.S. strategies and foreign policies
1946	Demobilization of forces	Unification controversy: army's Collins Plan defeated, National Security Act passed	Atomic monopoly and strong industrial economy; strategic deterrence
		Universal Military Training defeated; Selective Service lapsed, reinstituted	
1948	"Iron Curtain"; the Czech coup and war scares; Berlin blockade	Tight budgets, 1946-1950	Containment policy (NSC-68); European defense (NATO); Truman Doctrine
	Russian atomic bomb; Chinese communists win	Interservice competition: "revolt of the admirals" to save aircraft carriers, with criticism of air force big bombers; congressional, air force support for 70 groups	
1950	Korean War and Chinese intervention	H-bomb development dispute	Rearmament of U.S. and military aid for allies; more alliances
		"The Great Debate" on U.S. troops in Europe	
	U.S. and later Russians drop H-bomb		
1952	Eisenhower elected		Continental defense; realization of U.S. vulnerability
1954	French defeat in Indochina; no U.S. intervention	New Look emphasized airpower; "more bang for the buck" (Charles Wilson); budget ceilings reimposed after Korea	"Massive (nuclear) retaliation" discussed; tactical nuclear weapons to be deployed
1956	Disarmament talks and testing ban proposals	More interservice rivalry: army vs. air force on control of land-based strategic missiles and ABM, 1953-1959	
	Sputnik: Russians first in space		"Minimum" or "finite" deterrence

TABLE FIVE, continued

Year	Events	Policy disputes involving Pentagon	U.S. strategies and foreign policies
1958		Army critical of deemphasis of conventional and limited war capabilities; army's budget small, force levels low	
1960	Kennedy elected	Air force, congressional Democrats, and Kennedy campaigners claimed "missile gap" existed	
		Defense spending increased	
		Influence of General Taylor and army increased	Limited war and counterinsurgency doctrines for the Third World
	Berlin crisis and reserve callup		Conventional and strategic buildup; forward defense posture; "flexible response", multiple options
1962	Laos crisis; Vietnam	Series of weapons controversies; McNamara shelved B-70, nuclear-powered airplane, Skybolt missile, Dynasoar; postponed MOL, ABM	Ann Arbor counterforce doctrine discussed
	Cuban missile crisis		
	Nuclear test-ban treaty		
	Johnson became president		
1964		Congressmen and Goldwater campaign criticized restraints on military and methods of civilian control	Stabilization of strategic force levels (toward parity)
	Vietnam buildup: troop reinforcements and air war		

Year	Events	Policy disputes involving Pentagon	U.S. strategies and foreign policies
1966		Criticism of war policy from hawks and doves; draft controversy	
	Chinese nuclear capabilities demonstrated	Charges of an "ABM gap"; limited system approved by Johnson	Various rationales for Vietnam policy: containment of China, domino theory, avoid U.S. humiliation, etc.
1968	Nixon elected	Nixon campaign charge: "security gap"	
	SALT talks; related to ABM and MIRV deployment	Congressional debates about ABM, C-5A, other weapons systems, and national priorities	Nixon Doctrine for Asia; "Vietnamization" of war
1970		Nixon's new New Look with return to hardware emphasis, reduced manpower; interservice conflict initially muted; end to draft vowed	Shift from "two-plus" to "one-plus" contingency planning: capability to fight one major and one minor war simultaneously

and the system by which ambiguous intelligence data was interpreted continued to bias the threat estimates. The ability of bureaucracies to fall back, adjust to, and then to absorb or ignore their conquerors should not be underestimated. As Franklin D. Roosevelt said of trying to change the "Na-a-vy": you can hit it and hit it until you are exhausted, but it is like a feather bed; when you are through punching, it is the same as it was when you started.

Some civilian and military critics charged that McNamara was a "civilian on horseback;" they said he embodied the threats to normal constitutional processes usually associated with a military usurper, without the supposed political liabilities. The Left charged that the relative efficiency and centralization McNamara brought to the Pentagon led not to stronger civilian control but to more power for the "militarists," both those in and out of uniform.

Some checks and balances probably were weakened. McNamara was believed to have such control of the Pentagon's budget that the Bureau of the

Budget in the White House gave up any serious attempt to oppose Pentagon proposals. Johnson administration Budget Director Charles L. Schultze said it would have been like tilting at windmills. With all other executive departments, BOB recommended to the president a given level of appropriations, and the departments then had the right of appeal. By contrast, the secretary of defense presented his own final budget, and BOB had the right of appeal to the president. The burden of proof thereby was shifted to BOB.

McNamara also increased the Pentagon's influence over other executive departments, e.g., by centralized procurement through DOD. Business was involved more intimately in Pentagon decision-making through establishment of the Industry Advisory Council and cooperation with industry associations. The Pentagon took on new social missions, e.g., Project 100,000 and a declaration that segregated housing was off-limits for servicemen. McNamara and Secretary Clifford lauded the educational and civic action potentials of the military. The military set up a headquarters in the Pentagon to deal with American ghetto riots in the late 1960s, and army troops were used several times. Using this domestic violence rationale, military surveillance of civilian dissidents was increased in the late 1960s. The Pentagon conceded that its civilian data bank included information on 25 million people, and the army's domestic "snooping" network was found in 1970-1971 to cover civil rights groups and elected political officials. Secretary Laird announced plans to put domestic military intelligence operations under direct DIA control, and to put DIA under closer civilian scrutiny: in part, to "make certain the constitutional rights of all individuals are protected" [3, p. 1-A].

In terms of bureaucratic relations it matters, for example, whether the Joint Chiefs start the strategic planning process or comment on others' plans later. But there may be less to the difference in structures than meets the eye. What accounts for different strategies, resource allocations, and influence weighting between civilians and the military are the preferences and expectations of the president and whichever advisers he trusts or fears, not formal structure or the chain of command. McNamara reduced the level of JCS influence, but he permitted its scope of influence to be broadened into new areas and over greater sums of money, with less internal division. By 1971 the chiefs had been returned to the level of their pre-McNamara prominence, but it was not clear whether the scope of their influence would revert to its previous state.

Presidents, like secretaries of defense, are reluctant to overrule military judgments. "Technical military decisions—yes—can, were, have always been questioned," Schultze said, but "in the basic environment of the cold war," presidents have not been willing to "question military judgments to the point where the President will possibly face a major attack on grounds of undercutting the security of the United States"[5, p. 73]. Presidents are reluctant to overrule but not unwilling to do so: Civilians can and usually have controlled the military at the highest echelons of the executive branch, even under Laird's participatory management. Most civilian acquiescence on new programs and policies has been voluntary, not forced upon them by the political leverage of the military chiefs. Within the Defense Department the most common civilian control problems (as discussed in Chapter 4) involve the activities of the military bureaucracy *below* the Joint Chiefs level.

REFERENCES

1. Art, Robert J., *The TFX Decision* (Boston: Little, Brown, 1964).
2. Burney, John C., Jr., "Yessir, Computer, Sir," *Army,*19 (September 1969), pp. 42-46.
3. Dobkin, Robert A., "Laird Sets DIA Changes," *The Atlanta Constitution,* December 24, 1970, p. 1-A.
4. Duscha, Julius, "The Pentagon Under Fire," *The Progressive,* 33 (September 1969), pp. 32-37.
5. Joint Economic Committee of the U.S. Congress, Hearings before the Subcommittee on Economy in Government, "The Military Budget and National Economic Priorities," (Washington: Government Printing Office, 1969).
6. Longley, Charles H., "McNamara's Impact on Civil-Military Communication," paper delivered to International Studies Association convention, San Juan, March 1971.
7. Masland, John W., and Laurence I. Radway, *Soldiers and Scholars* (Princeton: Princeton University Press, 1957).
8. Nieburg, H. L., *In the Name of Science* (Chicago: Quadrangle, 1966).
9. Norman, Lloyd, "The Chiefs," Part I, *Army,* 20 (April 1970), pp. 24-30.
10. "Pentagon Widens 'Do-Gooder' Role," *Business Week,* no. 2041 (October 12, 1968), pp. 79-80.
11. Stone, I. F., "McNamara and the Militarists," *The New York Review of Books,* 11 (November 7, 1968), pp. 5-10.
12. Stone, I. F., "Nixon and the Arms Race: The Bomber Boondoggle," *The New York Review of Books,* 11 (January 2, 1969), pp. 5-10.
13. Wolf, Charles, Jr., "Military-Industrial Complexities," *Bulletin of the Atomic Scientists,* XXVII (February 1971), pp. 19-22.
14. Yarmolinsky, Adam, "How the Pentagon Works," *Atlantic,* 219 (March 1967), pp. 56-61.

CHAPTER NINE

The Military and Foreign Policy

The rationale for the military's size and power is the defense of the nation's security and international interests. The military exists to deter or to defend against enemy attacks, and to carry out national policies abroad, including the prosecution of wars.

Foreign policy involves military affairs—whether it be policy on Berlin and the North Atlantic Treaty Organization; the balance of payments and U.S. troops abroad; nuclear weapon proliferation and sharing; arms limitations and disarmament; nuclear testing and test bans; joint weapons developments with allies (e.g., the Main Battle Tank of the 1970s with West Germany); bans on weapons in the ocean beds and outer space; foreign aid; military bases; counterinsurgency training for Third World nations; U.S. arms for authoritarian regimes, Nigeria-Biafra, India-Pakistan, Turkey-Greece, and Israel; relations with Latin America and the Middle East; or the Vietnam War.

The concern about military participation in foreign policy-making has been that the military viewpoint may dominate that of the diplomat, because of the military's size, crisis orientation, and ability to determine the outcome of international clashes by supplying or using armed might. The charge that the military has exceeded its proper role in a democracy sometimes indicates that civilians have acquiesced too easily, not that soldiers have pushed their advice too hard. The corollary charge is that military men are responsible for an overemphasis on the use of force and violence in international affairs. Thereby, military men presumably show themselves to be narrow in their conception of what the national interest is. Since military force is instrumental, it must be provided a purpose by higher civilian authority, supposedly drawing upon knowledge of and concern with broader interests.

Critics say the military is so socially and intellectually isolated from civilian society that it is unable to comprehend nonmilitary values, i.e., the political, cultural, and economic context in which military advice must be judged. The desire to civilianize military perspectives has been especially strong in areas affecting the national economy and in dealings with foreign nations. Secretary of Defense Wilson in 1954 directed the Joint Chiefs of Staff, in giving advice, to "avail themselves of the most competent and considered thinking that can be obtained representing every pertinent point of view, including military, scientific, industrial and economic" [14, p. 395]. Subsequent administrations have expected the chiefs to restrict themselves to "military" advice while considering all of the factors that the president must consider. The military tries to satisfy these contradictory wishes.

The military also "has been considered deficient in its ability to judge the political consequences of its conduct" [15, p. 13]. It has sought to meet these criticisms through a broader form of military education, especially at the high-level war colleges where strategic and foreign-policy thought is encouraged, and by moving cautiously toward development of a cadre of officers with political and foreign-policy skills. Some want the military to move more decisively; Col. Louis Waple of the Military Assistance Officers Program said, "The object is to get the military into the political. Whether an operation is GO or NO-GO is as often as not a political decision. You cannot separate the two. ... We take abuse from the press and the public for decisions in which we have taken no part. So we must have men on our staff who have got all the tickets, and who are going to make their recommendations in military terms and in . . . political terms. We want a voice in our own destiny" [17, p. 77]. Waple's view of the desirability of political officers along Stilwell's lines has not been accepted by military leadership, but the Joint Chiefs in the 1960s was getting its political estimates and its caveats on paper prior to any commitment of forces. Although designed to protect it from subsequent scapegoat-hunting, if things went wrong, the secrecy of JCS recommendations limited the value of such protection. Of course, if the military moves too far to improve its political sophistication and to broaden what it considers in rendering advice and administering policies, it faces the objection that it has overstepped its proper role.

Military men advise on the "military" dimensions of foreign policy at the highest levels in Washington, and influence policy-making at locations throughout the world: in U.S. and allied commands, aid and training missions, embassies, and intelligence operations. The manner in which policies are interpreted and carried out by the military, especially in crises and wars, also has a profound impact on the meaning of those and future policies.

WASHINGTON

The increasing influence of the secretary of defense has made him a rival to the secretary of state and to special presidential assistants. The DOD Office of

International Security Affairs was the channel for conducting foreign-policy business with State and for providing foreign policy guidance within DOD itself. Under McNamara ISA was concerned with military aid and training programs (formally operating under guidelines set by the secretary of state), regional security alliances, United Nations relations, negotiations regarding U.S. forces abroad and arms limitation, and other strategic-political questions. McNamara's assistant secretary for ISA, John T. McNaughton, played a vital role in making and articulating civilian DOD recommendations on the Vietnam War. In the 1960s "ISA's mixture of political civilians, career civilians, and career military (from a variety of staff and command backgrounds was) typical of the Office of the Secretary of Defense," although the military often kept their best-trained officers to do international affairs work within the service staffs [28, p. 178].

The highest-level input from the professional military comes from the Joint Chiefs of Staff. The president, vice president, secretaries of state and defense, and director of the Office of Emergency Preparedness are statutory members of the National Security Council. The chairman of the Joint Chiefs is a statutory adviser to the NSC, which was important during the Eisenhower and Nixon administrations and less so under Kennedy and Johnson. The chairman also serves on lower NSC planning bodies and various interagency policy committees, e.g., the post-1966 Senior Inter-Departmental Group (with the deputy secretary of defense, the directors of the AID, CIA, and USIA, White House representatives, and the undersecretary of state who served as chairman). On the 1966 structuring Gen. Maxwell Taylor commented, "Thus, for the first time, the Joint Chiefs organization has been fitted by executive authority into the planning and implementation process of foreign affairs, and the military voice has been given a forum in which it can be heard and its influence exercised in an environment conducive to effective integrated action" [3, p. 12]. General Wheeler attended President Johnson's important Tuesday luncheons, and General Taylor was involved in informal decision-making groups during the Kennedy administration.

A state department representative also has met periodically with the Joint Chiefs, and on routine business service staffs may deal directly with State. As late as 1950 Pentagon staff personnel were expressly forbidden to communicate directly with their State Department counterparts. In the 1960s, however, close working relationships between the departments became routine. "No day passes that at least 30 military officers from . . . DOD are not in the State Department attending meetings" [4, p. 231]. As the State and Defense departments cooperated on Vietnam plans, the traditional suspicion between the two eased somewhat despite their continuing policy differences.

Crucial to the Joint Chiefs' influence is its position at the apex of the intelligence network. In crises "the military often are first with the intelligence reports and the prepared position papers." A defense official told reporter Norman, "When it comes to crisis planning, the JCS usually can beat the State Department to the punch with concise, clear-cut proposals. The military command posts are on the alert around the clock and they have their staffs ready to move fast. When General Wheeler goes to the White House, the President gets a prompt, succinct report and a quick tickoff of alternatives" [24, p. 38]. In listing these alternatives, of course, the chiefs are as thoroughly enmeshed in political estimates as civilian policy-makers. The military says it focuses on enemy capabilities, rather than on intentions, but it must also evaluate the probability of enemy and neutral actions occurring.

The influence of the Joint Chiefs on foreign policy has varied considerably. In the late 1940s and early 1950s the JCS was widely believed to have played a leading role in making policy. The chiefs were "fully consulted" on matters such as the Japanese peace treaty (which the military helped to write). Gen. George C. Marshall said in 1951 he could "recall no occasion when Mr. Truman has acted adversely to the Chiefs of Staff and Secretary of Defense in relation to the State Department"[1] [33, p. 142]. Although the chiefs' influence may have declined in the 1950s and 1960s, it continued to be substantial. "Despite the buffers of whiz kids and civilian strategists" during the McNamara years, the chiefs had "a massive and fundamental impact upon foreign policy and strategy. Not only do they have their brainiest and best-prepared senior officers participating in the highest policy-making committees but the military build the foundation upon which politico-military policy is constructed" [24, p. 38]. Peter Beckman [3, pp. 4, 10] operationalized military influence on foreign policy ("the degree that the military is able to have its preferences included in foreign policy decisions") as the number of times per 1000 lines of foreign policy statements in the *Department of State Bulletin* made by the president, secretaries of state and defense, and the presidential national security assistant, in which the military or a member of the military is mentioned. By this measure military influence has declined. (See Fig. Four.) Measuring influence by other methods is difficult, since one cannot create a laboratory situation in which the question "What would have happened in foreign policy crisis 'A' if the Joint Chiefs had *not been present* in policy-making councils?" can be answered. The "chameleon problem" also is troublesome: (1) the military favored a containment policy; (2) civilian policy-makers favored a containment policy; so (3) who influenced whom, and who was decisive in getting the policy adopted? In the crises and wars to be examined later in this chapter JCS positions will be compared with positions taken by civilians and with policies adopted.

---

[1] In 1954 Sapin and Richard Snyder [29, p. 29] felt that JCS views were accepted too uncritically by civilians. In the 1960s Huntington [3, p. 10] believed that "the power of the military profession 'in the councils of government' has decreased steadily since World War II. It has reached its postwar nadir under the vigorous leadership" of Kennedy and McNamara.

FIGURE FOUR

The Influence of the Military Establishment on American Foreign Policy 1945-1970—One Measure

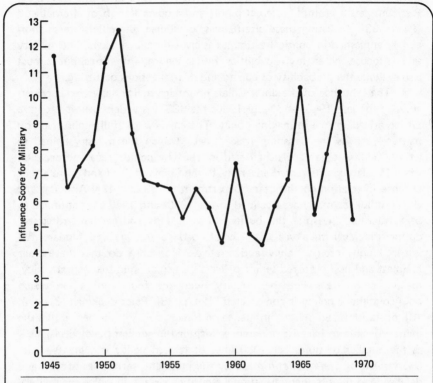

Source: Peter Beckman, "Influence, Generals, and Vietnam," a paper presented to the International Studies Association Convention, 1971.

ALLIANCES, COMMANDS, AND BASES

In varying degree the United States is allied with more than 40 nations. Even where formal commitments may be ambiguous, administration officials have conceded that the presence of U.S. bases or forces within a nation suggests American concern for that country.[2] Relations with neighboring countries

[2] Military forces abroad can lead to difficult foreign policy situations short of committing or provoking armed encounters: For example, the Japanese and Okinawan anti-American demonstrations during the 1960s, and other protests against the housing and transportation of nuclear weapons and nerve gas in Pacific islands; an air collision over Spain in 1966 in which two nuclear bombs broke apart, spreading radioactive plutonium over a wide area; and racial conflicts involving American soldiers in Germany in 1969-1970.

thereby are affected. In 1969 the Senate Foreign Relations Committee expressed concern about "de facto commitments" caused by bases and joint military maneuvers (aimed at suppressing a hypothetical rebellion) in Spain, and by the presence of 50,000 U.S. troops in Thailand. Referring to a 1963 agreement with Spain, which declared that an attack on joint bases would be regarded as a "matter of common concern," a committee report said, "In practice, the very fact of our physical presence in Spain constitutes a quasicommitment to the defense of the Franco regime, possibly even against internal disruptions. At some point, the distinction between defending American lives and property and defending the host government would be likely to become academic, if not to disappear altogether. It is not difficult to envision a situation in which the need to protect American servicemen would lead to large-scale military intervention in Spain"[7, p. 11].

Pentagon leaders used foreign commitments to justify the size of the defense establishment; to cut the defense budget, they said, the nation first must reduce commitments, and there had been few moves to do that in the quarter century after World War II. The United States has been committed by treaty to the defense of (1) all Latin American nations except Cuba (under the Rio Pact, 1947); (2) Canada, Turkey, Iceland, and 11 European nations (under the North Atlantic Treaty, 1949); (3) the Philippines (1951), South Korea (1953), Taiwan (1954), under mutual defense treaties, and Japan (1960) under a "treaty of mutual security and cooperation"; (4) Australia and New Zealand (under ANZUS, 1951); (5) five Asian nations, plus France and Britain (under SEATO, 1954), and South Vietnam and Cambodia under a protocol to the much-ignored treaty; and (6) nine countries (some covered previously by treaties) under executive agreements between 1951 and 1965. Since 1945 there have been five congressional resolutions supporting presidential actions in Taiwan, the Middle East, Cuba, Berlin, and Vietnam (Tonkin Gulf), and more than 30 executive branch policy declarations and communiques issued jointly with foreign governments.

America had almost 3000 minor military installations and at least 400 major bases overseas. Of the major bases 123 were in Germany and more than 150 were in Vietnam, South Korea, and Japan. The 1969 Nixon Doctrine proclaimed that Asian nations must be prepared to defend themselves, because U.S. troops were unlikely to be committed in future ground wars. To strengthen Asian self-defense capabilities Nixon promised more arms and training aid; even under this doctrine some kind of military involvement was viewed as necessary. Outside Vietnam the largest number of U.S. troops were stationed in Germany, at an annual maintenance cost of $2.2 billion. In 1971 the Nixon administration blocked an effort by Senate critics to reduce American forces in Europe by half, but it was expected that some troops would be withdrawn in the early 1970s. The possibility of negotiated East-West troop cuts in central Europe also was being discussed. Some bases were to be abandoned by the Nixon administration for economic reasons.

With the exception of a few in the Pacific, all bases had been opened since World War II began. Twice since that war, during the Korean and Vietnam wars, more than a million Americans have been stationed abroad. Before Vietnam 745,000 men were stationed abroad, and in 1969 the U.S. had more than 1.2 million military personnel in more than 30 countries and foreign possessions and in the Pacific and Mediterranean fleets. In addition, well over 600,000 American civilians, dependents, and foreign nationals were attached to U.S. overseas bases.

These people work under U.S. and Allied military commands which require high-ranking American officers to deal directly with foreign political leaders in the implementation of U.S. policies. Service in the Supreme Headquarters (SHAPE) of NATO, for example, has been politically sensitive: "The allocation of key commands to one nationality or another is so delicate from a diplomatic point of view that General Eisenhower's first tasks as SHAPE Commander were almost more diplomatic than military. . . . There were the politically explosive questions of Spanish bases and Spain's participation in Western defense, and of Balkan defense. Finally, the need to arrange for East-West supply lines across France . . . was a major diplomatic problem" [8, p. 142]. In the sixties France's determination to withdraw its forces from NATO provided continuing diplomatic problems for NATO commanders. During the Vietnam War service in the Pacific unified command headquarters was similarly important. Every ranking U.S. commander[3] stationed abroad, in fact, is a political agent responsible for amicable community relations and more. Unified commanders responsible for geographic areas usually are in close touch with ambassadors in those regions, in "relationships of equals" [28, p. 266]. These commanders and their staffs coordinate military aid for their regions, and also are concerned with alliance administration. The same working relationship with ambassadors is necessary for commanders of U.S. forces in any country.

Appointment of military men to diplomatic and other civilian positions was widespread immediately after World War II but has been less prevalent

---

[3] A foreign policy initiative warned of by the military's more extreme critics was that a field commander could precipitate an international crisis or war on his own, perhaps using some of the 7000 nuclear warheads the United States positioned in Europe alone. This had not been attempted, and the Pentagon maintained that nuclear weapons could not be used without the president's authorization.

In 1970 a Coast Guard admiral was subject to contrary criticism: that he had been unduly reluctant to confront the Russians. During a rendezvous off Cape Cod to discuss fishing rights, a Russian seaman jumped to a Coast Guard cutter, and asked for asylum. The U.S. commander was ordered by the admiral, without consulting the State Department or other Washington officials, to return the seaman, and if he jumped overboard to give the Russians the first opportunity to pick him up. Six Russians who were permitted to board the American ship beat the seaman before carrying him back to their ship. The admiral, his chief of staff, and the commander were suspended, and President Nixon condemned their actions.

since then. During that war, in addition to the broad discretion allowed field commanders, soldiers were used for advisory and diplomatic missions. Gen. Joseph Stilwell served as Chiang Kai-shek's chief of staff, as well as commander for the China-Burma-India campaign. Having spent most of his life in China, speaking Mandarin, and knowing many of the rival Chinese leaders, Stilwell was recognized as the War Department's China specialist. He clashed frequently with Chiang, pressed President Roosevelt to withhold Lend-Lease supplies until the Chinese put more forces into battle against the Japanese, and in 1944 was recalled because of Chiang's animosity. General Marshall was sent to China in 1945 as the president's special envoy, one of three generals sent on such missions after Stilwell's departure. The administration felt that a man of Marshall's standing was needed to calm its political critics. Marshall sought a coalition between the Communists and Chiang, and was charged by his critics with blocking a military aid policy which would have permitted Chiang to defeat the Communists. During this period three ambassadors to the U.S.S.R. were military men; under Truman 12 military officers served as principal State Department officers and ambassadors. Other active and retired officers served in high positions in the CIA, the Atomic Energy Commission, the aviation agencies, the Selective Service Administration, the Veterans Administration, the Foreign Operations Administration, the Office of Defense Mobilization, and the Justice Department's Immigration and Naturalization Service. Generals also directed military governments in Germany (Lucius Clay), Austria (Mark Clark), Japan (Douglas MacArthur), Korea, and Trieste, in which they were expected to supervise virtually all facets of national life, including "democracy-building."[4] Naval officers were involved in extramilitary administrative tasks in determining the status of the mandated central Pacific islands. In the late forties, the high point in using military men in civil government, they occupied an estimated 150 of 3000 top U.S. policy-making posts. A significant number of active-duty officers continued to be assigned to civilian agencies and diplomatic posts through the early fifties, but the percentage since has declined.[5]

[4] General MacArthur's officers helped to revise the Japanese constitution and laws. They supervised the press, schools, trade unions, and political parties. They changed the monetary and financial system, and determined the structure of industry. In Germany, U.S. and Allied officers purged the civil administration of Nazi leaders, and were closely involved in economic and political organization questions. General Clay said he neither sought nor received advice from the State Department before taking over in 1945. When Clay directed the sensitive Berlin airlift in 1948, he took his orders from the Defense Department, whereas his British and French counterparts took their orders from their countries' diplomatic departments.

[5] Early in the Nixon administration seven of the top nine officials in the Office of Emergency Preparedness were active or recently retired military officers. During the Johnson administration all nine posts were held by civilians. The OEP was designed to advance a civilian viewpoint in NSC discussions, and to oversee contingency planning at all levels of government.

Military men trusted by the president can play a special role in foreign policy-making at any period. Admiral Leahy served as ambassador to France, and then as chief of staff to Presidents Roosevelt and Truman. General Taylor was special military adviser to Presidents Kennedy and Johnson and he had a continuing hand in Vietnam policy.

There was more to American commitments in Spain and Thailand than the presence of bases and troops. U.S. military men were accused by congressional critics of exceeding their authority to make agreements committing the United States to the defense of those nations. The negotiations prior to a 10-year 1953 agreement on U.S. base rights in Spain were begun in 1951 by the American chief of naval operations. The next year they were conducted in large part by a military mission headed by Air Force Chief of Staff Gen. Nathan F. Twining, accompanied by the civilian secretary of the air force. Secretary of State Dean Rusk negotiated an extension in 1963, but in 1968-1969 military men again were involved. The chairman of the Joint Chiefs, acting under Secretary Rusk's instructions, apparently provided Spanish military authorities with a secret memorandum asserting that the presence of U.S. forces in Spain constituted a more significant security guarantee than would a written agreement. Gen. David A. Burchinal, deputy chief of U.S. forces under NATO, was assigned by the Joint Chiefs to begin discussions with Spanish military commanders on "purely" military matters. The New York Times [31, p. 10] reported that the general "had agreed with the Spanish representatives on various formulas that would have committed the United States to help defend Spain from imprecisely defined 'threats' from the Arab countries of North Africa." These negotiations, which Senator Mansfield suggested may have been started without the president's knowledge, went beyond the 1963 agreements. Burchinal's agreement was approved by the JCS chairman, altered substantially by Pentagon civilians, and the Spanish base rights were renewed. Whether Burchinal went beyond his authority was debated inconclusively.

A secret contingency plan was negotiated in 1964-1965 by the prime minister of Thailand and Gen. Joseph W. Stilwell, Jr., commander of the U.S. military advisory group in Thailand. Subsequently it was approved by the Joint Chiefs. When the agreement came to light 5 years later, the vice president said it did not require ratification by the president, State or Defense Departments, or the Senate. Secretary of State Rogers said the United States had hundreds of similarly secret contingency plans, none of which were binding on the governments involved. The State Department did not even have a copy of the Thailand plan. Senator Fulbright charged that the agreement again demonstrated the trend toward DOD domination of foreign policy. His charge that the agreement went beyond SEATO commitments was denied by the State Department. The plan reportedly provided for the United States to send troops to help Thai troops resist a Communist attack on Thailand launched through Laos.

AID, ARMS, AND ATTACHÉS

Almost 80 countries received U.S. military aid between 1950-1970. Military grants and loans for this period totaled over $38 billion, and some economic assistance supported military programs indirectly. In 1970 DOD administered the Military Assistance Program[6] and the Foreign Military Sales program under an air force general who was a deputy assistant defense secretary. Both programs were designed to strengthen anti-Communist military forces and provide opportunities for close contacts between U.S. and foreign military personnel. Various financial arrangements were possible, including "off-set" arrangements where nations (e.g., Germany) bought weapons from the United States to balance the cost of maintaining U.S. troops there. FMS aided the U.S. balance of payments, the Pentagon frequently pointed out. Up to $4 billion a year worth of arms has been given or sold to foreign nations by the United States, making America the world's leading arms seller and total exporter. Between 1945-1970 the United States exported more than $50 billion worth of military equipment, compared to $16 billion for the rest of the world combined.

Overseas, MAP and FMS were administered in 1969 by over 7000 military men attached to Military Assistance Advisory Groups (the most common aid arrangement), more narrowly defined military missions, and embassies in 50 countries. The MAAG works "very closely with the armed forces of the local government in: developing and assessing the latter's military requirements; evaluating local requests for assistance; advising and assisting in training local forces to use the material supplied; and screening and recommending local candidates proposed for military training in the United States" [28, p. 267]. The head of the country military aid group, like the attaché, is usually a key figure in the "country team," since military aid is an important matter of negotiation between the ambassador and the host country. MAAG officers negotiate on their own when they estimate the forces or equipment needed by the recipient country, but agreements must fit into the broader policies made in Washington. The ambassador is supposed to supervise MAAG operations in his resident country but, as with other departments' representatives, independent MAAG lines of communications to Washington and regional commands reduce the ambassador's control.

Military assistance goes to some nations not covered by formal defense agreements. For example, almost $170 million in U.S. military aid was

[6] The Senate Foreign Relations Committee and the General Accounting Office sought for more than 2 years to persuade the Pentagon to supply a 5-year plan for MAP which the committee said DOD had. As had happened with documents on the Tonkin Gulf incident and the Vietnam War, the Pentagon refused either to supply the material or to invoke executive privilege. The committee in August 1971 invoked a provision to cut off all military aid unless the plan was supplied; however, a reduced aid bill later was reported out.

provided (through the air force as executive agent) to support United Nations operations in the Congo (now Zaire) between 1960-1964, as well as bilateral military aid beginning in 1962. Military men led several U.S. investigating teams sent to the Congo, including one in 1962 to appraise the condition of the Congolese army. That team recommended negotiation of a series of bilateral aid plans between various nations and the Congo, under UN authorization. Although the UN secretary-general retracted his approval of the plan, the United States and several other Western nations began providing significant aid. The United States offered training for Congolese soldiers here and in the Congo, and provided airlift capability. One instance of emergency airlift assistance, to help the government put down a mercenary uprising, sparked cries of "another Vietnam" from Senate critics.

Military personnel also have been involved in more direct "advisory" functions, such as training and accompanying combat units. The 1960s Laotian "secret war" involved unannounced U.S. CIA and military forces. The elite Army Special Forces, or Green Berets, in Vietnam organized a Civilian Irregular Defense Group. They trained 200,000 Southeast Asians to fight as conventional soldiers, spies,[7] saboteurs, and propagandists. The Special Forces also provided counterinsurgency training in a number of Asian, African, and Latin American nations; they trained the Bolivian troops who killed Ché Guevara in 1967.

Many military men believe that in the underdeveloped nations the only hope for stability rests with the local military. The Pentagon so justified its training programs: "While military equipment and hardware may deteriorate in time, an understanding of American technology and management techniques, and most importantly, of American culture, carries over long after the foreign national returns to his own country. Such an understanding and appreciation of the United States may be worth far more in the long run than outright grants or sales of military equipment" [6, p. 43]. It was hoped by the Pentagon that among the 10,000 foreign military personnel trained annually by the United States at 175 domestic bases and centers overseas were future leaders of their nations' armed forces and perhaps governments. In 1969 in Latin America, for example, the president of El Salvador, the president of Nicaragua, the "strong man" of Panama, the president and foreign minister of Peru, and the war minister of Brazil were MAAG trainees.

---

[7] A 1969 Green Berets murder case involved a controversial intelligence mishap in Vietnam. A former Beret commander and five other officers were charged by the army with conspiracy and second-degree murder in the case of an Asian agent who vanished after being suspected of betraying Green Beret secrets. The Berets worked with the CIA on undercover assignments, and to maintain the secrecy of intelligence operations, the charges were dropped under congressional and administration pressure. Apparently the agent, involved in U.S. espionage in Cambodia, was not working for the Communists, but a CIA order to save him came one day after he had been "terminated with extreme prejudice."

Two of the five Indonesian coup-makers in 1965 had received U.S. Army training. In 20 years preceding 1969 more than 287,000 soldiers had been trained, in addition to those trained through FMS; even in a sensitive area such as chemical and biological weapons, several hundred were trained. Instruction was provided in operation and maintenance of U.S. equipment; general strategy, tactics, and military management; and counterinsurgency.[8]

The House Foreign Affairs subcommittee on national security policy in 1971 discussed one long-term training relationship:

The United States played an important role in advising and instructing the Japanese Self-Defense Forces during the 1950s and early 1960s. From 1954 to the present almost 10,000 Japanese officers and enlisted men have received U.S. training and some 71 senior officers have been graduated from U.S. command and general staff schools. ... Japanese military doctrine and procedures bear a distinct kinship to U.S. doctrine and procedures. American diplomatic and military personnel in Japan view as very important this rapport between the Japanese and American military establishments.

As the Japanese achieved self-sufficiency ... the U.S. MAP program was reduced and finally terminated in 1967. Some training has continued, purchased under the ... FMS. ... As a nation which has become largely self-sufficient in training its military forces under U.S. tutelage, Japan provides a prototype of what might be expected in other nations if the Nixon doctrine is carried through. ... Self-sufficiency. ... seems to have had these effects:

(1) An increasing unwillingness to send Japanese students to U.S. military schools. ... (They) are sending almost no one. ... (2) The time is fast approaching when the United States will no longer have the advantage of having trained the military leadership of Japan. The majority of men in the top echelons of the Japanese Self-Defense Forces have had at least one training tour in the United States, speak English, have been exposed to American life and institutions, and have formed friendships with their American counterparts. In the next few years, however, these men will be retired and their places are likely to be taken by men who have not been U.S. trained, who do not speak English, and who do not have personal ties with America and Americans. ... (3) Increasing divergence by the Japanese from U.S. military doctrine may be expected [35, pp. 2-3].

In addition to field forces and assistance programs, several hundred military attachés serve in American embassies around the world. Except in wartime most intelligence comes from public sources, rather than cloak-and-dagger work, and attachés provide this kind of intelligence. They advise the ambassador and report to military superiors on the military situation in the host country. (Like many weapons procurement officers, attachés are not specialized, and most serve only once.)

[8] Trainees came from several dozen countries, but in 1970 (due to Nixon's "Vietnamization" policy) the largest number were Vietnamese: 5000, or three times the 1969 figure. Congress cut back the program in 1970.

CRISES AND WARS

In addition to two major wars in Asia since World War II the United States has been involved in confrontations with the U.S.S.R. (e.g., Berlin 1948 and 1958-1962, and Cuba 1962), limited expeditionary operations (e.g., Lebanon 1958, and the Dominican Republic 1965), and situations where serious military escalation was considered (e.g., Taiwan 1950s, Indochina 1954, and Laos 1961). Here we will describe the nature of military influence over selected decisions on critical international events.

Korea, 1950-1953

In the first meeting of presidential advisers, including DOD officials, after the North Korean invasion of South Korea (June 25, 1950), there was general agreement that something had to be done, as President Truman himself already had decided. He authorized Gen. Douglas MacArthur, American commander-in-chief in the Far East, to use air and naval power to assure delivery of supplies to the South Korean army and to protect the evacuation of American dependents. On June 29 MacArthur reported that Korea would be lost unless U.S. ground forces were employed.[9] When Army Chief of Staff Lawton Collins told MacArthur that Truman was reluctant to commit troops to combat, the field commander demanded an immediate answer.

Norman reported, "The Chiefs were slow to propose use of U.S. military forces to repel the North Korean invasion. . . . Secretary of State (Dean) Acheson initiated the proposal to send U.S. forces to Korea. The Chiefs had considered South Korea eliminated from their defense responsibility as the result of a presidential policy decision that South Korea was not vital to U.S. defense" [24, p. 39]. On June 30 Truman authorized the use of U.S. ground troops then stationed in Japan, along with more to follow. MacArthur's request that a Nationalist Chinese offer of troops be accepted was denied the same day, however, on Acheson's recommendation and with all the chiefs concurring. The first major policy decisions were these: (1) to request a UN Security Council meeting, and to call for a North Korean pull-back; (2) to intervene with air and naval power, and to request assistance from other UN members; (3) to decline the Nationalist Chinese offer; (4) to commit U.S. ground troops; (5) several months later to cross the 38th parallel, and to seek reunification of Korea by military means; and (6) after November 1950 *not* to widen the war in various ways. Decisions 2 and 5 were the key political decisions altering existing U.S. policy.

Although he was later to be refused authorization to expand the area of

[9] The Joint Chiefs, one day earlier, had authorized the use of ground troops to insure retention of a port and air base in the Pusan area. The demarcation between air and naval involvement and ground troop involvement was not clearcut. Similarly, the first order to cross the parallel actually was given several days after the fighting began, when the chiefs authorized air and naval strikes across the parallel.

military operations, MacArthur's first requests were approved: commitment of U.S. ground troops; the Inchon offensive;[10] and crossing the 38th parallel. The decision on sending ground troops across the parallel separating the two Koreas came up in September after MacArthur's successful Inchon landing and counteroffensive. The Joint Chiefs notified MacArthur on September 27 that his military objective was the "destruction of the North Korean Armed Forces," although he was cautioned not to cross the Manchurian or U.S.S.R. borders. A month before, the chiefs and MacArthur had initiated the plan for MacArthur (in Truman's words) "to conduct the necessary military operations either to force the North Koreans behind the 38th parallel or to destroy their forces. If there was no indication of threat of entry of Soviet or Chinese Communist elements in force . . . (he) was to extend his operations north of the Parallel and to make plans for the occupation of North Korea" [26, p. 99]. MacArthur already had been given wide latitude by the president, who greatly admired MacArthur and his secretary of defense, General Marshall. Truman and the NSC approved the cross-the-parallel plan 4 days after it was presented as a JCS recommendation. The approval of the United Nations then was obtained.

As MacArthur crossed the parallel and advanced northward, he was cautioned by the Joint Chiefs to do nothing which might bring the Chinese in, but he was not ordered to stop. In November the Chinese launched a major offensive, and by early 1951 had almost pushed MacArthur's forces off the peninsula, after the longest retreat in American history. MacArthur requested reinforcements, but was told that none were available. To save his forces and to cripple China's capability to wage aggressive war and "thus save Asia from the engulfment otherwise facing it," MacArthur proposed an all-out effort: a naval blockade of China; air and naval bombardment of China's industry, communications, supply depots, and bases; and "unleashing" Nationalist Chinese troops to reinforce his own and to engage in "diversionary action" possibly leading to invasion of the mainland. He urged that the United States take advantage of the situation to alter the strategic balance in Asia, confident that American atomic might would deter Russia from intervening directly.

At least three times MacArthur's escalation proposals were turned down, but he continued to urge Truman and the chiefs to lift restrictions such as those against bombing hydroelectric plants or engaging in "hot pursuit" of planes across the Yalu River. "The development of the limiting process in the Korean War seems to have been the work, on the whole, of the civilian decision-makers . . . in rejecting or approving requests by the military to engage in military operation which would have (expanded) the war" [10, pp. 36-37]. An exception was the atomic bomb; few military men opposed

---

[10] The Inchon decision was almost entirely a military one; proposed by MacArthur, the plan was opposed by and then reluctantly accepted by the Joint Chiefs.

the prohibition on use of atomic weapons, and the military never requested permission to use them. But most military leaders opposed the limits on the geographic scope of the war. No previous war matched the unanimity of military field dissent manifested in Korea; with the exception of MacArthur's successor, Gen. Matthew Ridgway, the commanders were uneasy with the political restrictions which they felt denied them military victory. It was the charismatic MacArthur, seeing himself as a symbol of the free world and also symbolizing the frustrations of the generals, who came into direct conflict with the president.

After Truman, on the advice of civilian and military advisers in Washington, had turned down MacArthur's proposals in January 1951, the general replied that unless he was permitted to follow his plans he would have to evacuate his troops to Japan. By March the situation had become less critical; UN troops were once more at the 38th parallel. MacArthur insisted that the aim of the war remained the fall objective of militarily reuniting Korea, but the Truman administration had decided to press for negotiations. On the eve of a planned public statement by the president stating willingness to negotiate (about which MacArthur had been alerted), MacArthur released a statement of his own to the press. It was a declaration to the enemy field commander that MacArthur stood ready at any time to confer about ending hostilities. The communiqué contained what the State Department interpreted as an ultimatum to China that the UN might depart from its "tolerant effort" to contain the war to Korea. What MacArthur saw as a simple offer to discuss military matters with his counterpart was made in spite of directives to clear important policy statements in Washington. It contained suggestions at variance with U.S. policy (amounting, Truman felt, to "open defiance"), and it altered the diplomatic situation facing the president.[11] Soon afterward Republican House Minority Leader Joe Martin released a solicited letter from MacArthur; it repeated the general's policy preferences, closing with his favorite phrase, "There is no substitute for victory." MacArthur had communicated with congressmen and veterans groups before, but now Truman's suspicion increased that his field commander was conspiring with

[11] MacArthur later claimed he was unable to get clear political guidance from Washington. He said he was made a scapegoat for unsuccessful policies. He later told Senate committees:

When all other political means failed, you then go to force; and when you do that, the balance of control . . . the main interest involved, the minute you reach the killing stage, is the control of the military. . . . (Then) there should be no artifice under the name of politics. . . . A theater commander in any campaign is not merely limited to the handling of his troops; he commands that whole area, political, economic, and military. . . . When politics fails, and the military takes over, you must trust the military. . . . (An indefinite "limited" war) introduces into the military sphere a political control such as I have never known in my life or have ever studied. . . . The concept that when you use force, you can limit that force (is) appeasement [22, pp. 481-483].

Republican leaders, and appealing to the public to overturn the policies of the commander-in-chief. Six days later the president dismissed MacArthur.

To the public the war, with its ambiguities and frustrations, became "Truman's War," and MacArthur returned home to a hero's welcome. Truman was threatened with impeachment, condemned by several state legislatures, and booed in public. In New York City 7.5 million people, twice the number that greeted the victorious General Eisenhower in 1945, lined the streets to see MacArthur; millions more turned out in other cities, and a Gallup poll showed 69 percent of the public supported him against Truman. His emotional speech to a joint session of Congress ("Old soldiers never die ... ") was received enthusiastically. In 1952 he gave the keynote address to the Republican convention which he hoped would nominate him for president; instead it nominated Eisenhower, who promised to go to Korea if elected. MacArthur said civilian supremacy was not in question in his dispute with Truman, and he did nothing directly, such as appealing for support from his men against the president, to create a more serious civil-military crisis.[12] But he did invoke the "higher loyalty" tradition of the Prussian military when he told the Massachusetts legislature:

I find in existence a new and heretofore unknown and dangerous concept that the members of our armed forces owe primary allegiance and loyalty to those who temporarily exercise the authority of the executive branch of the government, rather than to the country and its Constitution which they are sworn to defend. No proposition can be more dangerous. None could cast greater doubt upon the integrity of the armed forces. For its application would at once convert them from their traditional constitutional role as the instrument of defense of the Republic into something partaking of the nature of a praetorian guard, owing sole allegiance to the political master of the hour [27, p. 315].

MacArthur's proposals had been opposed not only by the State Department, concerned about Allied opinion and about Russia, but by the Joint Chiefs on grounds of military effectiveness. The conflict was military-military as well as civil-military. Gen. Omar Bradley, JCS chairman, warned that MacArthur's plan would tie down too much of American resources "in an area that is not the critical strategic prize."[13] The chiefs' support for Truman and a limited war strategy in Korea, led Republicans to call them the

[12] Despite the public support symbolized by 2850 tons of ticker tape showered on MacArthur in New York, few officers rallied to his side. General Ridgway said: "It was a boon to the country that the issue did arise and that it was decisively met by the elected head of the government within the ample dimensions of his own high moral courage"[26, p. 154].

[13] The United States had to conserve its strength to check its principal enemy, the USSR, in the principal arena, Europe; Bradley felt MacArthur's expansion of the war to China would involve America in the wrong war, in the wrong place, at the wrong time,

"Democratic Joint Chiefs." The chiefs had been active proponents of Truman administration containment policies; they appeared before congressional committees to support foreign aid, treaties, deployment of American troops to Europe, and administration force level and budgetary policies. For a while, Huntington said, the Joint Chiefs succeeded as advocates, "capitalizing upon the combined prestige of military hero and technical expert. Congress listened to Bradley when it ignored Acheson. Eventually, however . . . the unpopularity of the policies . . . lowered the personal and institutional prestige of the men who were advocating them" [14, p. 386]. The Joint Chiefs' political position was not enhanced by their involvement in the Senate hearings on MacArthur's dismissal and in the 1952 presidential campaign, e.g., Bradley's criticism of the "Gibraltar theory" of defense advocated by Senator Taft.

That nations, including the United States, had been fighting wars with limited means for limited objectives for centuries prior to 1914 did not make Korea any less frustrating for American military leaders.[14] A few years earlier they had been fighting with almost unlimited resources for the goal of unconditional surrender. To political and military leaders the initial lesson of Korea was "never again," never again would the United States fight a large-scale but limited conventional war. When Vietnam nevertheless turned into such a war, political leaders sought mightily to avoid the public opposition and civil-military conflict which had characterized Korea. However, civilian control of the military again was to become controversial.

Indochina, 1954

Just as the military leadership was not the first to urge military action in Korea, so it has been cautious in its advice at the inception of other crises. In the Indochina crisis of 1954 and the Laotian crisis of 1961 elements of the military opposed U.S. involvement on the basis of (1) insufficient military capabilities to intervene, while meeting obligations elsewhere; (2) logistical difficulties; and (3) lack of a strong indigenous government to support.

The Eisenhower administration seriously considered intervening in Indochina in 1954, near the close of the French-Viet Minh war, to prevent a French defeat or withdrawal. That year the United States was paying 78 percent of the French war budget. Secretary of State John Foster Dulles, with the support of Adm. Arthur W. Radford, chairman of the Joint Chiefs, favored intervention to achieve a military victory. Radford suggested carrier

---

with the wrong enemy. Here again were the intra-military disagreements between the group Janowitz [15, pp. 285-291] called the "Europeans," including Bradley and Marshall, and those who favored greater attention to Asia, led by MacArthur.

[14] A reporter asked Gen. James Van Fleet, "What is our goal?" "I don't know," Van Fleet responded. "The answer must come from higher authority." Reporter: "How may we know, General, when and if we achieve victory?" Van Fleet: "I don't know, except that somebody higher up will have to tell us" [23, p. 185].

air strikes against Viet Minh forces at Dienbienphu, and the use of nuclear weapons also was discussed. The debate within the administration centered on questions of military feasibility, rather than basic national interests, and here the military was divided. Army Chief of Staff Ridgway opposed intervention, arguing that airpower would not be effective and that sufficient ground forces, due to Eisenhower's New Look reductions, were not available. Even if they were, the former Korean War commander felt involvement in a new Asian land war was undesirable. Congressional leaders, the British, the civilian and military intelligence community, and Eisenhower agreed.

Several months after the French withdrew from Indochina and the administration decided to support the Saigon regime, Eisenhower's personal emissary in Vietnam, General Collins, recommended that the Saigon premier be removed or U.S. plans for assisting Saigon be reevaluated. But the State Department and the CIA supported the premier, and he retained U.S. backing.

The Joint Chiefs recommended noninvolvement in the Hungarian revolt, the British-French Suez Canal campaign of 1956, and the Congo crisis of 1960, and opposed any action to tear down the Berlin wall in 1961 [24, p. 39]. Military leaders usually were hesitant to recommend armed intervention in crises in the 1940s and 1950s,[15] when U.S. conventional forces were relatively weak. With the Kennedy-McNamara conventional rearmament of the 1960s, however, sufficient forces existed to intervene in Third World crises, and existence of such forces seemed to create pressure to use them.

Cuba I (1961) and Cuba II (1962)

The unsuccessful Bay of Pigs invasion by Cuban refugees in April 1961 was CIA-sponsored. The explanation from Kennedy partisans is that the new president was reluctant to overrule the recommendations of the veteran, high-level experts he had inherited from the Eisenhower administration. The lesson which President Kennedy apparently believed he learned was to be more skeptical of advice from his experts, the Joint Chiefs, as well as the CIA.

In addition to the two top CIA officials, Hilsman identified the third sponsor of invasion plans as Gen. Lyman L. Lemnitzer, JCS chairman. Lemnitzer and other chiefs were involved in meetings with the president and other officials between November 1960 and April, and military personnel were present at the Guatemalan training camps of the refugees. However, because of the extreme secrecy of preparations, the Joint Chiefs may have been "required to give a judgment without benefit of the advice of experts on their own staffs"[12, p. 31]. The planning was CIA's and the execution was

[15] Not always. Radford's JCS, with Ridgway dissenting, recommended that the United States bomb the Chinese mainland if necessary to defend Quemoy, after U.S.-sponsored raids on the mainland had contributed to a crisis in the Formosan Straits.

CIA's. Overall, military involvement was minor; the military did not insist upon a thorough study of the improvised CIA-refugee plans prior to approval, and was not closely involved in tactical decisions involving air support and selection of landing sites. That did not save it from being implicated in and, to some extent, blamed for the disaster that occurred when the landing was attempted. Four of the five chiefs were gone within a year.

Cuba II, the missile crisis of October 1962, was the closest the United States and the U.S.S.R. had come to a direct nuclear confrontation. Where advisers had gone unchallenged in Cuba I, in the missile crisis the president meant to control events himself. Despite criticism from the Left and Right, Cuba II has been widely acclaimed as the finest example of "crisis management," with carefully calibrated responses to secret Russian implacement of missiles on the island and to subsequent events.

The initial American response was decided upon in days of secret meetings of the executive committee of the NSC: five representatives of the State Department, Secretary McNamara and two other Defense Department civilians, two or more presidential advisers, the director of the CIA, General Taylor (JCS chairman), several others, and the president's brother, Attorney General Robert Kennedy. The viewpoints represented were much more diverse than those involved in planning the 1961 invasion. The president had decided to do something; the executive committee was to recommend what that would be. McNamara and Robert Kennedy favored a naval blockade or "quarantine" of Cuba. Hilsman said:

One major obstacle—not objection, but obstacle—to a blockade was that the JCS still wanted an air strike or an invasion. The President met with the chiefs . . . and came out of the meeting annoyed. . . . The President was waiting to make his decision final mainly because of this continued opposition of the JCS to blockade and preference for more violent action. . . . It is elementary prudence for a president to protect himself from the charge that he had overruled his military advisers on a 'military' issue. . . . Some of the memoranda being written were not so much to present this or that case to the President—since he had already heard them all—but to build a record. If something went wrong, many of these papers would obviously begin to leak [12, p. 205].

The president, Robert Kennedy said,

. . . was distressed that the [military] representatives with whom he met, with the notable exception of General Taylor, seemed to give so little consideration to the implications of steps they suggested. They seemed always to assume that the Russians and the Cubans would not respond, or if they did, that a war was in our national interest. . . . On that fateful Sunday morning when the Russians answered they were withdrawing their missiles, it was suggested by one high military adviser that we attack Monday in any case. Another felt that we had in some way been betrayed. President Kennedy was disturbed by this inability to look beyond the limited military field. . . . This experience pointed out for us all the importance of civilian direction and control and the importance of raising probing questions to military recommendations [18, p. 97].

Despite military objections a blockade was decided upon.[16]   Since the manner of execution of this "controlled response" could have changed its meaning to the Russians, civilian officials involved themselves in details of execution. Pointing to the "delicacy" of the situation, they engaged in direct administrative supervision amounting almost to civilian command. The president himself decided what ships would be stopped, when and where. Some officers charged that the military chain of command was being bypassed, that the secretary was telling admirals where to place their ships and was giving other specific orders to ships at sea. In the navy's operations center McNamara questioned Adm. George W. Anderson, chief of naval operations, "sharply and in detail—who would make the first interception, were Russian speaking officers on board, and so on" [12, p. 215]. Anderson protested and subsequently was replaced and sent to Portugal as ambassador.

Dominican Republic, 1965

In the Dominican crisis of April 1965 the Joint Chiefs were not closely involved in making the initial decision to send 400 troops to safeguard evacuation of U.S. nationals, but they approved the subsequent decision to commit ships and 22,000 marines to prevent a Communist takeover. The MAAG chief in Santo Domingo contributed pessimistic reports on the situation to the decision-making process, and General Wheeler of the JCS advised on how many troops would be needed after the reinforcement decision had been made. This operation reflected the Joint Chiefs' belief that if the United States becomes involved in Third World conflicts, superior force should be applied quickly, even in the face of political protests abroad and at home.

Vietnam

Through the 1960s and early 1970s Vietnam was a war fought in the second act; the date and reason for its beginning were uncertain, and few believed it would have an early conclusion. Even its advocates had difficulty describing what victory would look like. It could be compared to the Thirty Years War or the Wars of the Roses; like George Orwell's "War in the West," it had been going on for as long as anyone could remember, a war seemingly without beginning or end.

---

[16] In "memoirs" attributed by *Life* magazine to then Soviet Premier Nikita Khrushchev, the author maintained that Robert Kennedy expressed fear that President Kennedy could not hold out much longer against his generals unless Khrushchev backed down [19, p. 52]. The missiles were withdrawn.

It also was a politically marbleized war; most decisions were military *and* political ones. Civilians made military decisions and military men ran civilian programs.

The first American soldier was killed in combat there on July 8, 1959.[17]

President Kennedy and General Taylor wanted to build a U.S. counter-insurgency capability, i.e., forces and strategies to meet limited Communist subversion or "wars of national liberation" in the Third World. The Army Special Forces received particular presidential support for this reason, in the face of much military skepticism, and conventional forces were built up. Under Kennedy the number of American advisers in Vietnam increased from the Geneva Accords level of 685 to 16,000. The guerrilla war there represented the type of challenge presumably amenable to a U.S. limited war response.

We will look at the war as a case of civil-military tension, and describe the locus of decision-making in the war's shadowy beginning and second act.

The Kennedy administration's decision to send in advisers and ground troops.   After an October 1961 fact-finding mission to Vietnam, General Taylor reported to the president that U.S. ground troops were needed. "The risks of backing into a major Asian war" by way of South Vietnam, Taylor said (according to *The New York Times* version of the Pentagon Papers, chapters 3 and 6-10, from which considerable material below is drawn), "are present but are not impressive." The Joint Chiefs figured that a maximum of 205,000 American ground troops would be needed. Whether it was Taylor's, Vice President Johnson's, or others' advice that proved decisive, the president did commit U.S. ground troops, while postponing a decision on a major troop commitment.

Military men often believe they are less eager for wars, and more reluctant to take on new commitments, than civilian leaders. Many U.S. officers did not like the idea of a land war in Asia; the Joint Chiefs discouraged intervention in Laos in the early 1960s unless the United States was willing to use almost unlimited firepower. Military men did not start the Vietnam War and it was not their job to stop it. Presidents start wars, of course, not generals—and in this case enthusiastic yea-saying was heard from the liberal intellectuals from the Harvard community (e.g., McGeorge Bundy), as well as from the conservatives of West Point. It was in the decisions to *continue* involvement, and to escalate the use of military force, that the influence of the professional soldier was most profound.

The Johnson administration's decision to bomb North Vietnam.   The Johnson administration, according to the Pentagon study, reached a "general

---

[17] American troops had been stationed in South Vietnam since 1954, and at least one was closely involved in Vietnamese politics: Edward Lansdale, an army colonel (CIA) who as the premier's closest adviser almost became U.S. ambassador in 1961 [12, p. 419].

consensus" on September 7, 1964 that air attacks against the North (as urged by the JCS) probably would have to be launched, although disagreement remained about when and to what extent.[18] The Joint Chiefs urged a "prompt and strong response" to the Viet Cong mortar attack on U.S. planes at Bienhoa airfield on November 1 (just two days before the presidential election), but the president decided, at least for the moment, to take no action.

Of three alternatives considered by the NSC, General Wheeler and the chiefs favored a "fast-full squeeze," i.e., bombing a large number of targets in the North within a short period of time for maximum military effect. Assistant Defense Secretary John McNaughton and several other civilians favored a "slow squeeze," i.e., gradual escalation of a modest bombing campaign, to weaken the North's ability to support the insurgents in the South.[19] This began a continuing dispute over bombing between the civilian DOD leadership and the chiefs. The strategy of 1965-1966 was largely the "slow squeeze," despite (1) the chiefs' warnings that the United States would have to show willingness to apply unlimited force against Hanoi, and (2) doubts expressed by the CIA and the DIA that bombing would break Hanoi's "will." Civilians were optimistic about their ability to secure concessions from North Vietnam through limited bombing, or calculated doses of force, in a step-ladder escalation.

By Christmas 1964 the Joint Chiefs and the Pacific military commander were pressing hard for reprisal and escalation, the study showed, although Johnson continued to hold back. General Taylor, then serving as U.S. ambassador in Saigon, and his nominal subordinate, Gen. William Westmoreland, urged going ahead with the air war even in the absence of a stronger Saigon government. In February 1965 the president approved Operation Rolling Thunder, sustained air attacks against the North. The Pentagon study concluded that the decision was due less to presidential enthusiasm than to a "lack of alternative proposals." Here the military's near-monopoly on strategic planning may have been decisive; no one else felt they had the experience or the resources to challenge the military version of reality, and the basic questions were not reopened for several years.

The decision to expand the ground war, 1965.   As it soon became clear that bombing would not save the Saigon regime, the president decided (April 1) to use American ground troops for offensive action in the South.

[18] According to the Pentagon study, McNaughton and the chiefs suggested a "provocation strategy" to provoke North Vietnam into actions which could be answered by expanded U.S. air operations, as in the Tonkin Gulf incidents. It was unclear, the study said, whether this strategy was ever adopted by the NSC.

[19] The Pentagon study said JCS proposals to destroy all major airfields and petroleum supplies in North Vietnam in three days were not forwarded to the president because civilian policy-makers considered them too costly and risky, just as plans which did not entail bombing the North were not formally presented to the NSC.

From a level of 27,000 General Westmoreland requested nearly 200,000 troops to hold off defeat long enough to permit a further U.S. buildup. As with the air war, the CIA warned that the planned ground war was unlikely to succeed. (Ambassador Taylor had once opposed additional U.S. troops for Vietnam, fearing that the Vietnamese would let the United States take over the prime combat role.) A month later President Johnson approved West-moreland's request—although as with most decisions discussed here he did not announce his decision.

Decisions to expand the bombing campaign, 1965-1967. The Joint Chiefs pressured for permission, the Pentagon study said, "to expand the bombing virtually into a program of strategic bombing aimed at all industrial and economic resources as well as at all interdiction targets. The chiefs did so . . . despite the steady stream of memoranda from the intelligence community consistently expressing skepticism that bombing of any conceivable sort (that is . . . except . . . population bombing . . .) could either persuade Hanoi to negotiate a settlement on . . . terms or effectively limit Hanoi's ability to infiltrate men and supplies into the South." Because Operation Rolling Thunder was "comparatively risky and politically sensitive," all bombing strikes were selected in Washington.[20] The number of sorties was gradually increased during 1965, and the list of targets lengthened, but McNamara continued to keep Hanoi, Haiphong, and the Chinese border area off limits. His program of military pressure against the North included occasional pauses (called "ratchets"), ostensibly to permit Hanoi time to offer to negotiate.[21] The study said the Joint Chiefs "were professionally

[20] During 1965-1966 civilians made important tactical decisions on bombing: avoidance of civilians; no bombing when weather was too poor to see targets clearly; initial use of supposedly less provocative B-26s instead of newer planes; and specification of bomb load, number of aircraft used, and altitude.

President Johnson and his senior advisers in Washington decided what targets could be attacked by given dates, and if attacks were not carried out by then the authorization lapsed. By contrast, the Nixon administration gave a list of authorized targets to the field commands, which then selected targets from the list. The field commands told Washington in advance what targets they intended to strike and by what date. This amounted to a decentralized system of command and control over the air war against southern North Vietnam, which was resumed at full-scale in April 1972. Although the Nixon administration maintained that civilian control was not being damaged, civilian officials and the Joint Chiefs remained dependent on what field commands told them. In June 1972 Gen. John D. Lavelle, former commander of the Seventh Air Force in Saigon, publicly acknowledged that he had falsified reports to cover up unauthorized raids. His forces had made at least 28 unauthorized air raids on the North between November 1971 and March 1972. Lavelle was dismissed from his command and retired.

[21] Like ratchets on a tennis net, pauses were designed to ease tension between each phase of increasing it; Hanoi's nonresponse permitted escalated bombing when it was resumed. Most soldiers probably disliked the idea of being used as ratcheteers. The term seemed part of the reification of which model-building civilian policy-makers were thought to be guilty.

distrustful of the diplomatic art and of the ability of the political decision-makers in Washington to resist the pressures from the 'peace movement' in the United States." Thus the chiefs, Westmoreland (who was initially skeptical about the value of the bombing), the Pacific command, and Secretary of State Rusk opposed even temporary halts in the bombing. They wanted to maintain pressure on the North and perhaps feared that Hanoi would offer to negotiate in exchange for a permanent halt without making major concessions.

By fall 1965 McNamara and McNaughton had begun to have serious doubts about the effectiveness of the air war, but the Joint Chiefs argued that the bombing had not worked only because of civilian-imposed restraints. Through the fall and winter the JCS pressed for permission to expand the bombing to include the North's oil tanks. The Pacific commander predicted that bombing the oil supplies would "bring the enemy to the conference table or cause the insurgency to wither from lack of support." The military also suggested closing the Haiphong port through bombing. In March 1966 McNamara finally accepted the Joint Chiefs' recommendation to bomb the supplies of petroleum, oil, and lubricants although the CIA again was pessimistic about the probable effects. The June execution message, the Pentagon study said, showed the "political sensitivity of the strikes." ". . . At Haiphong avoid damage to merchant shipping. No attacks authorized on craft unless U.S. aircraft are first fired on and then only if clearly North Vietnamese. Decision made after SEC-DEF [McNamara] and [Chairman] JCS were assured every feasible step would be taken to minimize civilian casualties." The strikes were accomplished, but intelligence reported that the flow of men and supplies was undiminished.

This was the last major escalation of the air war recommended by McNamara, the study said. He was increasingly troubled by the discrepancy between optimistic military predictions on effects of bombing[22] and troop reinforcements, and the results. However, through 1966 he continued to recommend that the president commit additional resources in search of "victory." McNaughton in the fall of 1966 suggested that the United States lower its sights from military victory to "compromise," but McNamara did not support this position, and administration policy remained unchanged.

Decisions to increase troop levels, 1965-1966.   Even if the United States did everything it reasonably could in Vietnam, McNamara had asked the Joint Chiefs earlier, could it win? "There is no reason," the chiefs replied, "we cannot win if such is our will." Where the military expressed confidence

[22]Later in 1966 a secret seminar of defense scientists judged the bombing campaign to have "had no measurable direct effect on Hanoi's ability to mount and support operations in the South," nor on its will, and suggested erection of an electronic barrier instead. The Pentagon study said this report had "a powerful and perhaps decisive influence in McNamara's mind," as he moved from "hesitancy" (winter 1965) to "perplexity" (spring 1966) to "disenchantment" with the war (fall 1966).

in the bombing, General Westmoreland usually was more reluctant to predict victory on the ground, although in July 1965 he told Washington that, by using a search-and-destroy strategy, he could defeat the enemy by the end of 1967.

The Pentagon study characterized President Johnson's approval of Westmoreland's July troop requests and endorsement of his strategy as an "open-ended commitment." It said: "Force levels for the search-and-destroy strategy had no empirical limits," since they depended on the enemy's response. From a request of 175,000 troops in June 1965, Westmoreland asked for 100,000 more for the "win phase" to begin in 1966. McNamara recommended that Johnson approve this request; the Pentagon study said of the secretary's remarks at this time: "Never again . . . would McNamara make so optimistic a statement about Vietnam—except in public." Westmoreland did not expect the enemy to build up strength so quickly, however, and he felt compelled to ask for more troops. McNamara in November 1965 began to express doubts about the ground war while continuing to favor meeting Westmoreland's requests. The general subsequently increased his force level requests several times, to 459,000 by January 1966.[23] In summer 1966, shortly after McNamara had approved a new deployment schedule (431,000 by June 1967), Westmoreland and the Joint Chiefs asked for 111,000 more. McNamara replied, "As you know, it is our policy to provide the troops, weapons, and supplies requested by General Westmoreland at the times he desires them, to the greatest possible degree. Nevertheless, I desire and expect a detailed line-by-line analysis of these requirements to determine that each is truly essential. . . . " McNamara was no longer willing to approve troop increases almost routinely. After his October trip to Saigon he recommended to the president that Westmoreland's troop request not be fully filled. Westmoreland then was asking for the projected troop level to be increased to 570,000 by the end of 1967, while the Joint Chiefs recommended mobilization of 688,500 reservists to provide more troops for an expanded war in Indochina and to build up the armed forces elsewhere.

For the first time, according to the Pentagon study, McNamara generated alternative strategies to those put forward by the military, and for perhaps the first time the president said no to Westmoreland. McNamara suggested that the United States should be "girding, openly, for a longer war," rather than pursuing Westmoreland's attrition or "meat-grinder" strategy of trying to kill more enemy troops than could be replaced. McNamara questioned the accuracy of body counts, and presented a discouraging picture of the military situation. He recommended: Limit the force

[23] The Pentagon study said it was possible that some military men felt that a meaningful victory would require a million men, but "knowing that this would be unacceptable politically," decided it would be better bargaining strategy to ask for the troops in increments. More likely, the study said, no one really foresaw what troop needs would be.

increase, install an electronic barrier, step up pacification, stabilize the bombing, and consider a bombing halt over North Vietnam as part of a more credible effort to reach a political settlement. The chiefs strongly criticized McNamara's proposals, as noted below.

Westmoreland reduced his troop request after finding that the president was reluctant to accept it; Johnson also was leery of politically risky cross-border and air operations. The new troop goal became 469,000 by June 1968, fewer than called for in Westmoreland's revised request or in McNamara's suggestion. The study noted: "From this time on, the judgment of the military as to how the war should be fought and what was needed would be subject to question." For the next year, until the president announced McNamara's departure from the Pentagon to become head of the World Bank, McNamara was constantly fighting with his generals on the war. His de-escalation suggestions in the spring and summer of 1967 almost certainly contributed to his removal.

The air war, again.   The Pentagon study identified three camps at the beginning of 1967: (1) The "disillusioned doves" led by McNamara, trying to set limits on the war; (2) the military, pressing for wider war; and (3) President Johnson and civilians in the White House, Air Force Department, and State Department, taking a middle position.

"In wartime," the Pentagon study said of the military, "their power and influence with an incumbent Administration is disproportionate." The chiefs responded to McNamara's proposals by recommending increased bombing, a "sharp knock" against the North, rather than cutting back on "the U.S. trump card." As with other escalation decisions the president moved more slowly than his military advisers desired, but eventually adopted most of their suggestions. Despite McNamara's opposition Johnson incrementally approved all but a dozen of the chiefs' 57 targets, including targets around Hanoi and Haiphong.

The chiefs said that McNamara's proposals would undermine the whole war effort; the air limitations, General Wheeler charged, would lead to an "aerial Dienbienphu." Chairman John Stennis of the Senate preparedness subcommittee agreed that the military was being unjustifiably shackled on bombing targets, and favored mobilization to meet Westmoreland's troop needs. Johnson may have approved new targets partly because of the scheduled Stennis subcommittee hearings. Even McNamara took his opposition to the air war to Congress in 1967, the first public evidence of his policy differences with the chiefs.

Decisions on troops and bombing, 1967.   The intensified debate within the administration in spring 1967 was spurred primarily by Westmoreland's request for 200,000 more troops. The Joint Chiefs endorsed the request, again called for mobilization of the reserves, again urged that the war be extended into sanctuaries in Laos, Cambodia, and possibly North Vietnam, and again asked permission to mine the North's ports. "When we add divisions, can't the enemy add divisions?" the president was reported to have asked Westmoreland and Wheeler. "If so, where does it all end?" Westmoreland conceded that the president's concern about possible Chinese intervention also was "a good question." The president refused to be pushed into asking Congress to mobilize reserve forces; the study said this became the "political sound barrier" he would not break.

Opposition of high civilian officials to the military proposals was more widespread than at any time in the war. The DOD systems analysis office produced a study purporting to show that U.S. troop increases did not produce corresponding increases in enemy losses. McNamara and McNaughton urged a bombing cutback to the 20th parallel (while recognizing its adverse morale impact on U.S. troops); an additional 30,000 troops; and acceptance of a sharply limited U.S. objective (perhaps including a coalition government with the Communists in South Vietnam). They expressed fear that granting Westmoreland 200,000 more troops would lead to "irresistible pressures" for carrying the battle beyond South Vietnam. In Congress, they predicted, "Cries would go up—much louder than they have already—to 'take the wraps off the men in the field.'"Eventually they feared pressures to use tactical nuclear and biological weapons. The president, the Pentagon study said, "did not promptly endorse the McNamara recommendations as he had on occasions in the past. This time he faced a situation where the Chiefs were in ardent opposition to anything other than a significant escalation . . . [and] in direct opposition to McNamara. . . . [This] created a genuine policy dilemma for the President." Seeing Johnson's hesitancy McNamara asked the JCS to do a new bombing study, which again supported bombing and criticized the secretary's "drastic" proposals. McNamara went to Saigon under Johnson's instructions to negotiate an agreement with Westmoreland on a troop figure well below that requested. The 525,000 ceiling agreed upon, and accepted by Johnson, was much closer to McNamara's position than to Westmoreland's 671,000.

Decisions on troops and bombing, 1968.   After the unanticipated Tet offensive of early 1968 the military again sought troop increases and a reserve call-up. McNamara ordered emergency deployment of 10,000 more troops, although the chiefs opposed deploying any more units to Vietnam without a call-up. The Pentagon study said, "The tactic the Chiefs were using was clear: By refusing to scrape the bottom of the barrel any further for Vietnam, they hoped to force the President to 'bite the bullet' on the call-up of the reserves—a step . . . they were determined would not now be avoided." Whether the president and General Wheeler pressed Westmoreland to ask for more troops, or Johnson merely asked for Westmoreland's recommendations, is open to question. (Later Johnson said, "it was the President who initiated this request"; Westmoreland said he did not *demand* more troops, and that his request was based on objectives and restrictions set down by civilian leadership.) At every previous critical point in the war, then Air Force Under Secretary Townsend Hoopes said:

... McNamara had flown to Vietnam to bargain directly with Westmoreland and other commanders regarding the manpower and discretionary authority required for the next phase. In every instance, he had reached his own conclusions before departing Washington. ... In every case he prevailed upon the military commanders to scale down their requests (called "requirements"); in return for their cooperation, he gave his public endorsement to the amended buildup. That pattern had been repeated at approximately 6-month intervals since early 1965 [13, p. 163].

Since McNamara was leaving the Pentagon soon, General Wheeler was sent to Saigon. This, Hoopes said, "produced an undiluted expression of the true military desideratum. ... This ... galvanized the Pentagon civilians, who were for the first time able to assert their strong anti-escalation position in a favorable psychological and managerial climate" [13, p. 165]. Wheeler returned with a request for 206,000 more troops, which would have meant a call-up of at least 280,000 reservists and the probable imposition of economic controls. This led to a series of meetings culminating in the reverse of what the military wanted.

The new secretary of defense, Clark Clifford, was assigned by Johnson to head a high-level group to decide on the means to provide the troops requested. As the group became involved in questions of basic war policy, Taylor (the only military member) aligned himself with the chiefs in opposing any change. The final Clifford group memo recommended "a little bit more of the same," according to the Pentagon study. But in private meetings with the president, where the chiefs could not engage in full and formal criticism, Clifford and others urged a different course. Former Secretary of State Acheson (like Clifford, a hawk much respected by Johnson) told the president that "the Joint Chiefs of Staff don't know what they're talking about," and that Westmoreland was attempting the impossible [13, pp. 204-205]. Clifford, convinced that more troops would not make victory any more likely, pressed for a partial bombing halt over the North. Johnson decided on a reserve call-up of 98,000, but then abandoned that plan and recalled Westmoreland from Saigon to become army chief of staff. In late March the president found that almost all of his informal Senior Advisory Group—all former government officials, including three retired generals—had turned against the war. After Tet optimistic military predictions sounded less credible than the continued pessimism of the CIA and DOD's ISA and systems analysis offices (which Johnson previously had discounted). Concern about domestic dissent and disillusionment, and about the American economy, also was growing.

On March 31, on television, the president announced a partial bombing halt and a token (one-tenth of requested number) troop increase—together with his own withdrawal from the presidential race—which reversed American policy. Three days later Hanoi announced its willingness to enter into negotiations.

After the bombing halt.   Later in 1968 Secretary Clifford sought a total bombing halt, limitations on the ground war, and a start on withdrawal of U.S. troops. But he said later, "I could not buck the Joint Chiefs any further. I could go no further than obtain the total bombing halt. The Joint Chiefs had the President convinced that he could take no more risks that would jeopardize our troops. He was listening only to the Chiefs and I did not believe I could get through"[24, p. 41].

President Nixon, who took office in January 1969, was determined to withdraw troops from Vietnam, and at a faster rate than the chiefs preferred. During 1969-1971 the chiefs, formally and informally, urged delays in announcing and making troop cut backs. The 150,000 troop withdrawal announced in April 1970 probably lacked the approval of the field commander and the chiefs.

The invasion of Cambodia in 1970, on the other hand, marked the temporarily increased influence of military advisers over those who wanted a fast pull out and negotiated settlement in Indochina. Similarly, the Laotian campaign of 1971 and the mining of the Haiphong harbor in 1972 met long-standing military desires.

Vietnam in Perspective

In addition to troop-level and bombing decisions made in Washington, opportunities for civil-military conflict and competition existed in the field. Technically the ambassador in Saigon had the power to overrule General Westmoreland, but "there was no evidence that Lodge, Taylor, or Bunker ever substantially did overrule him; it no doubt would have seemed too great a risk to interfere with the judgments of a general responsible for the safety of American troops in combat"[5, pp. 97-98]. Where MacArthur had to deal with the political complications of a United Nations Command in Korea, Westmoreland had few allies; expenses of most allies were being paid by the United States, and none were as politically significant as Britain in Korea. It has been an American tradition to delegate extensive powers and entrust enormous resources to field commanders, and this was done with Westmoreland as it had been with Eisenhower and MacArthur.

Initially the pacification program (the political or "other war") was directed by civilians. It was part of unprecedentedly large-scale and continuous theater-of-operations cooperation between the State and Defense departments. The civilian-run Operations Mission and successor USAID, however, had neither the financial nor manpower resources, neither the doctrine, "discipline," nor chain of command to direct such large advisory and pacification programs[17, p. 75]. The "other war" was restructured in 1966 by a presidential special assistant (who became civil supervisor under Westmore-land), to make the military chiefly responsible. The military believed its CORDS (civil operations, revolutionary development support) was more successful. In another advisory program, lack of manpower forced the CIA early in the war to give primary responsibility for training and leading mercenaries to the Army Special Forces.

Civilians were closely involved in air tactical decisions: Johnson person-ally selected targets in North Vietnam for bombing, and Pentagon civilians overruled Westmoreland's request to bomb Russian surface-to-air missile sites when they first appeared. Later, however, more planes were sent on armed reconnaissance (with permission to fire at anything) and "free fire zones" were enlarged.

The major limits set by the Johnson administration were: (1) no invasion of North Vietnam because of fear of Chinese involvement; (2) no mining of the Haiphong harbor, because of fear of hitting Russian ships; and (3) no pursuit of enemy troops into Laos and Cambodia, to avoid widening the war. Limitations on bombing did not prevent the air force from dropping more bomb tonnage in Vietnam by 1968 than had been dropped in all theaters of World War II, saturating possible targets in the North. In terms of men and material on the ground in the South the army got most of what it said it needed, much more than it said it would need when the war began. It is difficult to agree with those officers who asserted that American political leaders wanted to fight the war on the cheap, given the enormous economic and political costs of the war.

More importantly, civilians did not *control* the ground war. Regiments could not be controlled by civilians in the way that bombing raids could be and were. It was on the ground, rather than in the air war, that most Americans and Vietnamese were killed. It was here that search and destroy, pacification, My Lai, and the "we had to destroy the village in order to save it" philosophy helped to erode American public support for the war. It was here that the war would have had to be won. And it was here that some junior officers and Pentagon civilians in the Johnson administration felt the war was lost by unwise military tactics.

Unlike the relationship between Truman and MacArthur, President Johnson and his field commander felt a "deep, and mutual, loyalty" to one another [5, p. 98]. Westmoreland felt comfortable with McNamara's quanti-tative approach to the war (e.g., body counts), and was aware of the political aspects of his mission in Saigon and at home. He insisted, for example, that Vietnam be made a 1-year tour of duty, and he worried early about the resolve of the home front. He was called back from Saigon in April 1967 to address a joint session of Congress, in political defense of Johnson's policies, and apparently was one of the very few in November to have been informed of the president's intention not to seek reelection. Johnson reportedly asked Westmoreland if his decision would be seen by U.S. troops in Vietnam as desertion; Westmoreland said they would understand. "Probably no field commander in our history had ever been presented such an opportunity to influence American politics . . . but he confined himself to a proper soldier's answer" [5, p. 98] .

• • •

Why did the United States become involved in Vietnam, and stay involved? Can the blame (or credit) for intervention be laid at the door of the military?

No major war in American history has been initiated by the military, although generals have been accused of exceeding their authority in wartime. The military has been cautious about becoming involved in wars, but once in them, has sought to stay involved and to bring more military force to bear until victory is achieved. It is in this latter sense that military men can be characterized as hawks. In the 1960s and early 1970s, however, American leaders saw themselves engaged in *continuous* warfare, sometimes cold and sometimes hot, which therefore lacked a clear prewar period. The nation's prestige and security was believed to be always and everywhere at stake. This, combined with the continued erosion of differences in outlook between civilian and military leaders, may have dulled the military's traditional caution. Involvement in Vietnam, with some oversimplification, also can be seen as reflecting the "liberal" beliefs of some civilian and military leaders that all things are possible through the rational use of power.[24] "The armed services," Westmoreland said of his task, "were not about to go to the Commander in Chief and say that we were not up to carrying out his instructions —as a matter of service pride." Although the overoptimism of the soldiers reinforced that of the civilians, it was the latter's which was most critical.[25]

As in earlier crises and wars the military won some policy disputes on Vietnam and lost others. Civilian officials had to negotiate with military leaders strengthened by the prior commitment of soldiers to the field. Through much of the war, civilian counterweights (e.g., the Office of the Secretary of Defense and the CIA) did not compete with the military as much as they cooperated argumentatively.

---

[24] Civilian liberals, in domestic affairs and foreign aid, tended to believe that no task was too great for a rationally directed government. McNamara-style systems analysis, war games, and strategic thought emphasized the *controlled* application of force. Military men, too, were characterized by a "Can do!" orientation, and may not have been as conservative or pessimistic as Huntington[14] believed: problems have solutions; questions have right answers; technology and organization can deal with anything; nothing is hopeless.

[25] Long-time State Department "house dove" George W. Ball wrote: "the military did not push us into Vietnam half so much as the civilian theoreticians with theses to prove—doctrines of counter-insurgency and guerrilla tactics all reeking of the lamp" [2; p. 48] .

The best explanation for why the Vietnam War continued so long seems to be not the Leninist one of industrialists seeking new markets, nor the Johnsonian one of a procession of steps required to defend freedom and meet commitments, but rather careerism, or a *bureaucratic* explanation [9, p. 17]. Once involved, commitments begot larger commitments, and careers required defense of positions previously taken. The self-interest of many civilian and military bureaucrats coincided, resulting in organizational inertia. For example, military officers in the field had reason to make their reports unrealistically optimistic; as advisers or commanders they were held accountable for what happened in their districts. Future advancement[26] depended on *successful* tours of duty in Vietnam.

During World War II General Marshall used to tell President Roosevelt that his advice was being given purely from a military standpoint; "at times, during the war," General Bradley said, "we forgot that wars are fought for the resolution of political conflicts" [15, p. 13]. No military leader in Vietnam claimed to be unconcerned about and uninvolved in political matters. Their involvement was not qualitatively different from that of previous wars but, as befitted America's first television war, it was more openly discussed. (Where the Vietnam War has been fought out on color television in American living rooms, in World War II it was not until D-Day 1944 that most U.S. newspapers published pictures of American dead.)

Given the likelihood of increased military influence and bureaucratic inertia during a war, early on in Vietnam whose job was it to factor in possible nonmilitary consequences? Officers "are expected to ask and answer questions 1 through 7; questions 8 through 10 they ignore" [20, p. 73]. Officers should and usually want to accept foreign policy goals as "given"; once informed of the goals, it is their job to recommend military means to accomplish them, or to report that there is no feasible way with the resources to be allocated. What use would generals be if they did *not* think in military terms, if they were *not* attentive to ways to meet potential threats?

On Vietnam, dovish Sen. Eugene McCarthy told a military audience, political authorities failed to make political decisions, "yet they have been quite ready to make military decisions." If the war was wrong or the wrong one, civilian policy-makers, not the military, were primarily to blame.

The experiences of Vietnam, and the subsequent search for scapegoats instead of "welcome home" parades, could drive professional soldiers in either of two directions. They could try to disengage themselves from

---

[26] Military careers are advanced more rapidly in wartime. In 1969 a competent army officer could expect to be promoted to major about 6.5 years after being commissioned; immediately prior to substantial U.S. involvement in Vietnam, it took about 11 years. The de-escalation of the war was forcing some officers out of the service, and probably would make advancement slower for those who remained.

Of course, any explanation (such as careerism) broad enough to deal with war causation also may be sufficiently vague to defy disproof.

contacts with civilian groups and from political decision-making, in search of an idealized apolitical tradition. Or, as some younger officers are inclined to do, they might attempt to develop more political skills and to position themselves warily in policy debates. In the latter case the military would be able to tell civilian leaders what military and political commitments it required before getting deeply involved in "another" Vietnam. Westmoreland was sent to Vietnam with the vaguest of instructions as to what his mission would be: Objectives were neither clear nor fixed. Bombing and geographic limitations were aggravating, but perhaps just as difficult for the military was the uncertainty among political leaders as to what they wanted to accomplish. How would the soldiers know victory when and if they saw it?

American experiences in Indochina can be compared to those of the French military there and in Algeria; both military forces suffered declines in public respect as a result. A lukewarm "stab-in-the-back" theory was accepted by some American officers: if it had not been for the meddling of McNamara ... if it had not been for the press ... But there was no immediate search for a military man-on-horseback. In the early 1970s there was no evidence that significant numbers of American soldiers wanted to follow the French military's example of direct political intervention. Any military force has enormous *potential* for political leverage, but it is unlikely that American military men will be involved any more directly than they have been in the past.

REFERENCES

1. Abel, Elie, *The Missile Crisis* (New York: Lippincott, 1966).
2. Ball, George W., "In Defense of the Military," *Newsweek,* 78 (July 5, 1971), p. 48.
3. Beckman, Peter, "Influence, Generals, and Vietnam," paper delivered to the International Studies Association convention, San Juan, March 1971.
4. Borklund, C. W., *The Department of Defense* (New York: Praeger, 1968).
5. Clark, Blair, "Westmoreland Appraised," *Harper's,* 241 (November 1970), pp. 96-101.
6. Congressional Quarterly Service, *Global Defense* (Washington: CQ Service, 1969).
7. Finney, John W., "Spain 'Commitment' Decried by Senators," *The New York Times,* April 18, 1969, pp. 1, 11.
8. Fox, William T. R., "Military Representation Abroad," in *The Representation of the United States Abroad* (New York: the American Assembly, 1956), pp. 120-153.
9. Galbraith, John Kenneth, *How to Control the Military* (New York: Signet Books, 1969).

10. Halperin, Morton H., "The Limiting Process in the Korean War," *The Political Science Quarterly,* 78 (March 1963), pp. 13-39.
11. Higgins, Trumbull, *Korea and the Fall of MacArthur* (New York: Oxford University Press, 1960).
12. Hilsman, Roger, *To Move a Nation* (Garden City: Doubleday, 1964).
13. Hoopes, Townsend, *The Limits of Intervention* (New York: David McKay, 1969).
14. Huntington, Samuel P., *The Soldier and the State* (Cambridge, Mass.: Harvard University Press, 1957).
15. Janowitz, Morris, *The Professional Soldier* (New York: Free Press, 1960).
16. Johnson, Haynes, *The Bay of Pigs* (New York: W. W. Norton, 1964).
17. Just, Ward, "Soldiers," Part II, *Atlantic,* 226 (November 1970) pp. 59-90.
18. Kennedy, Robert F., *Thirteen Days* (New York: W.W. Norton, 1969).
19. "Khrushchev Remembers: Playing for High Stakes," *Life,* 69 (December 18, 1970), pp. 19-25, 47-54.
20. Lapham, Lewis H., "Military Theology," *Harper's,* 243 (July 1971), pp. 73-85.
21. MacArthur, Douglas, *Reminiscences* (New York: McGraw-Hill, 1964).
22. Millis, Walter, ed., *American Military Thought* (Indianapolis: Bobbs-Merrill, 1966).
23. Mills, C. Wright, *The Power Elite* (New York: Oxford University Press, 1956).
24. Norman, Lloyd, "The Chiefs," Part II, *Army,* 20 (May 1970), pp. 37-43.
25. *The Pentagon Papers as published by The New York Times* (New York: Quadrangle, 1971).
26. Ridgway, Matthew B., *The Korean War* (Garden City, N.Y.: Doubleday, 1967).
27. Rovere, Richard H., and Arthur M. Schlesinger, Jr., *The General and the President* (New York: Farrar, Straus and Young, 1951).
28. Sapin, Burton M., *The Making of United States Foreign Policy* (New York: Praeger, 1966).
29. Sapin, Burton M., and Richard C. Snyder, *The Role of the Military in American Foreign Policy* (Garden City, N.Y.: Doubleday, 1954).
30. Sarkesian, Sam C., "Political Soldiers," *Midwest Journal of Political Science,* 16 (forthcoming May 1972).
31. "Senate to Study Talks in Madrid," *The New York Times,* February 26, 1969, p. 10.
32. Sorensen, Theodore C., *Kennedy* (New York: Harper & Row, 1965).
33. Swomley, John M., Jr., *The Military Establishment* (Boston: Beacon Press, 1964).
34. Thayer, George, "American Arms Abroad,"*The Washington Monthly,* 1 (January 1970), pp. 62-73.

35. U.S. House Committee on Foreign Affairs, Hearings before the Subcommittee on National Security Policy and Scientific Developments, "Military Assistance Training in East and Southeast Asia," (Washington: Government Printing Office, 1971).
36. Wilensky, Harold L., *Organizational Intelligence* (New York: Basic Books, 1967).

CHAPTER TEN

Conclusion

In the previous chapters we have attempted to shed light on the questions raised in Chapter 1. On the first set of questions we have found that economic dependence on defense spending is indeed widespread, and that the military is involved closely with many civilian groups in support of a continued large defense budget. There is a community of interests. As in Shaw's armorer's code, industry and military can agree that "If God gave the hand, let not Man withhold the sword."[1]

But press and congressional concern often is misplaced. The opportunities for conflicts of interest are no greater in the defense complex than in a domestic program such as health. The ineptness of defense contractors is difficult to exaggerate, but this too is not the most important factor. The defense establishment is an economic colossus, and one whose allocative decisions may be motivated as often by desires to extend or consolidate its domestic empire as by international considerations. But the headquarters of the empire are in Washington. The problem is not corporate dominance of government, as widely asserted; rather, it is extension of the influence of loosely controlled governmental (military and civilian) bureaucrats over the economy. And it is in a cold-war setting, not a shooting war, that profits are higher and this bureaucracy's influence can be extended in a more orderly manner.

On the third set of questions, involving militarization of American life, the empirical support for normative concern is uneven. The growth of the military establishment between the Neutrality Act of 1935 and the Tet offensive of 1968 was a widely approved response to the dangerous international setting in which Americans saw themselves. But now traditional public acquiescence is hedged by concern about high defense spending, and the previously supportive upper strata is the most concerned. On the basis of

---

[1] This was the first principle of the Undershafts in George Bernard Shaw's *Major Barbara* (1905). Undershaft said he, the armorer, called the tune and paid the piper.

I am the government of your country. . . . You will make war when it suits us, and keep peace when it doesn't. . . . When I want anything to keep my dividends up, you will discover that my want is a national need.

Whether he was master or slave, however, was in dispute.

available data the military has not been successful (if indeed it was trying) in "hardening" society and the socialization institutions. Knowledge-producing institutions have been reoriented by defense monies, just as corporations have been, but the military has found the universities and the scientific community to be unreliable allies. The strength and absorptiveness of American society may have been underestimated by those who feared the coming of a garrison state.[2] They also may have exaggerated the extent to which military men can be distinguished attitudinally from other Americans. The military reflects the attitudes and values of the broader society, certainly as well as most bureaucracies.

The second set of questions involves control; control means initiative, influence, and more. Congress provides its critics with considerable grounds for charges that it enthusiastically has abdicated policy-making responsibility to DOD and has given the military a "blank check." Congress has the constitutional power to control defense policy, but it acquiesces because leading congressmen have wanted to go by the path set out for them by military leaders. In the executive branch the answer to the civilian control question is more ambiguous; different presidents, defense secretaries, and budget directors have dealt with the military in different ways. Despite the tremendous growth in military responsibilities, it does not appear that civilian control is in serious danger at the highest levels. Since "military" styles of coping with foreign policy crises have been adopted by many who do not wear military uniforms,[3] whether the content of American foreign policy is militaristic will be left to others to answer. Insofar as we have examined military factors, it was with the aim of learning more about the part military men as a group, in competition with other groups, have played in making policy.

● ● ●

What are our national priorities? Discussing new priorities does not bring them into existence, any more than discussion of the anticipated

[2] Lasswell's garrison state and the complex of the sixties and seventies differ in at least one important way. The garrison state envisioned a more total upheaval in societies, in which the businessman, as well as the politician, loses power to the military man. The complex usually envisions a cooperative arrangement between soldiers, industrialists, and selected political leaders. The complex is slightly less gloomy in its conception of what happens to the national life style.

[3] The distinction between civilian control on the one hand and the predominance of "foreign policy" over military considerations on the other is basic. "During the . . . period of policy dominance in the Pentagon by Secretary McNamara and certain key civilian aides . . . the requirement that their decisions reflect foreign policy desiderata . . . is just as great, and sometimes as hard to accomplish, as if some military body like the Joint Chiefs of Staff were in fact the dominant policy influence in the Pentagon"[1, p. 176]. Nor are military considerations synonymous with the Defense Department; Secretary of State Rusk and White House advisers sometimes sided with the military against McNamara.

post-Vietnam budgetary "peace dividend" has made that materialize. The battle over resources between military and domestic claimants was in no sense decided in 1969-1971. It simply submerged. The end of the war will not end the resources battle; rather, it is likely to *strengthen* the military's hand in competition within the administration and Congress by reducing public and nonspecialist congressional concern about the military. The military budget was moving up again in the early 1970s; it will never return to its prewar level. President Nixon announced arms-control agreements with the Russians in 1972, but then requested a $6 billion increase in the military budget for fiscal 1973. Unless there are additional international arms-control agreements or sweeping changes in military organization and procurement practices, new weapons and increased pay for the military will absorb much of the economy's "growth dividend," as well as the peace dividend. Although our analysis does not support the more alarmed appraisals of military influence over American government and society, the military's size and strength do act to prevent any sustained redirection of resources into domestic programs.

REFERENCES

1. Sapin, Burton M., *The Making of United States Foreign Policy* (New York: Praeger, 1966).
2. Shaw, George Bernard, *The Works of Bernard Shaw,* Vol. 11 (London: Constable, 1930).

Index

73 74 75 76   9 8 7 6 5 4 3 2 1